Legal Blunders

By the same author

Business Blunders

Legal Blunders

Geoff Tibballs

Robinson
LONDON

Constable & Robinson Ltd
3 The Lanchesters
162 Fulham Palace Road
London W6 9ER

First published in the UK by Robinson, an imprint of
Constable & Robinson Ltd 2000

Reprinted 2000, 2001

A copy of the British Library Cataloguing in Publication data is
available from the British Library

ISBN 1-84119-020-9

Printed and bound in the EU

10 9 8 7 6 5 4 3

To Carol

Contents

Contents

Introduction

Every lawyer in the land could make some small contribution to Geoff Tibballs' extraordinary range of Legal Blunders. Practice in the law has provided me with my own repertoire of stories with which to regale any willing audience. It usually only takes a little encouragement and a few glasses of wine.

Sometimes the tales lawyers tell are apocryphal; sometimes, though based in fact, they have benefited from embellishment; and sometimes they contain the horror or hilarity of absolute truth. The combination of the courts' pomp and circumstance juxtaposed with inevitable human frailty create the perfect recipe for endless anecdotes.

Usually the blunders to which we lawyers admit are harmless. The legal gaffe based on youthful inexperience. I remember so well my days of pupillage, when a member of chambers burst into the room in which I was quietly working in a corner. He launched into a very personal conversation with my pupil master, 'My wife is having a torrid affair with the chap downstairs. They are at it day and night. I could take no more. I broke into the flat and caught them in flagrante . . .' I did not wait for more. To save his embarrassment, I quickly made my presence known and crept apologetically towards the door. I only later discovered that this was an example of the legal shorthand which barristers would use in conversation with a colleague. 'I am a golden hearted whore', our head of chambers once announced, when he was acting for a brothel keeper. And before long I too was inducted into the formula of using the first person.

Many stories are about judicial foibles. As a young woman in practice, at a time when there were still comparatively few of us in the criminal courts, I learned the hard way to circumnavigate judicial sensitivities. In one of my first appearances at the Old Bailey I was acting for a sixty-year-old offender who was pleading guilty to a series of sex offences which had happened some years previously. In mitigation I sought to persuade the judge that by virtue of his great age my client was no longer sexually active and, therefore, no danger to the public. The judge looked over his spectacles and asked me whether it was my understanding that men of this age had lost their libido. I looked carefully at the judge and quickly calculated that I was on very dangerous ground. In hasty retreat I assured him that I was not seeking to generalize as I understood there were many old people who were still active in all kinds of ways but my client was not one of them. The joy of being twenty-three!

For some reason the legal profession seems to be a magnet for the eccentric, or perhaps eccentricity becomes a refuge for some, to enliven the duller aspects of the job or to disguise their own angst about the responsibility of it all. There have been many larger-than-life characters about whom tales abound. Part of my own pupillage was spent in the chambers of Billy Rees-Davies QC who was a legend in his own lifetime. One of the more notorious blunders he made was to persuade a court to rise in the middle of a serious trial on the pretext of illness only to be seen on the nine o'clock news at the Ascot races.

When cross-examining a witness at the Old Bailey, a note was speedily passed to him from his client in the dock. The usher tried to press the missive into his hand but he brushed it away and continued his verbal parry with the witness. The defendant became very agitated in the dock. The judge intervened to draw Billy Rees-Davies' attention to the communication. 'I am sure, my Lord, it is but a billet-doux,' said Billy. 'I fear, Mr Rees-Davies, it may be a Billy don't.'

Many of the blunders turn on failure of communication, often where judges insist upon the grandiose phrase in pursuit of gravitas. The bewildered, gum-chewing defendant who is told not to masticate in court, insisting he had his hands on the dock the whole time. Or the famous story told of the Scottish sheriff:

Sheriff: 'Although I find you a fecund liar, I will not on this occasion sentence you to prison.'

Prisoner: 'Thank-you, Your Honour, you're a fecund good judge.'

Sometimes, judicial blunders happen because judges get bored with the judicial role, missing the fun of being down there in the arena with the advocates. I remember well the occasion when His Honour Judge Cassels listened to some questions about the injury caused to a prisoner's wrists by the ratchets on police handcuffs. He insisted that the policeman come up to the bench and handcuff him, which the officer did. The judge triumphantly showed the jury his snugly cuffed hands and then sought their release. No key was available. It was back at the police station. He struggled with the irons, only to make the ratchets close yet tighter. He unceremonially rose from the bench and scuttled off to his chambers, where he miserably awaited his liberty.

The laugh is not always at the expense of judges. As barristers we are always advised at the beginning of practice never to ask a question to which we do not know the answer, an injunction which is often honoured in its breach. Another golden rule is to avoid the last question which goes too far. The classic example was in a Victorian poisoner case, where the defendant was accused of boiling up commercial flypaper to obtain a broth of strychnine, which he administered to his wife with fatal consequences. Counsel had a successful run of answers from the salesman in the local hardware store.

Counsel: The weather was warm at this time, was it not?

Witness: Indeed it was.

Counsel: There were many flies?

Witness: They were around in abundance.

Counsel: Can we take it that many people were buying flypaper?

Witness: Droves.

Then the one question too many.

Counsel: Well, how can you be sure that the accused bought flypaper from you?

Witness: Because he was the only one who asked if it contained strychnine.

Lawyers love to introduce a little drama to the proceedings: the surprise witness, the revealing photograph, the forgotten exhibit. In the trial of O.J. Simpson, there were gasps from the jury when O.J. was asked insert his hand into the incriminating glove from the scene of the crime: it clearly did not fit. However, my guess is that the display had been carefully rehearsed away from the public gaze.

Those *coups de grace* can sometimes turn into *coups de foudre*. A tale is currently told of a barrister seeking to expose as liars the policemen who claimed they had arrested his client in the act of applying a flame to a piece of crack cocaine.

Counsel: You were with me earlier, officer, when I examined the cigarette lighter which you claim was the source of the flame, were you not?

Officer: I was, Sir.

Counsel: You saw that I tried more than twenty times to get that lighter to work and it was incapable of producing a flame.

Officer: I saw that you had difficulty, Sir.

Counsel: Will you now show the jury that the lighter in question is incapable of producing the flame you claim you saw?

Whereupon the officer flicked the lighter with ease, producing a flame of at least six inches.

There is a famous Bateman cartoon of shock and horror created in a courtroom when the accused admits his guilt. Though not exactly on all fours, a colleague experienced a similar sense of dismay when he finished examining his own client in chief with the final flourish 'And are you guilty of these offences?' Whereupon the interpreter answered 'I think he is!'

However, legal blunders are not always a source of humour. The miscarriages of justice sent tremors through the legal world, reminding us that there can be dire consequences when blunders are made.

I am always suspicious of lawyers who claim they have never had misgivings about their conduct of a case. Frequently lawyers have to make carefully calculated tactical decisions and it is inevitable that there will be occasions when one will wonder about the course chosen. Might the outcome have been different had I called a certain witness or not called another? Such judgments are often finely balanced and they are made more confidently when we have acquired experience and greater professionalism. However, none of us are immune from error and we should never again succumb to the arrogance which allowed the profession and the judiciary to deny for so long that the system had failed a large number of people.

One of the most poignant and shocking failures of justice was the case of Stefan Kiszko, who was convicted of the sexual assault and murder of a little girl. Stefan, who was profoundly backward, had an alibi for the time of the crimes. He had been with the mother and aunt, two decent, honest people; yet in a sceptical court their account was dismissed.

After seventeen years spent in gaol, he was cleared by the Court of Appeal when it was discovered that swabs from the body of the child, available at the time of the trial, disclosed active sperm, whereas Stefan was completely infertile. More than one person screwed up badly in that case but the price was paid by a sad, slow-witted man and his aged mother. He died within months of his release, tragically followed by his mother only six months later.

Some of the most telling blunders have happened because of misidentifications. The famous case of Adolf Beck was used in my own student days as the dire warning on wrongful identification. This was a man hanged for crimes he did not commit because the real offender, who ultimately confessed, was so physically like him, a true doppelganger.

The trouble with mistaken identifications is that the errant witness is often very convincing, certain that THIS is the person who was earlier seen. They can be absolutely sure and absolutely wrong.

Only a few years ago I acted for the woman charged with bombing the Israeli embassy. She was identified on an identification parade by a single police officer, who was convinced she was the woman who parked a bomb-laden car close to the scene. There were significant differences between his original description of the bomber with the Harrods bag and the woman he selected many months later. The only reason she had come to be considered at all for inclusion on the parade was that she was Palestinian and the mother of a student, who was an acquaintance of another suspect. The policeman was adamant that he was right. The judge rejected the case against my client at the end of the prosecution case and virtually everyone involved in the trial, senior police officers, lawyers for the prosecution as well as those for the defence, became satisified of her innocence. However, the toll that was taken upon her life can never be redressed.

People ask lawyers how they feel about acting for someone they think might be guilty but they have many more sleepless nights representing someone they think is innocent.

The lessons we have learned from the great legal mistakes of our time is that justice requires constant vigilance. There has to be a willingness to self-examine and admit when the system or its servants might have failed. And the terrible blunders in the cases of Christie and Evans and that of Derek Bentley have surely convinced us that we can never again countenance the use of the death penalty.

Thank God, most of our errors and follies are inconsequential and recounting them helps prick the pomposity and hubris that so readily creeps into the legal system. Geoff Tibballs' book covers the terrain with great style, including not just the mistakes of lawyers and judges but those of policemen, prison officers and others in the system as a whole. He also has not omitted the blunders of our clients, without which most of us would have no practice.

Geoff's book entertains, informs and whets the appetite for more. Most of us who are involved in the legal system are able to see the mirth in our activities. These yarns of our failings remind us that in the midst of the serious stuff of life, there is the important need to laugh.

Helena Kennedy

Chapter 1

Here Comes the Judge

Colin Ferguson: A Crazy Case of Self-Defence

The only thing which was balanced about Colin Ferguson was that he had a chip on both shoulders. Despite an eminently middle-class upbringing in Kingston, Jamaica, he had developed into one of life's losers – a paranoid schizophrenic convinced that the world was against him. Every stage of his life – school, college, work and marriage – had ended in disappointment, causing him to resent bitterly anyone who had the things for which he craved, such as a good job, money or a family. In particular, he despised white people and also those blacks who he thought treated whites with too much respect. He was a time bomb waiting to explode.

On the night of Tuesday 7 December 1993, Ferguson was just another anonymous passenger on the packed 5.33 p.m. rush-hour train from New York's Penn Station to Hicksville. All around him, he saw the embodiments of his hatred: white well-paid office workers, able to afford the early Christmas presents which some had balanced on their laps. And they were bound for their neat suburban homes on Long Island where they would be greeted by loving families. It was too much for Ferguson to bear.

Sitting sullenly in the corner of car number three, unnoticed by the weary commuters, he began loading his semi-automatic pistol. He was intent on eliminating everyone in that carriage and had armed himself with over 100 rounds of ammunition –

lethal, hollow-point bullets, designed to inflict maximum damage. Between New Hyde Park and Merillon Avenue stations, he silently rose from his seat and coolly and methodically began firing into the heads of the unsuspecting passengers. At first, some thought it was nothing more than an imitation gun firing caps – perhaps some kind of joke – but as people began slumping forward in their seats and falling to the floor in pools of blood, it quickly became apparent that this was for real. Mass panic broke out. A few tried to make a run for it through the connecting doors to the next carriage. Others simply threw themselves on the gunman's mercy, cowering under seats or out of his line of vision, praying that they would be spared. One passenger, Kevin Zaleskie, put his briefcase over his head in the hope that the thick pile of paper would save him from any bullet. He said later: 'As I sat there I could feel him walk past me as he was shooting, but I wasn't hit. I think if I had run up the aisle I would have been a goner. I just lay very still and tried not to draw attention to myself. It was a nightmare scenario.'

Ferguson forged on down the aisle, mainly selecting whites for target practice. He seemed to be on another planet – he wasn't ranting or raving, just calmly gunning down complete strangers in cold blood. After pausing to reload, he was overpowered by three have-a-go heroes, Michael O'Connor, Mark McEntee and Kevin Blum. As they forced him down into a seat, Ferguson dropped his gun and muttered: 'Oh my God, what have I done, what have I done? Whatever happens, I deserve what I get. I deserve whatever I get.' Michael O'Connor recalled: 'He also said, "God will treat me well." It was all gibberish. He was a big guy and he could have put up far more of a struggle, but it was like he was glad in a way it was all over.' Ferguson's solo spree had succeeded in wounding 25 people, six fatally.

The trio held Ferguson until the police arrived. He was

arrested on the spot. At first, he refused to give the police any indication as to his motive. Their only clue came from a series of incomprehensible notes found on his person and at his home. In these, he cited white racism, which he claimed was rife in New York and, for good measure, he blamed 'the sloppy running of the no. 2 train'. It seemed an open and shut case. After all, he had been caught red-handed in front of numerous witnesses. He also confessed on tape to the police. His lawyers made no attempt to suggest that anybody else had pulled the trigger but instead came up with a bizarre defence of 'black rage' whereby they suggested that white racism had rendered Ferguson temporarily crazy. Psychiatric experts called in to assess his state of mind concluded that he was 'paranoid and delusional', seemingly a perfect basis for a plea of insanity. There was a distinct possibility that he would be declared unfit to stand trial.

However, Ferguson himself thought differently. He certainly didn't believe he was crazy and wanted to proceed with the trial so that he could draw the nation's attention to his plight. Twice he rejected a plea of insanity.

But his masterstroke was deciding that, despite the overwhelming evidence, he was not guilty after all. Upon reaching this conclusion, he sacked his lawyers, changed his plea to not guilty and announced that he would be conducting his own defence, almost unheard of in a major murder trial. To help him, his perplexed former defence team gave him a book, *Fundamentals of Trial Technique*, which enabled him to brush up on legal jargon, the presentation of a case and the art of cross-examination. While awaiting trial, Ferguson also read books in the prison library and watched old episodes of *Perry Mason*. He clearly hoped that Mason's invincibility would rub off.

Yet not even an inventive brain like Mason's could have conjured up the defence which Ferguson offered to the court.

Pursuing the claim that he was a victim of white racism, he acknowledged that while he owned the murder weapon, he had not pulled the trigger that evening. He said that the real Long Island Railroad killer was a mysterious white man who stole the gun which Ferguson was carrying at the time to a 'place of safety'. In his opening statement, Ferguson (who always referred to himself in the third person either as 'Mr Ferguson' or 'the defendant') told the court: 'The evidence will show that Colin Ferguson was in fact a well-meaning passenger. Like any other passenger, he dozed off. At that point someone took the weapon out of the bag and proceeded to shoot.'

His former lawyer Ronald Kuby was amazed by Ferguson's explanation of events. He told journalists: 'The reason we have a deranged man with a crazy defence representing himself in open court is that Ferguson and the prosecution want the same thing – a show trial. This is going to be six months of mental illness theatre.'

Ferguson wasted no time in proving them correct. He immediately objected to the jury because it contained whites and when Judge Donald Belfi refused to allow him to handle the pistol used in the killings, Ferguson demanded a retrial, insisting that the judge's decision 'sent a negative signal to the jury'. His reaction to being charged on 93 counts, ranging from murder to gun violations, was that the number of counts had been dictated solely by the year in which the crime had taken place. 'There are 93 counts only because it matches the year 1993,' he maintained. 'If it had been 1925, it would have been a 25-count indictment.' Prowling the courtroom like a seasoned campaigner and occasionally barking 'objection' at the most inappropriate moments, Ferguson went on to demand that President Clinton take the stand as he had heard that the President had commented on the case. When the request was refused, he turned to cross-examining the prosecution witnesses. This was when things really threatened to get out of hand.

He asked the first prosecution witness whether she had ever seen 'Mr Ferguson' before. 'Yes,' replied Maryanne Phillips who, a year after being shot in the chest, was wearing a cast and was due to undergo a third operation. 'I saw you shoot me.' Time and again, Ferguson's carefully constructed questions elicited the same response – answers which did little to help his case. Another witness, Robert Guigliano, who was shot several times in the course of the massacre, lunged towards Ferguson in court after describing how he had watched the death of a fellow passenger. 'This man is an animal,' screamed Guigliano. 'Just give me five minutes alone with him and I'll show him what pain is.' At this, the immaculately attired Ferguson straightened his tie uncomfortably.

Relatives of those killed also gave evidence. As the horrific details of the shootings were relayed to the court, many present were reduced to tears. Even Dennis Lemke, Ferguson's court-appointed lawyer, began to weep.

Ferguson was not impressed. 'I see you crying,' he snapped at Lemke.

'It has nothing to do with your guilt or innocence,' replied the lawyer. 'These people have suffered.'

As the trial drew to a close, Ferguson promised to produce a mystery witness who would apparently confirm his innocence. The mystery man never did take the stand but held a bizarre press conference outside the court at which he accused the CIA of planting a computer chip inside Ferguson's brain.

In a rambling, incoherent three-hour closing speech (during which survivors of the shootings and relatives of the victims stormed out of the court in a mass protest), Ferguson claimed to have been victimized by the media, the judge, the jury and American society. Having antagonized the jurors, he waited for their verdict. Not surprisingly, he was found guilty. Undaunted, he rose to his feet and declared himself to be a 'great man', comparable to John the Baptist. 'He was beheaded by a criminal justice system similar to this . . . as much as I am hated in Nassau County and America, I believe there are people who are strengthened by me and my stand.' At that point, Judge Belfi cut him off. He had heard enough.

The judge ordered Ferguson to serve six consecutive life terms of 25 years for each of the murders, as well as a minimum of eight and a third years on each of 19 counts of attempted murder, to run consecutively after the murder sentences. Judge Belfi said: 'You, Colin Ferguson, will never again return to society, but will rather spend the rest of your natural life in prison.'

Although sentenced to over 300 years in prison, Ferguson was not finished yet. Immediately after being convicted, he asked the lawyers whom he had previously sacked to launch an appeal. He instructed them to argue that he had never been mentally fit to stand trial and should not have been allowed to defend himself. For once, Colin Ferguson had got it right.

The O.J. Simpson Trial: A Bungled Prosecution?

It was the trial which gripped the United States. From the moment on 12 June 1994 when the butchered bodies of Nicole Brown Simpson and Ronald Goldman were found in the exclusive Los Angeles suburb of Brentwood, speculation was rife about the involvement of Nicole's former husband, legendary football star O.J. Simpson. Public opinion was split in two – those who couldn't believe that a sporting icon was capable of such an atrocity and those who studied the evidence and thought he was guilty as hell.

Over a period of ten months, nine national television stations covered the daily courtroom scenes at O.J.'s trial. CNN virtually transformed itself into the O.J. network and saw its ratings quadruple. Just as the cameras had been present five days after the killings to record the dramatic low-speed car chase along an Orange County freeway which led up to O.J.'s arrest, so they were present for the final act in this most public of trials, on 3 October 1995. The verdict, due at 10 a.m. Los Angeles time, brought the nation to a standstill. It was estimated that over 100 million people watched it live. In New York alone, it was to be screened live on no fewer than 21 channels with commercials running immediately before or after the big announcement selling at six times the standard rate. Restaurants on the East Coast ordered extra TV sets so that diners could tune in and even added special O.J. cocktails to their lunchtime menus. James Baker, former US Secretary of State, was forced to postpone a lunch to promote his new book following a stream of cancellations by journalists. And in the Oval Office, President Clinton interrupted his daily affairs to tune in to the verdict.

The jury of nine black, two white and one Hispanic had actually reached their verdict the previous afternoon following less than five hours' deliberation, but the speed of their decision-making had taken the court by surprise. So, in an act of suspense befitting events of the previous 12 months, Judge Lance Ito ruled that the envelope containing the verdict should remain closed until 10 a.m. the following morning to allow the major players on both sides to be present. When the envelope was finally opened, it revealed that O.J. Simpson had been found not guilty.

Simpson immediately broke into a triumphant grin, patted his heart and hugged his lawyer. He then mouthed a 'thank you' to the jurors, one of whom offered the Black Power salute in return. While O.J.'s mother, Eunice, leaned back in her wheelchair and raised her arms to the ceiling in jubilation,

Fred Goldman, Ronald Goldman's father, cried out: 'No, no, no! Murderer, murderer, murderer!'

While O.J. was shuffled home to Brentwood, his supporters celebrated and his son Jason read out a prepared statement in which O.J. vowed to catch the real killers. 'When things are settled a bit,' the statement went, 'I will pursue as my primary goal in life the killer or killers who slaughtered Nicole and Mr Goldman. They are out there somewhere. Whatever it takes to identify them and bring them in, I'll provide somehow. I can only hope that some day, despite every prejudicial thing that has been said about me publicly both in and out of the courtroom, people will come to understand and believe that I would not, could not, and did not kill anyone.'

As defence lawyer Johnnie Cochran proceeded to milk the occasion, the prosecution team were left to lick their wounds. Los Angeles Police Chief Willie Williams declared that he had no plans to reopen the case and Gil Garcetti, the city's District Attorney, affirmed that he still believed in the evidence against Simpson. Their dismay was understandable. At the outset of the trial, it had seemed an open and shut case. So where had it all gone wrong?

The O.J. Simpson trial was, of course, not just any trial. The defendant was a hero to millions, arguably the most famous and popular individual ever to have been charged with murder in the United States. Nicknamed 'Orange Juice' (from his initials) or simply 'The Juice', he was universally acknowledged as the finest running back in the history of American football. His charisma was such that his star continued in the ascendancy even after his playing career ended. He became a TV football commentator, sponsored athletic shoes and, inevitably, orange juice, and became the smiling face of the Hertz car rental commercials. He also turned his hand to acting, appearing in movies like *The Klansman* with Lee Marvin and Richard Burton, *Killer Force* with Telly Savalas,

The Towering Inferno with Paul Newman and Steve McQueen, and as the hapless Detective Nordberg in three of the *Naked Gun* films. That Simpson should play a bumbling cop was not without irony.

Not only was the defendant high-profile but he also carried the race card. It wasn't one which he himself particularly chose to play – his wife was white and he lived in a white district – but the case was seen in some quarters as a trial of the entire American judicial system with regard to justice for blacks. Views as to O.J.'s guilt were largely determined by skin colour. An ABC poll conducted shortly before the verdict showed that 77 per cent of whites thought that he was guilty while 72 per cent of blacks thought he was innocent. Against such a volatile background and faced with a predominantly black jury, the prosecution should have made doubly sure that its procedures were watertight and that there was no question of racial prejudice from any prosecution witnesses. That it failed to fulfil either of these criteria virtually guaranteed its downfall.

Nicole Brown was O.J. Simpson's second wife. He had divorced his first wife, Marguerite, in 1979 and married Nicole six years later. Up until their divorce on 15 October 1992, the charming O.J. and the beautiful Nicole were regarded as one of Los Angeles' most prominent celebrity couples, and even after the split they were frequently seen in public together, fuelling stories that a reconciliation was just around the corner.

But it was not to be. O.J. had a new girlfriend, Paula Barbieri, and a $2 million mock Tudor mansion on select Rockingham Avenue, Brentwood, where his neighbours included Meryl Streep. The house boasted a tennis court and swimming pool as well as a play area with swings and climbing frame for the visits of daughter Sydney and son Justin, his children by his marriage to Nicole. By June 1994, Nicole was living in a townhouse at 875 South Bundy Drive in Brentwood, some two miles from the home of her ex-husband. On the afternoon of Sunday, 12 June, Nicole bumped into O.J. at a school recital. According to witnesses, they sat together but there was a definite air of tension between the two. After the concert, O.J. asked to talk to her in private but she insisted that anything he had to say could be said in front of her parents who were also present. At that, he left. Nicole and her family moved on to one of her favourite haunts, the Mezzaluna restaurant on San Vincente Boulevard, where she had befriended one of the young waiters, Ronald Goldman, a former Armani model. Aware of the gossip, Goldman had always insisted to enquirers that he and Nicole were just friends. The dinner party finished around 8.30 p.m. 'Nicole was so happy that night,' her sister Denise said later, 'so vivacious, so full of life. She had just gotten it all together and it was so exciting. For the first time she was able to have her own friends. She had finally broken up with O.J. a week and a half before and was going to start her life over. She still loved O.J. She just could not live with him.'

About 9.15 p.m., Nicole telephoned the restaurant to say that her mother had lost her glasses. The owner said they had been found and that Ronald Goldman had offered to drop them off at her house when he finished his shift. Goldman duly left the restaurant at 9.50.

O.J. was due to fly to Chicago overnight to appear at a function sponsored by Hertz. A limousine arrived at his house at 10.25 p.m. to take him to the airport. The driver repeatedly rang the buzzer on the wrought-iron gates but received no reply. He waited and waited until, at 10.55, he said he saw a tall black man of Simpson's build entering the house. Then O.J. finally came on the intercom, said that he had been asleep and that he would be out in a moment. At 11.45, O.J. checked in for American Airlines flight 668 to Chicago. Some witnesses subsequently remarked that he looked agitated; others said he seemed perfectly normal. Conflicting testimony was to be a recurring theme of the O.J. Simpson case.

Meanwhile shortly after 11 p.m., a Brentwood resident found a white Akita dog wandering the street with blood-stained paws. The man had no idea that the dog was Nicole Brown's Kato and asked a neighbour, Sukru Boztepe, to look after it and take it to the dog pound the next morning. But the dog was so distressed that, shortly after midnight, Mr Boztepe and his wife decided to take it for a walk. Straining at the leash, the dog led them to 875 South Bundy Drive. There they discovered a scene of appalling carnage. Slumped against a tree on the tiled path by the gate lay the body of Ronald Goldman, the victim of a multiple stabbing. A trail of blood led inside the house to the body of Nicole, lying at the foot of the stairs with her throat sliced open. Both children were fast asleep, unharmed.

On hearing the news, O.J. returned from Chicago to Los Angeles. He was questioned by police for three hours but released without charge. Nevertheless the Los Angeles Police Department were certain they had got their man, particularly as a more violent side to O.J.'s personality began to emerge. Details were released of a late-night emergency call made by Nicole Brown Simpson on New Year's Day, 1989. Detective John Edwards had arrived to find Nicole, wearing only a bra and sweat pants, running out of the house, screaming: 'He's going to kill me. He's going to kill me.' Detective Edwards said he had asked: 'Who's going to kill you?' According to his later testimony, Nicole replied: 'O.J.' The detective also stated that Nicole had bruises on her throat and face and a split lip. Suddenly the clean-cut O.J. was being portrayed as a wife-beater.

A warrant was issued for his arrest but, in order to spare him the humiliation of handcuffs, police agreed to a request from his lawyer, Robert Shapiro, for Simpson to surrender himself at police headquarters at 11 a.m. on Friday, 17 June. O.J. failed to show. He had vanished without trace. At 1.50 p.m., the California Highway Patrol was obliged to issue an all-points bulletin: 'Suspect wanted for double homicide. Suspect Orenthal James Simpson. Suspect possibly armed, use caution.'

A worried Shapiro appealed to his client to surrender and revealed that O.J. had written three letters before his disappearance – one to his children, one to his mother, and one to the American people. When the contents of the third letter were released for general consumption, they read alarmingly like a suicide note.

The letter began: 'To whom it may concern. First, everyone understand I had nothing to do with Nicole's murder. I loved her, always have and always will. If we had a problem it's because I loved her so much. Recently we came to the understanding that for now we were not right for each other, at least for now. Despite our love we were different and that's why we mutually agreed to go our separate ways. It was tough splitting for the second time, but we both knew it was for the best. Inside, I had no doubt that in the future we would be close friends or more. Unlike what has been written in the press, Nicole and I had a great relationship for most of our lives together. Like all long-term relationships, we had a few ups and downs . . . As I leave, you'll be in my thoughts. I think of my life and feel I've done most of the right things, so why do I end up like this? I can't go on. No matter what the outcome, people will look and point. I can't take that. I can't subject my children to that. This way they can move on and go on with their lives. I've had a good life. I'm proud of how I lived. My mama taught me to do unto others – I treated people the way I wanted to be treated. I've always tried to be up and helpful. So why is this happening? I'm sorry for the Goldman family. I know how much it hurts . . . Don't feel sorry for me. I've had a great life, great friends. Please think of the real O.J. and not this lost person. Thanks for making my life special. I hope I helped yours. Peace and love, O.J.' Those who saw the letter said that he had drawn a happy face at the bottom just as he did when signing autographs.

At 5.56 p.m., as rumours circulated that O.J. had taken, or was about to take, his own life, he was spotted holding a gun to his head in a white Ford Bronco driven by his friend Al Cowlings. Wary of spooking O.J. still further, a cavalcade of police cars followed the Bronco along the freeway towards Los Angeles at a sedate 45 mph. For the next two hours, the events on the freeway were relayed to millions of homes in America by networks contemplating the very real possibility of a first prime-time, on-air celebrity suicide. NBC, which had paid a vast sum to cover that evening's national basketball final, relegated their coverage of the game to a small corner of the screen. At airports across the US, passengers chose to miss their planes rather than tear themselves away from the TV screens in the terminal. At 7.55 p.m., the Bronco turned off the freeway onto Sunset Boulevard and, a few minutes later, into the drive of O.J.'s house. Al Cowlings got out and was hustled away by police, but O.J. remained in the back seat with the revolver, refusing to move. After a tense hour-long dialogue with a police negotiator, Simpson surrendered quietly and emerged from the vehicle clutching two framed photographs of his family. He was then taken down to police headquarters where he was formally charged with the murders of Nicole Brown Simpson and Ronald Goldman. Appearing in court on 22 July, O.J. pleaded 'absolutely 100 per cent not guilty'.

The prosecution were supremely confident of a conviction, maintaining that the freeway pursuit was the action of a guilty man desperate to avoid capture. Simpson's expensively as-sembled lawyers – to be known thereafter as the 'dream team' – countered that O.J. had been driving to Nicole's grave where he had intended to commit suicide. The defence tried everything to bring the public around to their client's way of thinking, using the media to paint him in a sympathetic light while simultaneously complaining that excessive press coverage was endangering his right to a fair trial. They also offered a $500,000 reward for information about 'the real killer or killers', the implication being that there was no doubt as to O.J.'s innocence. At this stage, the prosecution certainly seemed to be holding all the aces, however. The forensic evidence against O.J. appeared damning. Blood had been found on the door handle of his Bronco and it was revealed that DNA tests showed that the defendant's blood had the same genetic make-up as samples from a trail of blood leading from the murder scene. But the first mistakes had already been made, notably a police search of Simpson's estate on the day after the killings. This had apparently unearthed a blood-stained glove, similar to one found at the scene of the crime. But the search had been made without a warrant. Such negligence would come back to haunt the Los Angeles Police Department and the prosecution.

Other difficulties were arising, caused by the huge amount of publicity devoted to the case. No sooner had O.J. been charged than two potentially key prosecution witnesses – Jill Shively, who claimed she saw Simpson speeding away from the scene of the crime, and knife salesman Jose Camacho, who claimed he sold a 15-inch German-made knife to Simpson some five weeks before the murders – seriously undermined their credibility by selling their stories to the tabloid press.

The trial of O.J. Simpson began in January 1995. It was originally to have been held in affluent Santa Monica but the prosecution agreed to a request to switch it to downtown Los Angeles. This was a grave mistake which immediately handed the initiative to the defence since the area was still scarred by the 1992 riots and its residents held a deep-seated resentment of the police. Thus downtown jurors were always more likely to view police testimony with suspicion, as the prosecution would find to their cost.

Assistant District Attorney Marcia Clark led the prosecution with Christopher Darden as her second-in-command. In his opening statement, Darden stated that O.J. had murdered Nicole 'for a single reason – a reason almost as old as mankind himself. He killed her out of jealousy. He killed her because he could not have her, and if he could not have her, he did not want anyone else to have her.' Darden added that O.J. had a sinister private face, 'the one Nicole Brown encountered almost every day of her adult life and the last day of her adult life. This was the face of a batterer, a wife-beater, an abuser, a controller.' Only hours before the murders, O.J. was said to have been angry with Nicole because she would not allow him to see their daughter. The motive was there.

To emphasize O.J.'s supposed dual personality, the jury heard a recording of a second emergency call made by Nicole to the police in October 1993. Nicole was heard to say: 'He's ranting and raving . . . he's crazy.' In a further call, made minutes later, clearly terrified, she told the police inspector: 'He's back . . . he's O.J. Simpson. I think you know his record.' She was then heard telling the operator that O.J. had 'broken the back door in, then he left, but he came back'.

Even with no murder weapon and no witnesses to the killings, the prosecution seemed to have a strong case. They spoke of Simpson's 'window of opportunity', a period of time during which he had no alibi and, they claimed, could have committed the murders. Time of death was estimated at 10.15 p.m. when Nicole's neighbour heard a plaintive howling from her dog. According to the prosecution, O.J. was last seen before the murders at 9.36 p.m. when he returned to the front gate of his house from a visit to McDonald's with his guest, Kato Kaelin, a bit-part actor and family friend after whom

Nicole had named her dog. Simpson reappeared at the front door at 10.54 p.m. to take a limousine to the airport but his movements between the two times were unexplained. Shortly after 10.40 p.m., Kaelin reported hearing three loud thumps outside his bungalow on the edge of O.J.'s compound. Seconds later, limousine driver Allan Park saw a tall black male wearing dark clothes and a woollen cap enter the main house and turn on the lights. The driver had been repeatedly ringing O.J.'s doorbell, but the next time he tried, O.J. answered.

It was behind Kaelin's bungalow that, the morning after the murders, LAPD detective Mark Fuhrman claimed to have found the bloody glove which matched the one taken from the murder scene, still sticky with both victims' blood and later linked to O.J. by one of his own hairs. Fibres from O.J.'s hair were also said to have been found on Ronald Goldman's shirt at 875 South Bundy Drive. In addition, the police said that they had discovered bloodstains on the driveway of O.J.'s mansion, part of a so-called 'trail of blood' leading from Nicole's house to her ex-husband's nearby home and vehicle. DNA analysis of blood found on Nicole's back gate, on O.J.'s car and on a pair of socks found in his bedroom was said to incriminate him with odds of more than a billion to one. Small wonder that Marcia Clark described the DNA tests as 'devastating proof of the defendant's guilt'.

And what did the defence have to offer? O.J.'s original claim that he had been asleep at the time of the murders was now replaced by a different version of events. According to Johnnie Cochran, O.J. had been practising his golf swing, knocking balls into the children's sandbox in the front garden. Cochran produced a potential alibi witness, Rosa Lopez, a neighbour's housekeeper, who said she had seen O.J.'s car outside his house at the time of the murders. But her evidence, which was not given before the jury, was pulled apart under cross-examination and she was forced to admit that she could not be sure of the precise time she had seen the Bronco.

In an attempt to suggest that the victims had been slain by an unknown gang, the defence called another witness, Mary Anne Gershas, who said she saw four men running from Nicole's house on the night of the killings. However Marcia Clark revealed Gershas to be an obsessive Simpson fan who had told a friend that she was nowhere near the building at the time. So she too was discredited. Another critical blow to the gang theory was that the police insisted that they found only one set of footprints at the murder scene.

The defence also tried to claim that O.J. would not have been physically capable of carrying out the killings. Ronald Goldman was a fit young man who put up a terrific struggle and O.J.'s football career had left him with scars on his knees, swollen legs and arthritic hands. But Marcia Clark came up with an exercise video which showed that O.J. was anything but frail.

Therefore, despite the fact that photographs of O.J.'s body, taken three days after the murders, showed no marks consistent with a struggle and that there was no sign of the killer's heavily blood-stained clothes, things still looked grim for the defence, all the more so when Denise Brown testified how O.J. had humiliated her sister and had once hurled her against a wall.

There appeared to be just one minor hurdle for the prosecution to negotiate – the evidence of Detective Mark Fuhrman, the man who said he had found the incriminating glove. But Fuhrman had a somewhat tarnished reputation. He had already committed the grave error of conducting his search of O.J.'s property without the necessary authorization and there were also widespread allegations that he was a racist. An internal police psychiatric report had hinted at his leanings as had, more forcibly, an article in the *New Yorker* in 1994. Given this knowledge and the fact that they were trying to convince a largely black jury, the prosecution should have avoided Fuhrman like the plague and concentrated on the other, equally compelling, evidence, but instead they decided to stand by their man. At first, it seemed that Fuhrman and the prosecution would get away with it. When he took the stand in March 1995, he withstood everything that the defence could throw at him and swore under oath that he had not used a racial slur in the past ten years. His words were to become the defence team's major weapon.

But cracks were starting to appear in the police evidence in general, notably the DNA, upon which so much store had been placed. In a devastating eight-day cross-examination of police criminologist Dennis Fung, DNA expert Barry Scheck tore much of the DNA evidence to shreds. It emerged that the police scientist sent to collect the crucial blood samples was a mere trainee and that a detective had been allowed to carry around a vial of O.J.'s own blood for a whole day before handing it over as an exhibit. What should have been the prosecution's strong point suddenly became a weak link amid accusations that bungling police technicians handled blood samples with such a degree of incompetence as to render the delivery of accurate and reliable DNA results almost impossible. If nothing else, the appalling inefficiency of the police, both at the scene of the crime and in forensic laboratories, certainly gave grounds for reasonable doubt. And with a jury distrustful of the police in the first place, that was all that was needed.

As the prosecution case threatened to fall apart before their very eyes, they decided to play their trump card – the glove. Nicole Brown had bought a pair of expensive, highly distinctive gloves for O.J. at Bloomingdale's department store in New York. The prosecution had the receipt and two bloodstained gloves. With supreme confidence, Christopher Darden invited O.J. to try them on in court. But as O.J. struggled and strained to slide his hands into the gloves in full view of the jury, mouthing 'they don't fit', it dawned on Darden that he had scored a spectacular own goal.

Just when the prosecution probably thought things couldn't get any worse, they did. A Los Angeles private detective by the name of Pat McKenna had been following up leads for the defence team and, one afternoon in July, he received a call from a confidential source who claimed that a woman called Laura had some tapes of Detective Fuhrman which might be of considerable interest. McKenna was put in touch with Laura McKinny, a North Carolina-based screenwriter who was trying to make a documentary film about the LAPD. At first, she was reluctant to hand over the tapes but O.J.'s lawyers took her to court and won access to them. On 5 September, the jury heard excerpts from the tapes which revealed Fuhrman as a committed racist. Despite his previous testimony under oath, he was heard to use the word 'nigger' 41 times. The jury also listened to him boast that, in his days as a patrol officer, he would routinely invent charges against black motorists and mixed-race couples. He went on: 'If you put a bruise on a nigger, it's pretty tough to see. I used to go to work and practice. Niggers, they're easy to practice my kicks . . . The only good nigger is a dead nigger.'

Robert Tourtelot, a lawyer who had stoutly defended Fuhrman on TV against allegations of racism, now promptly and publicly disowned him, saying that he was 'profoundly disgusted' by the tapes.

The next day, Fuhrman was recalled to the stand, branded a racist and a liar. Defence lawyer Gerald Uelman asked: 'Did you plant or manufacture anything in this case?' The disgraced Fuhrman answered: 'I wish to assert my Fifth Amendment privilege', thereby invoking his constitutional right to avoid incriminating himself. He went on to give the same replies to questions regarding whether his earlier testimony had been truthful and whether he had ever falsified a police report. With those three answers, Detective Mark Fuhrman had effectively wrecked the case for the prosecution. The open and shut case had been slammed in their faces.

Desperately trying to cling to the gloves, the prosecution asserted that the reason they did not appear to fit was that they had shrunk after having been soaked in blood. Glove designer Richard Rubin was called to give evidence and testified that the gloves, identified as Aris Lights, a brand produced exclusively for Bloomingdale's, were of the same design as those worn by O.J. as a television commentator at football games.

As the chances of convicting Simpson of first-degree murder receded, the prosecution asked the judge to make a second-degree murder instruction to the jury. However, the defence vigorously opposed such a move, knowing full well that the prosecution blunders meant that it was unlikely that O.J. would be found guilty of first-degree murder, thus leaving the only other option as a 'not guilty' verdict. But the judge told jurors that they could consider a verdict of second-degree murder, noting that while evidence had been presented to support the premeditation required for a verdict of first-degree in the killing of Nicole Brown, there was no evidence of premeditation in the stabbing of Ronald Goldman who had simply been 'in the wrong place at the wrong time'.

Marcia Clark's closing speech lasted for eight hours. With each phase of her argument, she added a piece to a jigsaw puzzle of O.J.'s face taking shape on an overhead projector. She conceded that Fuhrman was racist but told the jury that 'it would be a tragedy if, with such overwhelming evidence as we have presented to you, you found the defendant not guilty in spite of all that, because of the racist attitude of one officer.'

Christopher Darden, roundly criticized for the blunder of allowing O.J. to demonstrate that the glove did not fit, tried to redeem himself with a stirring closing speech in which he pinpointed 'pathological jealousy' as O.J.'s motive. He claimed that 'the fuse was burning' throughout their marriage and that O.J. had stalked Nicole after their divorce. Darden reminded jurors of a safe deposit box in which Nicole had left photographs of the wounds allegedly inflicted on her by O.J., along with a will. 'She's leaving you a road map,' said Darden, 'to let you know who it is who's going to kill her.'

Adopting the style of a manic street preacher, O.J.'s black lawyer, Johnnie Cochran, did not pass up the opportunity to play to the fears of the nine black jurors. With fiery rhetoric, he put Fuhrman on a par with Hitler – a move which angered American Jews – and spoke of the 'conspiracy, contamination and corruption' in the LAPD. 'You have heard lie after lie', he yelled at the jury. 'Stop this cover-up!' He told the jury that they were a bulwark against racism throughout the United States and, reminding them of the glove episode – as if they needed reminding – he repeated over and over: 'If it doesn't fit, you must acquit.' It is not often that a murder trial spawns a catchphrase.

The 'not guilty' verdict infuriated many in the white community who saw the acquittal as proof that black jurors were not prepared to convict a fellow black despite a mountain of evidence, the fact that Simpson had no convincing alibi and had also declined to give evidence in his own defence, thus rendering him safe from cross-examination. The view was that the jury had ended up trying the Los Angeles Police Department on a charge of racism instead of O.J. Simpson on a charge of murder.

As the publishing world went into overdrive – including a book from an author who claimed to have made telepathic contact with Nicole Brown's dog – Simpson repeated his denial of murder. He did, however, confirm that he was the 'shadowy figure' seen by limousine driver Allan Park on the fateful night, adding that he had walked some five yards from his front door to deposit his bags in readiness for being picked up for the drive to the airport.

In his own book, *Murder In Brentwood*, the disgraced Detective Mark Fuhrman was highly critical of the handling of the case, both by the police and the prosecution. In particular, he blamed senior detectives for crucial mistakes made in the first 14 hours of the investigation. Fuhrman said that he and his partner, Brad Roberts, while searching O.J.'s home, found a pair of socks on the floor of his bedroom. These socks later turned out to contain blood from both O.J. and Nicole. Yet the socks did not feature on the police videotape shot to show the state of the house and so the defence were able to question whether they had been planted. Even when it was proved that the video had been shot after the socks had been removed, the doubt still remained in the minds of the jury. Unaccountably, Detective Roberts was never called by the prosecution to back up Fuhrman's story.

Fuhrman also criticized the handling of the blood evidence on the Bronco. Fuhrman wanted the Bronco impounded but Detective Philip Vannatter rejected the request and decided that the car should stay in the street, guarded by just two officers. With sightseers swarming all over the place, this was woefully inadequate and led to allegations of evidence contamination. And when the Bronco was finally impounded, security was so lax that an employee at the car pound was able to sneak inside the vehicle to take a receipt from the glove-box as a souvenir. Again, the defence was able to claim that the evidence on the Bronco was contaminated. Fuhrman said that Vannatter blundered once more by ordering Nicole's body to be covered by a blanket from her house. The defence was able to turn this to its advantage with yet another claim of crime scene contamination.

But, according to Fuhrman, the biggest blunder of all

surrounded a bloody fingerprint on the gate at Nicole's house, the discovery of which he had written up in his notes. He maintained that Detective Tom Lange ordered criminologist Dennis Fung to test and recover the blood on the back gate on 13 June but failed to confirm that Fung had actually done so. As a result, the blood was not recovered for another three weeks and the actual print was never photographed or lifted. Fuhrman wrote: 'Had the bloody fingerprint been properly handled and analysed, it alone could have put the case away. But there was only superficial mention of the fingerprint at the trial. What happened to this crucial piece of evidence? Somehow, the fingerprint was lost, and so, eventually, was the case.'

Of course, to point the finger at other officers for losing the case is to play down Mark Fuhrman's own role in snatching defeat from the jaws of victory.

Undeterred by the prosecution's inability to secure a conviction for a crime for which there was no other suspect, the families of Ronald Goldman and Nicole Brown filed civil lawsuits against Simpson. In February 1997, a civil court jury found Simpson liable for the death of Ronald Goldman and for battery against Nicole Brown. The ruling effectively found him liable for Nicole's death too, although the Brown family had not been seeking such a verdict. Simpson was ordered to pay the families of the survivors $33.5 million. The civil court may not have been empowered to take away O.J. Simpson's freedom but the ongoing interest in the case ensures that he will never be truly free again.

Courtroom Capers

After defendant Bill Witten had sworn at him for refusing to reduce his bail on a charge of grand larceny, Judge Joseph Troisi of St Mary's, West Virginia, took off his robes, stepped down from the bench and bit him on the nose. Judge Troisi resigned from the bench shortly after the 1997 incident. He was said to have had a history of courtroom outbursts.

*

A juror at Newcastle upon Tyne Crown Court was barred from the July 1998 trial of a man charged with grievous bodily harm after requesting the defendant's star sign in order that he could reach a verdict. The pony-tailed man in his twenties scribbled a note to the judge asking for the accused's exact time and date of birth so that he could draw up an astrological chart to see what it foretold. But after consulting with barristers, Judge Esmond Faulks discharged the juror on the grounds that consulting such a chart fell outside the terms of his oath to consider only the facts before the court. The juror had said he needed the information because he was unable to come to a decision without drawing up a chart and was puzzled as to why the judge frowned upon this. The deputy court manager explained later: 'Jurors are told not to allow themselves to be swayed by any outside influences. Obviously the judge took the view that this man was capable of being so influenced.'

*

The jury at a trial at Lewes Crown Court, East Sussex, had been considering its verdict for four hours when the judge was told: 'The foreman had handcuffed himself.' The month-long trial in January 1998 was of four men accused of planning a jewel robbery. After hearing that the gang planned to use a pair of handcuffs on a Brighton shop assistant before raiding the safe, the foreman of the jury – a middle-aged man – decided to experiment with the evidence while deliberating a verdict. Unfortunately he got his hand stuck and there was no key to free him. Judge Simon Coltart quickly sent for the fire brigade but then he remembered that the law prevented firefighters from entering the jury room or speaking to jurors.

The matter was further complicated when the fire officer in charge of the rescue operation realized that his sister-in-law was on the jury. As the red-faced foreman sat in pain and firefighters waited outside the court for orders, legal minds wrestled with the tricky issues raised. Finally, barristers agreed that the courtroom should be cleared. All 12 jurors then trooped back into the jury box and the trapped foreman was freed with bolt-cutters. The judge admitted: 'Perhaps I should have warned the jury not to experiment with the handcuffs.'

*

A hearing at Guildford Crown Court in 1997 had to be stopped in the afternoon because both the prosecution and defence counsel fell ill after eating curry in the court canteen at lunchtime.

*

In April 1992, a bench of magistrates dismissed themselves from a public order trial after the barrister for the defence claimed that two of them had fallen asleep during proceedings – one in the morning and afternoon and the other just in the afternoon. Presiding magistrate David Boswell and his colleagues, Pamela Kings and Terence Dunn, duly stepped down. The clerk to the justices at Hull magistrates' court denied that they had dozed off but said that they had agreed to a retrial because 'justice had to be seen to be done'.

*

A 1978 murder trial in Manitoba had been under way for two days when one juror confessed that he was completely deaf and didn't have the faintest idea what was going on. The judge, Mr Justice Solomon, asked him whether he had heard any evidence at all and, when there was no reply, dismissed him. Then a second juror, a fluent French speaker, revealed that he didn't understand a word of English and expressed great surprise that he was attending a murder trial. Proceedings were finally abandoned when a third juror said that he too spoke no English and, for good measure, was almost as deaf as the first juror. The judge ordered a retrial.

*

In March 1995, Judge Bentley was forced to make a formal apology in open court after saying that a defendant did not 'need to stoop so low' as to employ the services of a solicitor-advocate rather than a barrister. He made the apology at Sheffield Crown Court following a complaint from solicitor-advocates.

*

In October 1992, Judge Lee outraged women everywhere by his comments at the end of a robbery case at Hereford Crown Court. The 65-year-old judge told the defendant, who had held up a solicitor's office because he wanted to be arrested to escape troubles with his girlfriend, that it was a woman's 'function in life' to upset men.

*

Judge Charles Guyer was sacked from the Pennsylvania bench in 1992 after a hidden video camera recorded him offering convicted men lighter sentences if they allowed him to shampoo their hair.

*

A pregnant woman juror at Exeter Crown Court in Devon was discharged by the judge after taking a call from her mother on her mobile phone while trying to reach a verdict. Deliberating the January 1999 case of four defendants accused of ill-treating residents at care homes, the jury had sent a question to Judge Graham Neville but when the bailiff returned to the jurors' room with the answer, he heard the mobile phone ring. The judge called the jurors back into court and told them: 'I have heard one of your number has a mobile phone. It is not permitted because the jury has to be completely sacrosanct.' After discharging the woman, he added:

'We do not know what to do about mobiles. You are told not to use them. They are everywhere.'

*

Back in the 1820s at the Old Bailey, Mr Justice Graham, a man with a reputation for courtesy, read out a list of 16 names of people to be executed. When informed that he had missed out the name of John Robins, the judge could not apologize enough. 'Oh, bring John Robins back,' he said, 'by all means let John Robins step forward. I am obliged to you, John Robins. I find I have accidentally omitted your name in my list of prisoners doomed to execution. It was quite accidental, I assure you, and I ask your pardon for my mistake. I am very sorry, and can only add that you will be hanged with the rest.'

*

Two English solicitors hit the headlines for the wrong reasons in 1996. One was convicted of assault and the false imprisonment of a client's wife following a dispute about his bill and the other was convicted of assaulting his clerk for failing to photocopy court papers.

*

In July 1993, a lawyer for death row prisoner Robert Drew, convicted of stabbing a teenager in Houston, Texas, complained after a judge had signed his client's execution order with a little 'happy face'. District Judge Charles Hearn said: 'It's just become part of my signature.'

*

At Luton Crown Court in 1997, Judge Alan Wilkie, QC, had to order a retrial for a man accused of supplying crack cocaine because juror Shane Smyth had shouted at the defendant: 'Why don't you plead guilty? You are f— guilty.'

*

An attorney in Burbank, California, representing a man charged with flying an aeroplane while intoxicated, was himself admonished by a Ventura County judge for being drunk in court. The attorney, 64-year-old Elmer O. Docken, arrived in the courtroom of Municipal Judge Lee Cooper Jr. in April 1987 over two hours late for the trial of a client charged with flying a private plane from Pacoima to Oxnard while under the influence of alcohol. Docken, who was wearing a crumpled suit, slurred a few words whereupon the judge ordered him to take a breath test. When he was found to be over the limit, he was told that he was in no fit state to represent his client. An hour later, Docken was arrested on suspicion of drunk driving.

*

An Old Bailey judge was forced to order a retrial when two jurors nearly came to blows after one had accused the other of burgling his flat. The row had been simmering from the very start of a burglary trial in November 1993 when, during a break for legal submissions, one juror accused the other of smoking in a 'no smoking' area. Two days later, the accuser arrived at court in a foul mood because his home had been burgled. He immediately blamed the other juror, calling him a 'swine' and claiming that he had taken his name and address from a label on his rucksack. As tempers threatened to boil over, the two jurors were paid off. A court official said: 'The man had a cast-iron alibi and was obviously being picked on as a scapegoat. There was no way the pair could be left to reach a verdict when there was such bad feeling between them.' The dispute cost £45,000 in wasted court time.

*

Italian lawyers were left with egg on their face when they invited newsmen to see the Italian legal system in action. The scribes discovered vital documents relating to forthcoming trials stacked in the public toilets at Rome law courts.

*

In October 1992, a murder trial was halted and a retrial ordered after a juror talked about the case at a Law Society ball. Linda Kelly, accused of killing her husband Mick at their home in Cramlington, Northumberland, was freed on bail after the jury at Quayside Crown Court, Newcastle upon Tyne, had retired to consider its verdict. Martin Bethell, QC, for the defence, told a reconvened hearing that the juror had spoken about the case to a barrister at a ball in Sunderland. The cost of the abortive 11-day trial was estimated at £100,000.

*

In April 1994, Judge Graham Hume Jones discharged the jury and ordered the retrial of a fraud case at Exeter Crown Court after two jurors complained that one of their colleagues was infested with fleas.

*

In 1985, one Dennis Newton stood trial for armed robbery in Oklahoma City. In court, the District Attorney asked the supervisor of the store that had been robbed to identify the culprit. When she pointed to the defendant, Newton leapt to his feet, accused the witness of lying and screamed: 'I should have blown your f— head off!' Following a moment of stunned silence, he added as an afterthought: 'If I'd been the one that was there.' Newton was jailed for 30 years.

*

A defendant at Cardiff Crown Court was mistakenly sentenced to two years in prison in April 1999, all because a juror happened to cough at an inopportune moment. Unable to stifle a tickle at the back of his throat any longer, the juror coughed just as the foreman was announcing a verdict of 'not guilty' . . . With the result that the noise drowned out the word 'not'. Judge Michael Gibbon, thinking that the defendant Alan Rashid had been found guilty on the charge of making a threat to kill, promptly jailed him for two years, thanked the jurors for their efforts during the two-day trial and released them. The puzzled jurors assumed that Mr

Rashid was being sentenced for other offences of which they were unaware until on the way out of the building, one juror asked an usher why Mr Rashid had been sent down after being found not guilty. The official realized there had been a blunder and called everyone back into the court. A confused Mr Rashid, who, minutes earlier was being consoled in the cells, was led back to the dock and told by the judge that he was free to go after all. His lawyer, Penri Desscan, said: 'It was pretty bizarre. One moment my client was facing two years' imprisonment, the next he was going home on the bus.'

The Hall–Mills Case: Willie Stevens Stands Firm

On the morning of 16 September 1922, a young couple walking in secluded De Russey's Lane on the outskirts of New Brunswick, New Jersey, stumbled across the bodies of a man and a woman lying on their backs under a crab-apple tree with their arms outstretched. Resting against one of the man's shoes was a card bearing his name. He was the Revd Edward Wheeler Hall, rector of St John's Episcopal Church, and he had been shot through the head with a single bullet. His companion, Mrs Eleanor Mills, wife of the sexton of that church, had been shot three times in the head and her throat had been cut.

Scattered in the lane were several cartridge shells from an automatic pistol and a collection of letters written by Mrs Mills to the minister. The nature of the correspondence told the police what most of the neighbourhood knew anyway: that the relationship between the man of the cloth and the woman who sang in his choir was physical as well as spiritual. The only people in the district who seemed unconcerned about the liaison were the respective spouses.

A number of people came forward as witnesses, notably a

local widow, Jane Gibson, who raised hogs and subsequently achieved fame at the trial as the 'pig woman'. She recounted how, at around nine o'clock on the night of 14 September, she had heard a wagon pass near her farm. Fearing the return of thieves who had been stealing her corn, she saddled her mule, Jenny, and set off in steady pursuit. Reaching De Russey's Lane, she saw four shadowy figures partly illuminated by the headlights of a car. Tying her mule to a tree, she heard raised voices, a mention of letters and then saw something glittering in one of the men's hands. The next thing she knew there was a shot, followed by three more shots and a woman moaning, 'Oh, Henry!'. At that, the pig woman rode home as fast as her mule would take her. But she had seen enough and identified three of the people in the lane as Mrs Hall and two of her brothers, Willie and Henry Stevens.

All three suspects were questioned at length but the investigation, according to one lawyer, had been an exercise in 'bungling stupidity'. The pig woman's testimony failed to convince the Grand Jury and as a result nobody was indicted.

And that was how it stayed for four years, by which time everyone outside New Brunswick had forgotten all about the affair. Then Louise Geist, who had worked as a maid in the Hall household at the time of the murders, issued an inflammatory statement. She said that she had been a confidante of the minister and claimed to know that he had intended to elope with Mrs Mills. As a result of her information, Governor Moore of New Jersey appointed Alexander Simpson as special prosecutor with orders to reopen the case. Soon Mrs Hall and the Stevens brothers were charged with murder.

The three stood trial at Somerville, New Jersey, in November 1926 and the proceedings rapidly developed into a head-to-head between Alexander Simpson and Willie Stevens. Simpson was an articulate, slightly built lawyer with a razor-sharp mind and a tongue to match. Willie Stevens was an ungainly 54-year-old with a heavy drooping moustache and a child-like mentality. He was known in some quarters as 'Crazy Willie', something of the town buffoon, the butt of all jokes. It seemed to be a no-contest. The press predicted that Stevens would 'blow up' on the stand, that he would be trapped into contradictions by the wily, resourceful Simpson and would ultimately be tricked into blurting out his guilt. In turn, Simpson, with his love of sarcasm and innuendo, was supremely confident that he would 'tie Willie Stevens into knots'. The outcome appeared a foregone conclusion.

Perhaps Simpson should have heeded the testimony of Dr Laurence Runyon. Called by the defence to denounce a prosecution witness's claim that Willie Stevens was a stuttering epileptic, the doctor said: 'He may not be absolutely normal mentally, but he is able to take care of himself perfectly well. He is brighter than the average person, although he has never advanced as far in school learning as some others. He reads books that are above the average and makes a good many people look like fools.' Alexander Simpson would soon be added to that list.

For the first 16 days of the trial, Willie Stevens sat impassively in the dock. When it was finally his turn to take the stand, there was a hush of expectancy around the courtroom in anticipation of the forthcoming confrontation. Stevens remained calm and composed as his own lawyer, Clarence E. Case, took him through his movements on the night of the murder, 14 September 1922. His testimony was precise down to the most minute detail. He explained quietly that he had come home for supper that night and had remained in his room until 2.30 in the morning when his sister had woken him up by banging on his bedroom door. She was worried that her husband, Edward, had not returned home. Stevens said he got dressed and joined his sister in a search of the neighbourhood. They started at the church and moved on to the Mills's house but, seeing no lights on there, they reluctantly abandoned the hunt and went back home. He went through every street name meticulously, concluding with how he opened the front door of his own house. He even offered to show the court the latchkey.

Now it was Simpson's turn to question the witness. Although renowned for his intimidating tactics, Simpson decided to opt for the softly-softly approach. He obviously thought there was more to be gained by appearing to be Willie Stevens's friend than by antagonizing him. In the belief that Stevens was slow on the uptake, Simpson thought he could lull him into a false sense of security and then pounce. His first question was a gentle loosener, but one calculated to undermine the witness's standing. However, in asking it, Simpson committed the lawyers' cardinal sin of asking a question to which he didn't know the answer. 'Have you ever earned your livelihood?' queried Simpson, certain that the reply would be in the negative. 'For about four or five years,' said Stevens, 'I was employed by Mr Siebold, a contractor.' Simpson was immediately thrown, all the more so when Stevens asked politely: 'Do you wish his address?' This elicited a huge roar of laughter from the spectators since Simpson was known for despatching teams of investigators to seek out anybody whose name was mentioned in connection with the case. Unwittingly, Stevens had drawn first blood.

Disarmed by Stevens's ready smile and by the fact that the gallery was clearly on the defendant's side, Simpson tried to impose his authority by demanding to know why, during their search of the locality, Stevens and his sister had not knocked on the door of the Mills house to see if Edward Hall was there. But in asking the question, Simpson mispronounced the name of a local boarding house. Stevens was quick to correct him. More laughter. Simpson then made the mistake of referring to the deceased as Dr Hall. Once again Stevens, courteously but firmly, pointed out the error. 'I am glad you corrected me on that,' said Simpson through gritted teeth.

Simpson was in danger of losing the psychological war altogether so he made another desperate attempt to shake Willie Stevens's testimony. Certain that the only way Stevens had been able to recall the exact details of the night-time search from over four years ago had been to learn them parrot-fashion, Simpson asked him to run through his movements one more time. He was expecting Stevens to repeat his testimony word for word but, to the prosecutor's intense frustration, while the meaning was identical, no sentence was the same as it had been first time round. Seething with barely concealed indignation, Simpson asked him to repeat it for a third time. The defence objected, but Stevens interrupted: 'May I say a word? All I have to say is I was never taught, as you insinuate, by any person whatsoever. That is my best recollection from the time I started out with my sister to this present minute.' Simpson realized there was no point in pressing the matter further.

Instead he wanted to know how Stevens could prove that he was in his room between 9 p.m. and 2.30 a.m. on the night of the murder. 'Why,' replied Stevens logically, 'if a person sees me go upstairs and does not see me come downstairs, isn't that a conclusion that I was in my room?' 'Absolutely', conceded Simpson. 'Well,' continued Stevens, 'that is all there was to it.'

Indeed it was. One of the servants had testified that she had seen Willie Stevens' door closed at around 10 p.m. (his door would only stay closed if he locked it) and Louise Geist had stated that she had not seen him that night after dinner. The one person who claimed to have seen him after he went up to his room was Jane Gibson, the pig woman. It was her word against his, and Willie Stevens had proved a far more impressive witness.

Alexander Simpson knew that he had failed miserably in his

quest to destroy Stevens's testimony. On the contrary, it was the prosecutor who was left feeling humiliated as the newspapers trumpeted Stevens's performance in the witness box. Simpson had gravely underestimated him. With Stevens refusing to cave in, it was inevitable that the jury would return a 'not guilty' verdict against all three defendants. The real killers of Revd Hall and Mrs Mills were never caught.

Dr. Robert Buchanan: The Witness Who Talked Too Much

Robert Buchanan has gone down in criminal history as one of the most notorious poisoners of the nineteenth century. Yet in all probability he would have got away with his crime had he not insisted, against the advice of his counsel, on giving evidence at his trial. And once in the witness box, he talked so freely, without any apparent thought as to the consequences of his words, that he sealed his own fate without too much help from the prosecution.

Scotland was a veritable breeding-ground for Victorian poisoners and some of the most dastardly – men such as Edward Pritchard and Neill Cream – were members of the medical profession. To this list can be added Robert Buchanan.

Although born in Scotland – in 1862 – Buchanan emigrated with his parents to Nova Scotia and landed a job as a clerk at a drugstore in Halifax. The desire to study medicine had obviously been in his blood from an early age for he then went to Chicago and graduated from the city's College of Physicians and Surgeons in 1883. From Chicago, he retraced his steps – first to Halifax where he just about had time to set up in practice and to marry Annie Bryce Patterson, and then back across the Atlantic to his homeland and a further year of study in Edinburgh. In 1886, he abandoned Scotland for the second time and decided to seek fame and fortune in New York.

That Buchanan should be lured by the bright lights of the big city was entirely in keeping with his personality. For although the bespectacled little medic looked every inch the meek and mild practitioner, he was in fact an inveterate womanizer. He lived a double life, running a successful practice by day and then frequenting clubs and brothels by night, frequently in the company of his close friends, tavern proprietor Richard Macomber and retired British army captain William Doria. One of their favourite haunts was a house of ill repute run by Anna Sutherland on Halsey Street, Newark, New Jersey. It was a train and ferry ride for the intrepid trio but they reckoned it was worth it to sample the pleasures of Mrs Sutherland's ever-willing girls.

Anna Sutherland was some 20 years older than Buchanan. Her hair was dyed a fiery orange and, by all accounts, the end of her nose was adorned by a prominent wart. It is fair to say that she stood out in a crowd. Brothel-keeping had proved a lucrative business for her and the healthy state of her bank account greatly endeared her to Buchanan who was constantly on the lookout for ways of bettering himself, financially if not morally. He worked his way into her affections by tenderly treating her for a kidney complaint and soon she had kicked out her lover of 14 years, odd job man James Smith, and replaced him with the young doctor. Smith was none too happy about the turn of events.

Buchanan wasted no time to getting his claws into Mrs Sutherland's money and Macomber was summoned to witness a change to her will in which she left virtually everything to her new love. The one condition was that they were to be married and so on 12 November 1890, Buchanan obtained a divorce from the long-suffering Annie, although the fact that it was on the grounds of her adultery suggests that maybe she had been playing him at his own game. Two weeks later, Dr Buchanan and Mrs Sutherland were married in Newark. The bride not only forked out the $1000 in legal fees required to rush through the divorce but also coughed up $9500 dollars to buy a house at 267 West Eleventh Street (in today's Greenwich Village). The deeds of the house were in Buchanan's name. He not only ran his practice from there but he also lived there with his mother and young daughter.

It seemed that the smooth-talking doctor with the impeccable bedside manner had landed on his feet – a position to which his new bride was distinctly unaccustomed. But once she moved into the house, things started to turn sour. Buchanan had always been at pains to keep his two lifestyles separate but now he found them overlapping uncomfortably. As a police surgeon and newly appointed Lunacy Commissioner, he had a certain standing in the community but this was regularly undermined by his new wife who, in her role as his receptionist, quickly managed to alienate most of his patients by her coarseness and vulgarity. She may have been ideally suited to running a brothel but lacked the social graces necessary for a doctor's receptionist. Buchanan's patients let it be known that if things did not improve, they would transfer to another practice. Suddenly his livelihood and reputation were at stake. Something would have to be done.

Buchanan then acquired an 18-year-old mistress and began staying out all hours. He started referring to his wife as 'an old hag' and generally treated her badly. He didn't want a divorce because she would surely change her will but since, as he told his friend Macomber, she had the symptoms of Bright's disease, he calculated that she would probably be dead in six months anyway. And then he would be free and rich. Just a year after the exchange of marriage vows, he was telling Macomber of his plans to rent the practice to another doctor and to return to Edinburgh to pursue his studies. But the scheme was scuppered temporarily when, on mentioning it to his wife, she had insisted on joining him. Getting rid of her was going to be tougher than he thought.

She may have been taken in by Buchanan at the start but the erstwhile Mrs Sutherland was beginning to see the devious doctor in his true colours. She consulted a lawyer to see whether there was any chance of recovering the money she had given him, but Buchanan was one step ahead. He paid the same lawyer $50 to put his own interests first and foremost. According to Buchanan, the lawyer told him: 'Don't give up a cent, but get rid of her any way you can.'

By the spring of 1892, the relationship between husband and wife was at an all-time low but Anna's health had not declined. Buchanan was still determined to go to Scotland alone and confided to Macomber that his wife was intending to go back to Newark and to re-open her brothel. He said that she had also threatened to poison herself whereupon he had replied: 'Why don't you? You know where my poisons are kept.'

Buchanan pressed ahead with his plans to leave the country but, in April 1892, just four days before he was due to sail, he cancelled his passage when his wife was suddenly taken ill. She had collapsed in the dining room and was suffering from severe head pains and was experiencing difficulty in breathing. Buchanan carried her to bed before, acting against type, summoning the best medical help available. He asked Ida Brockway, wife of the dentist to whom he was going to rent the house in his absence, whether she knew of a good nurse. Mrs Brockway recommended Sarah Childs and the two women arrived at the ailing woman's bedside just as Buchanan was giving his wife medicine from a spoon. There would later be a discrepancy as to the size of the dose administered by Dr Buchanan: Mrs Brockway said that it was two spoonfuls but Nurse Childs saw only the one. However the nurse did observe that Buchanan's hands were trembling as he gave the medicine.

On 22 April, Buchanan enlisted the help of two eminent

physicians, Burnette McIntyre and Henry Watson. Dr McIntyre arrived to find Mrs Buchanan in a hysterical state, complaining that she was dying and wanted to see a lawyer. He diagnosed a straightforward case of hysteria and prescribed bromide of sodium. Nurse Childs remembered him sniffing the medicine bottle but assumed from his calm reaction that he had found nothing untoward in the contents. Anna Buchanan's condition deteriorated rapidly although Dr McIntyre, on his second visit, still did not appear unduly alarmed and prescribed nothing stronger than chloral, a mild anaesthetic. By the time of his third visit, in the evening, the patient was in a deep coma. He wondered whether she was allergic to chloral but Buchanan assured him that an earlier doctor had prescribed considerably larger doses for her. Doctors McIntyre and Watson then settled on a cerebral haemorrhage, Buchanan helpfully revealing that her father had died from the same illness.

The following morning her temperature, which had been perfectly normal 24 hours earlier, had risen to 105 degrees and her face was almost the same colour as her hair. This was consistent with a cerebral haemorrhage. It was clear that nothing could be done for her. That afternoon, Buchanan informed Nurse Childs that he had to go out on urgent business. Shortly after his departure, his wife died.

Despite his apparent attention to his wife's medical care, Buchanan hadn't exactly been grieving too much. His 'urgent business' was a trawl of the local taverns with Richard Macomber, presumably in celebration of his impending freedom. When he eventually returned home to learn of his wife's demise, he promptly checked into a hotel rather than spend the night in the same house as a corpse. After the funeral, he again went out celebrating with Macomber, having learned that his late wife had not amended her will. She was still warm when he gleefully collected the $50,000.

But when James Smith, the man Anna had dumped for Buchanan, heard about her death, he was immediately suspicious. He contacted the coroner, Dr Schultz, and told him that Buchanan had only married her for her money. And now, just 18 months later, she was dead. Schultz was unimpressed by the allegations, however, pointing out that the death certificate had been signed by two of New York's most eminent physicians.

Enter Isaac White, a reporter with the *New York World*. Still fresh in his mind was the trial in New York a couple of months earlier of Carlyle Harris, a 23-year-old medical student ultimately convicted of murdering his wife by morphine poisoning. Harris who, like Buchanan, was a seasoned womanizer, had substituted morphine for quinine in some capsules for insomnia and had administered it to his wife, of whom he had grown tired. Experts argued as to the presence of morphine in the body but this was determined by the dead woman's pin-pointed pupils – a sure sign of the presence of morphine. Listening to Smith's tale, White was struck by the similarity in the two cases and relayed his suspicions to Dr McIntyre who admitted that some of Mrs Buchanan's symptoms were consistent with morphine poisoning but that her pupils had not contracted.

White wasn't going to be thrown off the scent that easily and hunted down Buchanan's drinking partners, Macomber and Doria. They were joyously indiscreet and White was intrigued to hear a comment made by Buchanan at the time of the Harris trial. 'Harris is a fool', Buchanan had said. 'An amateur. He just didn't know how to disguise the symptoms of morphine. Every acid has its neutralizing agent.' Buchanan had added that it would not present too much of a problem for an accomplished medical man to come up with an undetectable poison. Further investigations revealed that Buchanan had secretly remarried his first wife, Annie, in

Nova Scotia just three weeks after the funeral of his second spouse.

Acting upon this information, the authorities ordered the exhumation of Anna Buchanan's body. The post-mortem showed that all of her organs were healthy, effectively ruling out a cerebral haemorrhage, but that there was no contraction of the pupils. The intrepid White tracked Buchanan down to Macomber's bar in New York where the doctor vehemently denied any accusations of malpractice. Besieged by the press, Buchanan tried to make a run for it but before he could do so, he was arrested and charged with poisoning his wife.

The trial of Dr Robert Buchanan began on 20 March 1893, by which time he had been imprisoned for the best part of a year. The prosecution was led by District Attorney Delancey Nicoll, who was able to field as his star witness none other than Richard Macomber, the man who had been privy to Buchanan's wildest indiscretions. Macomber recalled a conversation between Buchanan and his lawyer in which the latter advised: 'If you did poison her, get out of New York and go as far as you can. If you did not, then stay here and face it out.' Soon afterwards Buchanan was enquiring about countries which had no extradition treaties with the United States and was planning to settle in Milwaukee under an assumed name. His anxiety to flee was seen as a clear indication of guilt. Buchanan had apparently bitterly regretted his decision to have the body embalmed before burial, a move which would preserve any evidence of foul play. 'My God,' he had told Macomber, 'if they dig the old woman's body up they will find it full of morphine. If only I'd had the sense to have the old hen cremated.'

That Buchanan was deeply concerned about what the body might reveal was further demonstrated by the fact that he had hired a private detective to check the grave on a daily basis to make sure that it had not been disturbed. It was looking grim for Buchanan, particularly when it was revealed that his wife's father had died of gangrene and not a cerebral haemorrhage as he had told doctors.

Professor Henry Loomis, the pathologist who conducted the autopsy, said that he had been unable to find any cause of death but his reputation was destroyed in a brilliant cross-examination .by young defence lawyer William J. O'Sullivan. As a consequence of O'Sullivan's probing questions, Professor Loomis had to admit that he had failed to make notes of his findings; that he hadn't known that the embalming fluid used on Mrs Buchanan contained arsenic and zinc which might have caused changes to the brain; and that he had not conducted a detailed examination of some of the organs until six months after the autopsy. O'Sullivan, who himself possessed a degree in medicine, had the professor rattled and Loomis was forced to concede that there were diseases which could have caused Mrs Buchanan's death but that he had simply not thought of them. O'Sullivan caused further embarrassment to the prosecution when T. Mitchell Pruden, a professor of pathology who had assisted Loomis, attempted to demonstrate the intricacies of the case to the jury via the use of a wax model of the brain. Complaining that the first model was unsuitable for his purposes, Pruden was handed a second brain by O'Sullivan. Pruden immediately denounced it as being 'a mere caricature', to which O'Sullivan pointed out that it was, on the contrary, a genuine human brain taken from the corpse of a man who had died from Bright's disease. Suddenly the expert testimony was beginning to look anything but.

To back up his claim that 'amazing amounts' of morphine had been found in the dead woman's stomach, the district attorney called toxicologist Professor Rudolph Witthaus to the stand. Feeding some of the contents of the stomach to a kitten, Witthaus succeeded in killing the poor cat in court, a demonstration which, thankfully, would be frowned upon these days. He went on to prove that the tell-tale pin-pointing of the pupils could be counteracted by putting drops of belladonna into the eyes, thus masking the presence of morphine. Buchanan's remark at the time of the Carlyle Harris trial about being able to disguise the symptoms of morphine now took on an even greater significance.

Despite this wealth of circumstantial evidence, O'Sullivan was more than a match for the prosecution witnesses and, by calling his own medical experts, was able to gouge huge holes in the district attorney's case. The morphine tests were shown to be hopelessly inconclusive and the prosecution was left licking its wounds, having failed to prove that Mrs Buchanan had died of morphine poisoning or, if she had, that it had been administered by her husband. If Robert Buchanan had left it at that, he would surely have been acquitted. His lawyers advised him not to give evidence but, mindful of the fact that Carlyle Harris had gone to the electric chair after electing not to testify, he ignored their warnings and took his place in the witness box. He was also motivated by his arrogance – the belief that he could handle anything the prosecution threw at him, that his medical knowledge outweighed that of all the experts combined, that he had outwitted them all.

Buchanan was not prepared to concede an inch. For a start, he flatly denied knowing that the house in Newark was used as a brothel, despite the fact that he was a frequent visitor and subsequently married the madame. He was either a complete fool or a brazen liar and, considering his status in the medical profession, he was clearly not lacking in intelligence. Therefore it was none too difficult for the jury to conclude that he was lying through his teeth. The prosecution lawyers could hardly believe their luck. They confronted him with all the incriminating evidence and, without giving his own counsel time to object, he responded with equally incriminating an-

swers. The more he denied what were obvious facts, the bigger
the hole he dug for himself. The jury was left with little doubt
that he would have sworn on oath that the earth was flat if it
meant that he could save his own skin.

Naturally, Buchanan thought that he had given a good
account of himself and was confident of an acquittal, particularly when the jury requested that some of the medical
testimony be read to them again. The jurors were obviously
confused by the complexity of the evidence and, if in doubt,
were bound to deliver a verdict of 'not guilty'. However, after
28 hours of deliberation, they found Buchanan 'guilty' of first-
degree murder.

The appeals process began almost straight away. Learning
that one of the jurors had suffered some form of fit during the
deliberations and had literally had to be carried into the
courtroom, Buchanan's lawyers claimed that their client
had been tried by '11 men and one lunatic'. When this plea
failed, further appeals were launched, each as unsuccessful as
its predecessor. Finally they ran out of ammunition and, on 2
July 1895, Dr Robert Buchanan was electrocuted in Sing Sing,
the New York state prison. Right to the last, he refused to
confess to his crime – the final act of an arrogant man.

Raymond Burr: The Case Perry Mason Lost

Perry Mason was all but invincible. Erle Stanley Gardner's
celebrated defence counsel lost only three of the 271 cases he
tackled on American television between 1957 and 1966. On
one of those rare occasions, when a defendant refused to
reveal the information that would have saved her, 30,000
Americans wrote to Raymond Burr, the actor who played
Perry Mason, urging: 'Don't do that again.' In Britain, a
Glasgow bookmaker claimed to have been tipped off that

Mason was going to lose that week's case and offered odds of 20–1 on him losing. In all, 600 punters took up the challenge, but the bookie's information was wrong and he graciously donated his £100 takings to charity. Even when Burr was ill for 'The Case of the Constant Doyle', Bette Davis stepped in to play a lawyer friend and duly triumphed. Like I say, Perry was a tough man to beat.

The trouble with playing a popular character for so long is that an actor tends to identify too closely with the role and that was how Raymond Burr came to learn that, where courtroom matters were concerned, he was considerably more fallible than his screen alter ego.

In September 1963, a court in Phoenix, Arizona, ordered Burr to pay $1085 to a creditor, Ward George Shaheen, who claimed that the actor had owed him the money since 1949. Judge Charles C. Stidham said that he would have dismissed the case because the debt was so old but, instead of answering the summons through a lawyer, as Arizona law required, Burr had followed the improper procedure of pleading his own case. Furthermore, Burr had failed to appear for a court-ordered deposition in June. This, remarked the judge, was not good law. Raymond Burr's decision to conduct his own case had proved a costly error.

Chapter 2

Law and Disorder

The Siege at Ruby Ridge: Fatal Error by the FBI

In August 1992, Randy Weaver's wife and 14-year-old son were shot dead by federal agents during a siege at the family's remote mountain cabin in Idaho. The shootings – the culmination of a succession of blunders by the FBI in the course of the operation – resulted in allegations of cover-ups and a 'shoot on sight' policy. Coupled with the Waco deaths at the Branch Davidian compound a year later, the Weaver case seriously undermined the Bureau's standing with the American people.

The FBI's interest in Randy Weaver began in the late 1980s after an informant had tipped them off that Weaver was involved in selling arms to the neo-Nazi Aryan Nations group which was based near his Idaho home. For his part, Weaver, who had no criminal record, steadfastly denied being a white supremacist associated with Aryan Nations and preferred to describe himself as a religious white separatist who interpreted the Old Testament to mean that different races should not marry. It was claimed that he and his wife were members of the Christian Identity Movement whose doctrine states that Europeans are the lost tribe of Israel and that Jews and blacks are satanic.

Following the tip-off, federal authorities started to monitor Weaver's movements in and around the isolated, self-constructed two-storey cabin on Ruby Ridge, near Naples, Idaho, where 44-year-old Weaver lived with his wife Vicki, son Sam and daughters Sara, 16, Rachel, 10, and 10-month-old Elisheba. Family friend Kevin Harris, aged 24, also made his home in the cabin which in truth was little more than a shack with no TV or radio and only intermittent electricity provided by a generator. The US government was determined to nail Weaver – if only for his beliefs – and, in a carefully planned sting, two agents from the Bureau of Alcohol, Tobacco and Firearms (ATF) persuaded him to sell them a pair of illegal sawn-off shotguns. With Weaver suitably compromised by what was perilously close to a case of entrapment, the agents tried to pressurize Weaver into spying on Aryan Nations despite his protestations that he had no connections with the group. When he refused to co-operate, the ATF carried out its threat and charged him with selling the guns.

A court summons to answer these charges was duly sent to his home but it bore the wrong date. The letter ordered Weaver to appear in court to face the shotgun charges on 20 March 1991 when the hearing was actually a month earlier, on 20 February. As a result, a memo was circulated within the US Marshal Service warning that, because of the error, the case was already a lost cause. In fact, Weaver had no intention of showing up on any date but, despite the internal misgivings about proceeding with the matter, he was still indicted for failure to appear. Officially he was now a federal fugitive and this gave the authorities a fresh incentive to hunt him down and bring him to justice.

Although Weaver's only crime was altering two guns, he was pursued with a vigour more befitting the search for the Boston Strangler. While Weaver remained in his mountain hideaway from where he refused to budge, the government drafted in more federal agents on a further surveillance operation at a cost of $13,000 a week. In an attempt to justify the exercise, they painted Weaver as an enemy of the nation –

racist and anti-Semitic. Like most mountain folk, Weaver kept a small arsenal but by the time government propaganda had done its job, he was depicted as having an armoury that would have been the envy of the Soviet Union.

Day after day, week after week, month after month, nothing much happened. It was a case of the irresistible force coming up against the immovable object. The agents were becoming increasingly frustrated. As the stake-out entered its sixteenth month and still with no end in sight, Marshal William Degan, a member of the Special Operations Group (the US Marshals' national Special Weapons and Tactics unit) was brought in with orders to bring the matter to a conclusion – one way or the other. On Friday, 21 August, the marshals, who were the men responsible for serving federal warrants, decided to arrest Randy Weaver. Degan and two other officers – all armed, masked and dressed in camouflage gear – set off from their base camp on the long journey up the mountain to the Weavers' cabin. Shortly after midday, they stumbled across Weaver, his son Sam and Kevin Harris at a junction of two dirt tracks. With the family was Sam's Labrador, Striker.

As the three marshals watched from the woods, the dog sniffed them out and began barking. The marshals immediately opened fire and shot the dog – a court later heard of their plan to take the dog 'out of the equation'. Seeing his dog gunned down and masked men emerging from the woods, Sam Weaver fired back. As he ran towards his father, he was fatally shot in the back by the marshals. In the ensuing gun battle, Marshal William Degan was also shot dead. Randy Weaver later testified: 'My kid was a good shot. He fired twice, low from the hip, and yelled, "I'm coming, Dad" when they cut him down, right through the heart.'

Randy Weaver and Kevin Harris retreated up the mountain path, leaving the two surviving marshals to radio back to headquarters that their colleague had been killed and that they were under fire.

The FBI was now called in and that evening sent its elite Hostage Rescue Team (HRT) to the site. There they immediately surrounded the cabin in which the rest of the family were holed up. It later transpired that the marshals had painted a mean picture of Randy Weaver. They told the FBI that he was a highly dangerous extremist who boasted an extensive knowledge of the mountains and who was bent on killing as many federal agents as he could. In charge of the FBI operation was Dick Rogers who, a year later, would lead the tactical team on the ill-judged assault at Waco. Acting on the advice of the other federal agents at the scene, Rogers concluded that Weaver posed a considerable threat and resolved not to take any undue risks. Accordingly, he asked Washington for permission in this instance to change the FBI's rules of engagement. Normally, agents were only permitted to use their guns in self-defence or to protect the innocent but now, instead of shooting merely to save lives, Rogers wanted his men to be able to adopt a policy of shooting Weaver – or any other threat – on sight.

It appears that the rules of engagement were indeed amended, although precisely how and by whom was to become the focus of a bitter debate. But HRT men on the ground said they were instructed that: 'If any adult in the compound is observed with a weapon after the surrender announcement is made, deadly force can and should be employed to neutralize the individual.' This had the effect of making Mrs Weaver fair game. The amendment allegedly added: 'If any adult male is observed with a weapon prior to the announcement, deadly force can and should be employed if the shot can be taken without endangering the children.' Eugene Glenn, an on-site FBI commander at Ruby Ridge, told the *New York Times* that he considered the children to be hostages – despite the fact that the marshals had already killed one.

Seizing the initiative on the afternoon of 22 August, a team of 11 HRT snipers crept into position around the cabin. At that stage, there had been no attempt to bring in trained negotiators to talk Weaver and his family into surrendering peacefully. Indeed there had been no verbal contact whatsoever with anyone in the cabin. Consequently, the occupants had no idea that they were circled by crack marksmen with high-velocity weapons trained on the building. One of the sniper units was commanded by Special Agent Lon Horiuchi, a former army officer with a reputation as an expert shot. Shortly after 6 p.m., just as Dick Rogers flew overhead in the HRT helicopter to assess the situation and the lay of the land, Horiuchi spotted Randy and Sara Weaver leaving the cabin in company with Kevin Harris. They were heading towards the shed where Sam Weaver's body still lay. According to his later testimony, Horiuchi thought that one of the men was about to open fire on the helicopter. Without warning, he shot Randy Weaver under the right armpit. As the men ran back to the cabin, Horiuchi fired a second shot just as they reached the porch. The bullet, apparently aimed at Harris, missed its target but smashed through a panel in the door and into the head of Vicki Weaver who had been standing on the other side, cradling baby Elisheba. Mrs Weaver, who was unarmed, died instantly and the same bullet ricocheted into Kevin Harris, smashing an elbow and two ribs. Miraculously, the baby was not injured.

The FBI later claimed to be unaware of the fact that Vicki Weaver had been shot but this contradicted suggestions that agents were equipped with listening devices which enabled them to hear conversations in the cabin. Over the next nine days, the cabin remained under constant siege from federal agents who were in turn reinforced by the presence of police and national guardsmen. The saying about using a sledge-hammer to crack a walnut comes to mind. If the troops hoped to starve the family into submission, they were sorely mistaken since local supporters succeeded in smuggling food into the cabin under the noses of the authorities. Randy Weaver had become a *cause célèbre*. Vocal neighbours and members of the Aryan Nation Group assembled at road blocks leading from the mountain to stage vigils and yell abuse at agents and police. In the space of just 24 hours, the planned arrest of Randy Weaver on a minor gun charge had escalated from a local incident to a national event.

Randy Weaver later described the scene inside the cabin. 'We were under siege, crawling around the floor, afraid to show our heads at the windows. The two girls freaked out if I stood up. Kevin lay in the kitchen in agony, begging me to shoot him in the head. I told him: "You've got one good arm left, buddy. If you want that, you do it and I'll see you in the next one." Vicki had been breast-feeding the baby. All we had was powdered milk. It kept her going, but she sure missed her mama.'

As the siege dragged on, James 'Bo' Gritz, a former lieu-tenant-colonel in the Green Berets who had known Weaver in the Army Special Services, was brought in to try and persuade him to surrender. Kevin Harris finally gave himself up on Sunday, 30 August, and the following day Gritz convinced Randy Weaver and his daughters that the best course of action was to surrender. Gritz said afterwards: 'He just cried his wife's name and his son's name.'

Harris and Weaver were flown to Boise, Idaho, where they were charged with the murder of the marshal and with con-spiracy to engage in armed confrontation with the govern-ment. Weaver had acquired hero status in the eyes of American racists and right-wing extremists who claimed that he had been framed by the FBI. However, the ATF countered that the action had nothing to do with Weaver's beliefs. 'You can believe anything you want to in this country,' it said, 'but it's when you start getting involved in the trafficking of illegal weapons that we get concerned.'

The trial of the two men took place in July 1993 and proved to be an unmitigated disaster for the FBI. Agents, marshals and police all gave contradictory evidence and HRT members admitted that they were shocked by the 'shoot on sight' rules which were in effect during the 11-day siege. The defence maintained that the position in which Randy Weaver was shot showed that he had no intention of firing his rifle at the helicopter. Asked about the killing of Mrs Weaver, Special Agent Horiuchi insisted that he hadn't seen her behind the door and had been aiming at Harris. Yet other evidence suggested that he had been lining up a second shot at Randy Weaver after initially wounding him. It emerged that the HRT team didn't even have a search or arrest warrant until 12 hours after Sam Weaver had been killed and that evidence had been deliberately tampered with. The crime scene photographs were fakes while physical evidence from the scene of the killings had been removed and replaced. Prosecutor Hoiwen, who knew of the deception but had withheld this information from the defence, was forced to apologize in open court. At the end of the trial, he collapsed mid-statement, telling Judge Edward Lodge, 'I can't go on.' The prosecution actually turned on the FBI after the trial, accusing the Bureau of closing ranks and of deliberately delaying the sending of vital evidence. Indeed, a court order had to be issued to force the Bureau to send its case file at all, but even then it was only despatched by fourth-class mail so that it conveniently arrived after Horiuchi had finished testifying. However, the irate judge wasn't falling for such blatant tactics and ordered Horiuchi to return to the stand. The FBI case collapsed in turmoil and, after hearing that the marshals fired first, the jury acquitted both defendants although Weaver did serve four months in jail on the gun charges.

Judge Lodge was openly critical of the Bureau's handling of the case, saying that it had covered up its misconduct of the affair and that its behaviour had 'served to obstruct the administration of justice'. For what he saw as prosecution misconduct, the judge ordered the government to pay part of the defence attorneys' fees – an almost unprecedented move.

The Justice Department of Professional Responsibility conducted an internal review of the Ruby Ridge confrontation. Central to the inquiry was the question of the alleged alteration to the rules of engagement to allow the marksmen to shoot on sight. Such orders would have been illegal since the FBI never opens fire without warning unless under direct threat. In explaining this discrepancy, Dick Rogers said that he had obtained approval for a change in the rules on that occasion from Larry Potts, the man responsible for supervising the FBI operation, and that Potts had discussed the matter with senior colleagues at Bureau headquarters. But Potts disputed this, claiming there had been a misunderstanding as to what he and Rogers had actually agreed upon.

Although censured for his poor supervision of the Ruby Ridge stand-off, Larry Potts was surprisingly promoted by FBI Director Louis Freeh to the post of Deputy Director in May 1994. Like Dick Rogers, Potts had also been involved at Waco and thus found himself facing two official inquiries in the summer of 1995. A few days before the Waco hearings were due to begin, Potts was suddenly demoted.

Meanwhile the Justice Department continued to investigate charges that key FBI documents, believed to shed light on Potts' orders during the Idaho siege, had been altered or destroyed as part of a high-level cover-up. Releasing the results of the FBI's own internal review, Louis Freeh said that the rules of engagement at Ruby Ridge were 'poorly drafted, confusing and can be read to direct agents to act contrary to law and FBI policy'. But he concluded that there had been no criminal conduct. However, Eugene Glenn charged in a complaint to the Justice Department that the FBI's internal investigation had been designed to protect Potts and to create scapegoats. He claimed that Potts had approved the new rules of engagement. Potts continued to deny the accusation.

With the Weaver case becoming an embarrassment for the FBI which refused to go away, five senior officials, including Potts, were suspended and placed under criminal investigation. Randy Weaver sued for $200 million. The US government agreed to pay $3.1 million – $100,000 to Weaver and $1 million to each of his three daughters. ATF agents continued to blame Weaver for the showdown and he did admit that he was partly at fault for having refused to surrender when the warrant was originally issued. He added that the shoot-out should never have happened, but had arisen out of a fatal clash of egos.

In September 1995, Weaver gave evidence to senators on Capitol Hill and spoke of the events surrounding the shooting of his wife. 'She was not wanted for any crime,' he said. 'She was standing in the doorway of her home. When the bullet crashed through her head, she slumped to her knees. We took the baby from her as she lay dead and bleeding on the floor.' Dismissing the claims of Lon Horiuchi, who fired the fatal bullet, Weaver said: 'He tried to murder me and he murdered Vicki.'

In 1996, FBI headquarters manager E. Michael Kahoe pleaded guilty to obstructing justice after admitting that he had destroyed the official report on the Ruby Ridge shootings. Other officials, including Larry Potts, escaped prosecution because the Justice Department maintained that there was insufficient evidence. Lon Horiuchi was charged with manslaughter but in May 1998 Judge Lodge ordered the charges to be dropped. An appeal against the decision is pending.

Amid protests that the FBI had got off lightly, a further chilling indictment of its bungled operation at Ruby Ridge occurred when reports stated that the anti-government paranoia of Timothy McVeigh, the man responsible for the 1995 Oklahoma City bombing in which 168 people were killed, had been partly fuelled by the shootings of Sam and Vicki Weaver.

The Hunt for the Yorkshire Ripper: A Botched Job

Between 1975 and 1980, a total of 13 women were butchered by Bradford lorry driver Peter Sutcliffe, the man christened the Yorkshire Ripper. At first he targeted mainly prostitutes in the seedy red-light districts of Leeds and Bradford but soon he spread his net further afield and began attacking perfectly respectable women who had the misfortune to stray into his path. No woman in West Yorkshire felt safe. In the face of massive publicity, the police pulled out all the stops in their bid to catch the Ripper but incompetence dogged their every move. Sutcliffe was questioned – and released – no fewer than ten times in the course of their inquiries and was eventually apprehended more by luck than judgement. It was no wonder that the mother of student Jacqueline Hill – Sutcliffe's final victim – tried to sue West Yorkshire Police for negligence in not catching the killer earlier.

Born in Bingley, a small mill town six miles to the north of Bradford, Peter Sutcliffe was the eldest of six children. He was a shy, weedy boy and was frequently bullied at school. He left school at 15 and landed a job as a grave-digger at a cemetery in Bingley. It was there that he later claimed to have heard the voice of God ordering him to go out on to the streets and kill prostitutes.

His first real girlfriend was the equally introverted Sonia Szurma whom he married after an eight-year courtship. For the first three years of their married life, they lived with her parents before moving to a house in Heaton, a middle-class suburb of Bradford, less than a mile from the city's infamous Lumb Lane, the heart of the Manningham red-light district. Sonia, a teacher by profession, kept the house spotless and remained blissfully unaware of the fact that her husband was seeking out prostitutes. Indeed, by the time the seemingly ordinary young couple had moved to their new home in September 1977, Sutcliffe had already killed five times.

His first known attack had actually been as far back as 1969 when he hit a Bradford prostitute over the head with a heavy stone in a sock following an argument over a £10 note. The woman survived, as did two more of his early victims. In July 1975, he struck in Keighley, attacking Anna Rogulskyj with a ball-peen hammer, the weapon which was to become his trademark. He was about to finish her off with a stab wound to the stomach when a passer-by panicked him. And the following month, he launched a vicious assault on office cleaner Olive Smelt in Halifax, again with a hammer. Her life was saved by approaching car headlights.

Then, on 30 October 1975, a Leeds milkman doing his rounds in the Leeds red-light district of Chapeltown found the body of 28-year-old Wilma McCann. She had been attacked from behind and bludgeoned about the head with a hammer. Her clothes were ripped away and, once she was dead, she had been stabbed 14 times in the chest and stomach. Sutcliffe had killed for the first time. Three months later, Sutcliffe struck again in Chapeltown, murdering 42-year-old Emily Jackson. Like Wilma McCann, her body was found with her breasts exposed. The only clue to her killer was the imprint of a size 7 Wellington boot on her right thigh – an unusually small shoe size for a man.

On 9 May 1976, Sutcliffe attacked coloured prostitute Marcella Claxton in Leeds, hitting her twice with a hammer and leaving her needing 50 stitches in the head. Claxton was educationally subnormal and the police decided to treat her account of the assault and of the 'black and crinkly bearded' man who had attacked her with scepticism. Consequently they did not immediately link it to the other recent attacks on women in the area. Little did they know that Peter Sutcliffe was often nicknamed 'Jesus' on account of his black, crinkly beard. After the attack on Marcella Claxton, Sutcliffe would go on to attack six more women, four fatally, before the end of 1977.

It was not until Sutcliffe's third murder – that of part-time Chapeltown prostitute Irene Richardson early in 1977 – that the police became aware that the same man was responsible for the attacks. The common denominator was his 'signature': multiple fractures of the skull, displaced clothing and mutilation of the lower abdomen and breasts with a knife or screwdriver. A team of 120 detectives was appointed to work around the clock on the Richardson case but the feedback proved disappointing. In a bid to trap the killer, Detective Chief Superintendent Jim Hobson, the head of Leeds CID, decided to put policewomen on the streets of Chapeltown disguised as call-girls. The move was not a success. Meanwhile information from the various attacks was clogging up a system which required individual officers to process considerable amounts of data in an inadequate amount of time. The attacks were becoming so frequent that the indexing and cross-referencing work on statements relating to previous murders often hadn't been finished by the time a fresh set came in. The inquiry was getting bogged down by the sheer volume of paperwork. This, plus the fact that the killer was starting to move around to pastures new, even led to speculation that he might be a police officer simply because he seemed to know how to stay one step ahead of the boys in blue. In April 1977, Sutcliffe struck in Bradford, killing prostitute Tina Atkinson in her flat just around the corner from the red-light district. A size 7 Wellington boot print was found on the sheet of her bed.

Up until June 1977, a different investigating officer had been assigned to each case but the murder of a non-prostitute, 16-year-old Jayne MacDonald, in Leeds caused a storm of public outrage and forced Ronald Gregory, Chief Constable of West Yorkshire, to put his most experienced detective, George Oldfield, in overall control of the hunt for the Ripper. The Ripper squad now boasted 304 full-time officers, painstakingly checking every avenue of investigation. After an attack on Maureen Long in Bradford in July 1977, Oldfield told journalists: 'The investigation is beginning to bubble. I feel we are getting nearer.' His words were to prove hopelessly premature.

The Ripper's sixth victim, prostitute Jean Jordan, was butchered in Manchester in October 1977. This was a close call for Sutcliffe. She had climbed into his new red Ford Corsair near her home in the Moss Side district of Manchester, taken £5 from him in advance and directed him to a patch of open land some two miles away – a spot where prostitutes often took their clients. There he bludgeoned her to death but, after dragging her into nearby bushes, the arrival of another car forced him to make a hasty exit. On his way back to Bradford, he realized that he had left behind the £5 note. Furthermore, it was a brand-new £5 note straight from his wage packet and therefore a clue which could link him to the dead woman. He waited anxiously for eight days until, with no newspaper reports of a body having been found, he chanced his arm and returned to the scene of the murder in a bid to retrieve the incriminating evidence. Unable to find Jean Jordan's handbag, he resorted to trying to disguise his familiar 'signature' on the body by attacking it with a broken pane of glass. But the glass was not sharp enough and in the end, he gave up in frustration.

The following day, Jean Jordan's naked body was found by an allotment holder. For once, the police had more luck than Sutcliffe and discovered the handbag containing the £5 note which they immediately set about tracing. It turned out to be one of £50,000 worth issued by a bank in Shipley. Sutcliffe worked as a driver for the haulage firm of T. and W. H. Clark (Holdings) Ltd of Shipley, one of the companies from where the note could have originated. Sutcliffe was duly interviewed at home but the police left satisfied as to his innocence. Sutcliffe and his wife were then questioned again by two different officers six days later. Once again, no suspicion was aroused. In February 1978, a senior detective with Manchester CID, who were in charge of the Jordan investigation, stated: 'I personally don't believe that we have yet met the killer in our multitude of interviews. When we do, I am positive we will realize and nail him.'

An ongoing part of the investigation was interviewing motorists whose cars had frequently been seen in the red-light districts of Bradford and Leeds. Among them was Peter Sutcliffe whose Ford Corsair had been seen in Bradford's Lumb Lane on as many as seven separate occasions. Accordingly in August 1978, by which time Sutcliffe had killed nine times, another officer, Detective Constable Peter Smith, called on Sutcliffe at his Heaton home. Sutcliffe quietly explained that his journey to work took him through Manningham every day and dismissed out of hand the suggestion that he used prostitutes. His wife Sonia supported his stories. Since the reports of the earlier police interviews with Sutcliffe were still, ten months on, part of the vast backlog of paperwork waiting to be processed at Ripper HQ in Leeds, DC Smith had no way of knowing that Sutcliffe had also been questioned in connection with the £5 note. If the two strands had been tied together, four lives might have been saved. As it was, the Yorkshire Ripper remained free to continue his evil mission.

Eleven days before the murder of building society worker Josephine Whitaker (Sutcliffe's tenth victim) in the spring of 1979, a letter was sent to Assistant Chief Constable George Oldfield's office in Wakefield. It bore a Sunderland postmark and was dated 23 March 1979. Handwriting experts stated that it was written by the same person who had sent two letters the previous year, both of which had also borne a Sunderland postmark and had been signed 'Jack the Ripper'. This third letter seemed particularly promising since it mentioned that Vera Millward (victim number nine) had recently been a patient at Manchester Royal Infirmary, the scene of her murder. The police jumped to the conclusion that such information could only have come from Vera Millward herself and that therefore the letter-writer was the Ripper. So desperate were they for a lead that they dismissed the possibility that the letters were the work of a crank even though curious misspellings such as 'curserred coppers' bore eerie echoes of the Jack the Ripper letters used to taunt the police nearly a century earlier. Instead the police launched a full-scale offensive on the Sunderland area which yielded nothing but another mountain of paperwork.

Then, on the morning of 18 June 1979, a buff-coloured envelope was sent to the police. Written in the same hand as the previous letters, the envelope contained a cassette tape. The voice on the tape was that of a Geordie and it was taunting George Oldfield. It began: 'I'm Jack. I see you are having no luck catching me. I have the greatest respect for you, George, but Lord, you are no nearer catching me now than four years ago when I started. I reckon your boys are lettin' you down, George. They can't be much good, can they?'

Oldfield was convinced the voice was that of the Ripper and voice and dialect experts traced it to Castletown – a small mining community on Wearside. Oldfield declared that he was '99 per cent sure' the killer came from Wearside and instructions were issued to all officers by the Chief Constable of West Yorkshire that any suspect who did not have a Geordie accent could immediately be eliminated from inquiries. Of all the blunders made by the police on the Ripper case, this was the most foolhardy.

The key beneficiary from the order-on-high was Peter Sutcliffe. He had a Yorkshire accent which enabled him to survive yet another police interview (his fifth) in July 1979. Detectives Greenwood and Laptew called at Sutcliffe's home, 6 Garden Lane, to talk to the owner of a Sunbeam Rapier (Sutcliffe had changed cars) which had been seen in Lumb Lane on 36 occasions. The detectives had no idea that Sutcliffe had previously been questioned about his old Ford Corsair or about the £5 note because his incident room file was almost two years out of date. However, in the course of the 90-minute meeting, Detective Constable Andrew Laptew sensed that there was something 'not quite right' about Sutcliffe and suggested that he be interviewed by a senior officer with the Ripper Squad. Laptew was particularly struck by Sutcliffe's similarity to descriptions given by two survivors of Ripper attacks – he was the same height and build; he had a beard, a Jason King-style moustache and collar-length black hair; he had a dark complexion and smallish feet; and a distinct gap between his two top front teeth. He was also a lorry driver – one of the Ripper's suspected occupations. Although Sutcliffe again denied using prostitutes, a search through records told Laptew that Sutcliffe had a prior conviction for 'going equipped to steal' back in 1969. This information, plus DC Laptew's suspicions, were relayed to senior officers on the case in a two-page report but, such was the burden on the system, it was a further nine months before they finally got to see it. And even then, when Sutcliffe's voice and handwriting didn't

Law and Disorder

match the Sunderland tape and letters, it was put in the files along with tens of thousands of others. A month after being visited by DC Laptew, Sutcliffe claimed his eleventh victim, student Barbara Leach.

By the summer of 1979, more than 150,000 people had been interviewed in connection with the Ripper murders. A total of 27,000 house-to-house inquiries had been conducted, over 15,000 vehicles checked, 22,000 statements taken and some £3 million had been spent. The police were convinced that the killer was among the 8000 questioned in connection with the £5 note but these names were never put on a computer system for swift recall. Instead of using modern technology, the West Yorkshire force relied on a cumbersome card index, wasting valuable man hours. One result of the frequently bungled Ripper investigation was that West Yorkshire resolved to use computers for all major investigations in the future.

The strain was taking its toll on George Oldfield for whom the case, particularly after the receipt of the tape, had become a personal obsession. He had been working 16 hours a day, six days a week for two years but was getting nowhere fast. In August 1979, he suffered a near fatal heart attack brought on by the pressure of the investigation and was told to stay away from work for a few months.

In his absence, disturbing news was starting to emerge. Voice experts at Leeds University had come to the conclusion that the Geordie tape was a hoax. To all but the most blinkered, it was hardly a startling revelation since none of the women who had survived a Ripper attack had noticed the slightest trace of a Geordie accent on their assailant. Indeed, at least one had stated quite categorically that he had a local Yorkshire accent. Some detectives harboured reservations about the authenticity of the letters because one had failed to mention a murder (that of Yvonne Pearson, victim number seven) which had taken place two months before it was written, but where the body was not discovered until after the letter had been received by the police. It seemed that the writer was one murder behind and was taking his information from other sources – namely the newspapers. Also, Detective Chief Inspector David Zachreson, who had been working on the Castletown line of inquiry, had taken the trouble to study the newspaper cuttings on the case and had realized that there was nothing in the Sunderland letters which had not been reported in the press at one time or another. The connection between Vera Millward and Manchester Royal Infirmary, in which the West Yorkshire police had placed such store, had actually been reported around the time of her death by the *Daily Mail*. These misgivings were passed on to the new men in charge but, amazingly, Chief Constable Gregory chose to ignore them. He remained certain that the tape was genuine and that the Yorkshire Ripper was a Geordie and, against the advice of some of his own senior officers, launched a media blitz on North-East England. The tape was played on radio stations across the region and over loudspeakers at football matches in the hope that someone would recognize the voice. A special four-page newspaper bearing a copy of the handwriting was delivered to every home in Yorkshire, Lancashire and the North-East. In all, some 50,000 calls were received but they conspired to do nothing more than jam up the system yet more. By the middle of November, the list of possible suspects had risen to around 17,000.

At the start of 1980, the Manchester police made a renewed attempt to track down the owner of the £5 note found in Jean Jordan's handbag. By a process of elimination, they managed to narrow down the number of firms who could have issued it from 30 to three. Among the three firms was T. and W. H. Clark (Holdings) Ltd of Shipley. The police also had the picture of a boot-print found close to Josephine Whitaker's body in Savile Park, Halifax. Sutcliffe was actually wearing the same boots on the morning of 13 January 1980 when he jumped down from the cab of his lorry to be questioned by police officers. The fact failed to register with the police. This was to be the first of three close shaves for Sutcliffe in as many weeks. On 20 January, police questioned him (for the eighth time in all) as part of the screening of all Clark's employees. He was taken home, his clothes were inspected and Sonia was questioned about his movements on specific dates and about any sexual deviations. Her answers were obviously to their satisfaction. Then on 2 February, Sutcliffe and another Clark's driver were taken to Bradford police headquarters for a handwriting test. Although Sutcliffe was shaking and sweating when he was taken in, he was released for the familiar reason that he didn't have a Geordie accent and his writing didn't match that of the letters. In any case, the Laptew report, submitted six months earlier, still hadn't entered the system so there appeared nothing in Sutcliffe to arouse undue suspicion.

While Ronald Gregory's North-East initiative was said by his press spokesman to have produced '100 per cent rubbish' and was thus a complete waste of time and manpower, Sutcliffe had his tenth brush with the law in June 1980 when he was breathalysed after being caught speeding on Manningham Lane, Bradford. The two constables involved suggested that the Ripper Squad might care to take a closer look at Sutcliffe but were subsequently informed that he had already been seen and eliminated from inquiries.

After the abysmal failure of the North-East blitz, the police tried a new tactic by starving the Ripper of publicity. And so when Marguerite Walls became victim number 12 in Pudsey in August 1980, the killing received scant coverage and was not even attributed to the Ripper. The following month, Sutcliffe attacked Upadhya Bandara, a doctor from Singapore, in the Leeds suburb of Headingley but was disturbed before he could finish her off. Again the attack was not considered to be a

Ripper job – as far as the public was concerned he had been quiet for 15 months. Then in November 1980, just a quarter of a mile from where Dr Bandara was attacked, student Jacqueline Hill became the thirteenth victim of the Yorkshire Ripper.

The West Yorkshire police were at their sloppiest in the case of Jacqueline Hill. A fellow student had found a handbag on the pavement, seen spots of blood and dialled 999. A banker's card inside the bag bore the name 'Jacqueline Hill' and so when two officers arrived, the student suggested that they find out where Jacqueline Hill lived and ascertain whether she was safe. Maybe the officers in question didn't like being told how to do their jobs, because they contented themselves with a cursory search of the area by torchlight which failed to spot a pair of spectacles, a woollen mitten or even the poor girl's body lying no more than 30 yards from her handbag. Back at the station, the bag was written off as 'lost property'.

The news of the killing nagged away at Trevor Birdsall who thought that the description of a brown car spotted nearby at the time of Jacqueline Hill's murder matched that of his friend Peter Sutcliffe's recently purchased Rover. Birdsall decided to pen an anonymous letter to the police. 'I have good reason to now (sic) the man you are looking for in the Ripper case. This man as (sic) dealings with prostitutes and always had a thing about them . . . His name and address is Peter Sutcliffe, 6 Garden Lane, Heaton, Bradford. Workes (sic) for Clarks Transport, Shipley.' Hearing no news of an arrest over the next 24 hours, Birdsall was persuaded by his girlfriend to go with her to Bradford police headquarters. There, he repeated what he had written in the letter, adding that he had been with Sutcliffe when the latter had got out of his car to go after a woman in Halifax on 16 August 1975. It was the night on which Olive Smelt had been attacked. Birdsall was thanked for his co-operation but heard nothing more from the police. His statement was never seen again.

At the end of 1980, the beleaguered Ronald Gregory announced the formation of a 'think-tank' of senior officers drawn from outside the West Yorkshire force. George Oldfield's deputy, Jim Hobson, was placed in charge. Oldfield himself was quietly dropped from the case. The new brains trust had no more joy than its predecessor. What was desperately needed was a stroke of luck.

It arrived on 2 January 1981 when Sergeant Bob Ring and Constable Robert Hydes were patrolling Melbourne Avenue in Sheffield's red-light district. They saw Olivia Reivers climbing into a Rover V8 and decided to investigate. The driver, Sutcliffe, gave his name as Peter Williams. He offered no resistance but said that he needed to go for a pee. Out of sight of the officers, he took the murderous ball-peen hammer and knife which he kept in a pocket of his car coat and hid them behind a small storage tank in a dark alley. The police were too busy calming down Reivers who was complaining about the threat to her earnings. But they did discover that the number plates on the car were false and, on that basis, took 'Williams' in for questioning.

At the station, Sutcliffe gave his real name but was still only being questioned for a minor traffic offence. However, dismayed at the poor groundwork in the aftermath of the Jacqueline Hill murder, Gregory wanted to make sure there were no repeat performances so when anyone remotely suspicious was picked up in a red-light district, the Ripper Squad were alerted. Sutcliffe was interviewed by Detective Sergeant Des O'Boyle at Dewsbury but nearly managed to slip through the net again. He freely admitted that he had been quizzed by the police in the past in their hunt for the Ripper and DS O'Boyle was about to write him off as another false alarm and to recommend his release when the Chief Superintendent at Dewsbury demanded that Sutcliffe be questioned further. So O'Boyle persisted and Sutcliffe reluctantly agreed to give a blood sample.

Back in Sheffield, DS Bob Ring, hearing that the man he had picked up 24 hours earlier, was still being questioned by the Ripper Squad, decided to return to the scene of the arrest. Remembering that Sutcliffe had gone for a pee, he searched the alley and, there, hidden in the bushes, he found the hammer and knife. It was pure chance that a passer-by hadn't picked them up and taken them home. This evidence, plus the news that Sutcliffe was blood group B – the same as the Ripper and one shared by only 6 per cent of the population – told the Ripper Squad that they had finally got their man. Sutcliffe quickly confessed.

At his trial, Sutcliffe pleaded not guilty to murder by reason of diminished responsibility but the jury decided that he was evil rather than insane and found him guilty on 13 charges of murder. He was sentenced to life imprisonment.

In 1992, Sutcliffe confessed to an additional attack – one with which he had not been charged. On 27 August 1975 – a few weeks before he killed his first victim, Wilma McCann – he had battered 14-year-old Tracy Browne about the head with a hammer in a lane at Silsden, to the north-west of Bradford, before throwing her over a fence. Aided by the presence of a full moon that night, she was able to give police a detailed description of her assailant. She said he had dark hair and a full beard, a gap between his front teeth and a local accent. When the ID picture was printed in the local paper, it looked so much like Sutcliffe that he even joked to his mother-in-law that it could have been him. In 1977 when the Ripper was front-page news in West Yorkshire, Tracy Browne told the police that it was the Ripper who had attacked her, but her claims were dismissed. Fifteen years later, she was proved right and the police were proved wrong. How much sooner he would have been brought to justice had the police paid more attention to her story and description instead of putting their total faith in the Geordie hoax tape to the exclusion of all other lines of inquiry, or improved their methods for collating information or simply been more observant, is a question which would haunt many of the Ripper squad for years to come.

The New York Subway Shoot-Out: Officers Wounded by 'Friendly Fire'

As a burst of gunfire echoed through the packed subway station at 53rd Street and Lexington Avenue, New York City, rush-hour commuters dived for cover. They thought it was a gangland feud, a drugs war or maybe an attempted robbery. What they didn't think was that it could be police officers mistakenly firing at each other.

In the early evening of 22 August 1994, Desmond Robinson, a 31-year-old black undercover officer with the transit police, was on pickpocket patrol at the station. Meanwhile Peter Del-Debbio, an officer with the New York City Police Department since 1988, was off-duty and travelling home on the subway towards Queens. Both men were dressed in civilian clothes. Apart from being law enforcement officers, the two men were not connected in any way, but soon their worlds would collide in catastrophic fashion.

Just before 7.10 p.m., with Robinson inside the station looking for likely suspects, two passengers making for the exit approached a pair of uniformed transit officers near the entrance to the station and told them that they had just seen two teenagers on the E train platform with guns. Armed with descriptions, the officers headed for the platform. While one man was arrested on an escalator, his accomplice tried to make his getaway on a Queens-bound E train, the one carrying Del-Debbio, which had just pulled into the station. But in doing so, the second teenager dropped the sawn-off shotgun he was carrying between the platform and the train and the weapon went off, injuring a bystander in the leg. Hearing the gunshot, Robinson ran towards the sound and chased the suspect with his gun drawn. Meanwhile, Del-Debbio, hearing the shotgun blast, saw the weapon and then spotted a man (Robinson) brandishing a gun. Putting two and two together, he immediately assumed that Robinson was the criminal and emptied his five-shot revolver at him, wounding him four times in the back. Seeing his colleague being fired upon, another transit officer, Joseph Fitzgerald, shot twice at Del-Debbio, hitting him once in the right arm.

As commuters panicked, dropping to the platform floor, hiding in the train or fleeing the station as fast as they could, the truth dawned on Peter Del-Debbio that he had shot a fellow officer by mistake. Desmond Robinson was left in a critical condition (he later recovered) after an incident described by the police authority as a 'friendly-fire situation'.

But there was nothing friendly about the reaction provoked by the shooting. Inevitably, the race card was played amidst claims that Del-Debbio, seeing a black man in civilian clothes with a gun, naturally thought him to be a villain. Robinson's supporters wanted to know whether Del-Debbio would have been so quick to pull the trigger had the man been white. Naturally the police department tried to play down any racial overtones, insisting that the shooting had just been a genuine mistake but there was also disquiet about the fact that Del-Debbio had shot Robinson in the back.

In 1995 a Manhattan grand jury indicted Del-Debbio for 'recklessly shooting' Robinson and the case came to court the following year. The defence insisted that the shooting was Robinson's fault because he wasn't wearing his badge of identification and Del-Debbio testified that it was a fear of being shot which caused him to empty his revolver into Robinson. Significantly, Robinson told the jury that he had been shot twice while upright and at least twice more after he had fallen to the platform and had lost control of his own gun. Much play was made of the fact that both men were in civilian clothes, that everything had happened so quickly and that there was the safety of the other passengers to consider, but at the end of the day Del-Debbio was convicted of second-degree assault. To his eternal credit, Robinson, who had refused to jump on the racism bandwagon, pleaded for Del-Debbio not be sent to jail because both men had been forced out of the job they loved. Del-Debbio was given five years' probation and 200 hours' community service. Summing up the case, Police Commissioner William J. Bratton said the shooting had resulted from 'two good cops doing their jobs'.

The incident was by no means the first between transit police and New York police. In December 1992, Officer Derwin Pannell of the transit police was shot three times by two New York police officers as he made an arrest in a subway station. The officers said they saw Pannell, who was in plain clothes, pointing a gun at a woman and thought they were seeing a mugging in progress. They claimed that they had identified themselves as cops and had ordered him to drop his gun and that they shot him only when he turned towards them, still holding the weapon. Pannell, who was left partly paralysed, countered that his gun wasn't drawn and that the two men hadn't identified themselves as police officers. The two officers were cleared.

Waco: A Sledgehammer to Crack a Nut

When agents from the Bureau of Alcohol, Tobacco and Firearms launched a disastrous attack on the compound of the Branch Davidian religious sect at Waco, Texas, in February 1993, they sparked a chain of events which would leave

82 cult members – 21 of them children – and four ATF agents dead. In its eagerness for a spectacular, high-profile raid, the ATF made many crucial errors, leaving the FBI to pick up the pieces. What should have been a straightforward mission developed into a tense stand-off from which neither the government agencies nor the religious fanatics, led by self-styled Messiah David Koresh, emerged with much credit. In short, Waco was a totally unnecessary tragedy.

The Branch Davidians can trace their history back to early nineteenth-century New England where carpenter William Miller believed that the Book of Revelation predicted the second coming of Christ in the immediate future. His followers called themselves Seventh Day Adventists. Then in the early 1930s, Victor Houteff, disillusioned with the materialistic direction which he thought the Seventh Day Adventist Church was taking, branched out and formed his own sect at Mount Carmel on the outskirts of Waco. The community became known as the Branch Davidians. Through a succession of leaders, the Davidians continued their search for salvation and eternal life. During the 1980s, one of the sect's most popular members was a young man by the name of Vernon Howell who took to referring to himself as the Lamb of God, having told anyone who would listen that he had spoken to God and that he alone could redeem them after the Apocalypse. He also claimed to be the only person able to reveal the spiritual mysteries of the Seven Seals. After a fierce struggle, the charismatic Howell took over as leader of the Branch Davidians in 1987, by which time he had changed his name to David Koresh – David after King David and Koresh after Cyrus, the Persian emperor who freed the Babylonian Jews from slavery.

Once in charge, Koresh began to break every rule in the book. He drank, he smoked, he swore and had sex with a number of the female cult members, claiming that God had instructed him to father many children. It was nice work if you could get it. To his followers, Koresh's word was final. He convinced them that they should prepare for the forthcoming Apocalypse. Stocks of food and water were brought in, along with gas masks, so that the Davidians would be ready for the final confrontation with the forces of darkness, represented in Koresh's mind – and therefore that of his disciples – by the FBI and, more specifically, the ATF. Koresh believed that the agents would eventually storm and kill everyone in the compound. Armageddon was just around the corner, he said, and only then would he be able to unlock the mystery of the Seven Seals that would end the world and ensure the salvation of the Branch Davidians.

In the meantime Koresh had developed a fascination with guns and began to amass a huge arsenal of weapons and ammunition. He ran his own gun business, buying a large number of semi-automatic rifles as an investment, in the belief that gun control legislation would force up the prices. Thus he came to the attention of the ATF.

Although officially run by the Department of Treasury, the ATF was essentially independent. Originally set up to investigate the smuggling of contraband cigarettes and whisky, it now tended to concentrate on the firearms industry and illegal explosives. The ATF's interest in Koresh stemmed from a tip-off by Larry Gilbreath, a United Parcel Service worker, who had made a number of deliveries of guns and weapon parts to Koresh's gun shop in the course of 1992. Most of these arms shipments were perfectly legal under the liberal Texas gun laws but, with the help of undercover agent Robert Rodriguez, who had infiltrated the Davidians, the ATF concluded that Koresh and his cohorts were also converting semi-automatic rifles to machine guns as well as manufacturing hand grenades and other explosive devices. These operations were all illegal.

The ATF began to compile search and seizure warrants in

readiness for a raid. In truth, the warrant could have been delivered simply by knocking on the front door of the compound – the local sheriff said later that he would have been perfectly happy to oblige. Alternatively, Koresh could have been picked up on one of his regular trips into town or while he was out jogging. But it seems that the ATF, anxious to add a spot of glory to an image which had become increasingly lacklustre in recent years, wanted a dramatic raid which would put the agency back in the headlines. The operation certainly did that – but for all the wrong reasons.

The raid was pencilled in for Sunday, 28 February, 1993. The local paper, the *Waco Tribune Herald*, had also been taking a close interest in the Branch Davidians and had interviewed former members as part of a series of exposés on the cult. The first article appeared on Saturday, 27 February – the day before the raid – and immediately served to put Koresh and his followers on red alert. On that same day, the ATF, determined to capture maximum publicity, tipped off the paper and a local TV station about the impending raid. By 8.30 the following morning there were over a dozen TV and newspaper journalists around the compound.

However, it was not only the newspaper article which had given Koresh reason to suspect that some form of attack was imminent. He had also become puzzled by the presence of a group of men in a nearby house who claimed to be students but were all over 40. They were, of course, part of a supposedly top-secret ATF surveillance team. It was like something out of *'Allo 'Allo*.

The crowning glory was when one of the Davidians, a mailman, was returning from his morning round and bumped into a TV cameraman outside the compound. The cameraman, unaware that he was talking to a Davidian, warned him to keep clear of the area as helicopters and agents would shortly be arriving on the scene. This news was quickly relayed to Koresh. While the Davidians took up arms, undercover agent Rodriguez managed to sneak out of the compound and ran to tell his superiors that the secret was out. Through its insistence on informing the media, the ATF had forfeited the crucial element of surprise. However, as Diarmuid Jeffreys noted in his book *The Bureau*, 'In spite of a standing order that the assault should be cancelled if secrecy was lost the field commanders, Philip Chojnacki and Chuck Sarabyn, decided to go ahead. They didn't even bother to modify their strategy.'

Shortly after 9.30 a.m., 91 armed ATF agents set off for Mount Carmel in a convoy of 80 vehicles to execute a search warrant for illegal weapons. Three ATF helicopters swooped over the compound. According to several survivors, the choppers opened fire with machine guns and killed three Davidians. The ATF maintained that no shots were fired by their men and that the Davidians fired first, although autopsy reports appeared to indicate that the men had been shot from the air. The question of who fired the first shots would continue to be aired for months to come. Immediately after the raid, one ATF agent told an investigator that a fellow agent may have fired the first shot when he killed a dog outside the compound. The agent later retracted the statement, sticking to the agreed line that the Davidians fired first. The Davidians have always strongly denied this.

The ATF then launched its ground assault. Almost immediately one of the Davidians made an emergency call to the sheriff's office. 'There are 75 men around our building and they're shooting at us,' he screamed. 'Tell 'em there are children and women in here and to call it off.' Believing that God's people were, as Koresh had prophesied, being attacked by the forces of darkness, the Davidians saw it as their duty to return fire. In the subsequent battle, four ATF agents and three more Davidians were killed, bringing the death toll to 10. Among the 28 wounded was David Koresh.

Koresh wasted no time in expressing his outrage. Dialling 911, he yelled at the police despatcher: 'You brought a bunch of guys out there and you killed some of my children. We told you we wanted to talk. How come you guys try to be ATF agents? How come you try to be so big all of the time?'

Having bungled its operation in such spectacular fashion, the ATF was obliged to hand over to the FBI. Many FBI agents had little regard for the ATF – they considered it to be a second-rate organization – and the Mount Carmel fiasco had done nothing to improve the agency's standing. Now the FBI was determined to show the world how such an operation should be conducted.

For the next 51 days, Mount Carmel was under siege. The FBI wanted to resolve the situation in a peaceful manner and hoped to persuade Koresh to surrender without any further loss of life. Meeting no response, two weeks into the siege the FBI embarked on a policy of what it termed 'stress escalation'. The electricity in the compound was cut off and all through the night, huge loudspeakers blasted out the sounds of sirens, crying babies, dying rabbits, roosters, bagpipes, Tibetan religious chants and dental drills, to ensure that the Davidians could not sleep. In a further bid to weaken the cult's resolve, agents bombarded the compound with the worst music they could find, including Andy Williams's 'Christmas Album' and Nancy Sinatra's 'These Boots Are Made For Walkin''. If only the FBI had been able to lay its hands on Dawn's 'Tie a Yellow Ribbon', the Davidians would surely have surrendered in their droves.

Over the ensuing weeks, some followers, including a number of children, did leave the compound, but the majority of the 130 chose to stay. Negotiations continued over the phone with Koresh who refused all medical attention for his bullet wound. He said that he would surrender if the FBI allowed him to address the nation. Accordingly, Waco's Christian radio station broadcast a 58-minute sermon from Mount Carmel, but at the end of it Koresh reneged on the deal. As Koresh dug himself in, federal agents tried to win over his followers, to prove that they were not the ogres Koresh had painted them out to be. They sent in videos, portraying themselves as caring Christians, but their cause was not helped when some Davidians discovered that concealed among gifts of stationery sent into the compound by the FBI were tiny transmitters, designed to give a clearer picture of what was going on inside. It was a clumsy move and one which merely served to widen the gulf with the Davidians who destroyed the transmitters straight away.

Koresh's stance appeared to be hardening. The FBI brought in tanks but Koresh made tapes showing the children inside the compound in order to deter agents from launching another military attack. Negotiations continued, however, and Koresh kept making and breaking promises. On 14 April, Koresh told his lawyer, Dick DeGuerin, that he would surrender when he had finished writing a manuscript which would explain the Seven Seals, but by now the authorities' patience was beginning to run thin. The stalemate could not be allowed to continue indefinitely. There was no possibility of the Davidians being starved out because they had bought thousands of army surplus ready-prepared meals and had stored sufficient water for a year. The FBI was particularly worried that the Davidians would commit mass suicide like the 914 followers of Jim Jones who had poisoned themselves in Guyana in 1978. On 18 April an HRT sniper spotted a movement in one of the compound windows. The view through his high-powered telescope showed that someone had propped a cardboard sign on the window ledge. It read 'Flames Await'. He passed on the information to the forward command post but their response was not recorded. They were probably too busy planning the final strategy.

The new Attorney-General, Janet Reno, was listening to advisers who wanted to storm the compound with CS gas to drive out the Davidians. The cult members did have gas masks but the filters would only last eight hours at the most. Reno remained hesitant about taking such drastic action. She contemplated erecting a cage-like fence around Mount Carmel to keep the Davidians penned in, but the risk to construction workers was deemed too great. Besides, to walk away from a group of people who had already killed four federal agents would make the FBI look hopelessly ineffective. The Bureau could not be seen to lose face. Image was everything.

Reno was persuaded that the longer the siege went on, the greater the risk of disease inside the compound. There were no flush toilets and members, afraid of HRT snipers, had long since stopped burying their human waste and had resorted to simply throwing it out of the door. She was also told that the FBI's hostage rescue team was fatigued but what really swayed her was being told by agents that the children in the compound were in danger of abuse at the hands of Koresh. And so, albeit reluctantly, she gave in to some of her more extreme advisers and approved the use of CS gas on the Branch Davidians. She subsequently stated that her main reason for approving the tear-gas assault was that 'babies were being beaten'. But several months later she revised her statement, agreeing that there was no evidence of ongoing child abuse by Koresh.

At 6 a.m. on 19 April, FBI tanks with large booms attached to the front rumbled in and knocked holes in the walls of the complex. At the same time, the authorities called the compound to say: 'There's going to be tear gas injected into the compound. This is not an assault. Do not fire. The idea is to get you out of the compound.' The gas was pumped in two minutes later and went on for six hours. But the planned exodus did not materialize. Instead, shortly after noon, smoke and flames were seen rising from the battered building. Within minutes, the whole compound was on fire. Only nine cult members – all adults – survived. Koresh was not among them. Just as he had promised, Armageddon had come to the Branch Davidians.

A total of 21 children died in the fire. Six were apparently crushed when a tank demolished the walls; some were shot, presumably by their parents, to put them out of their misery; others choked to death on the gas. Harvard professor Alan Stone later published a report attacking the US government for exposing the children to the gas when it was known that gas masks were available only to adults. All the children had to protect them against such a prolonged attack were wet towels and blankets.

In the aftermath of the tragedy, Janet Reno held her hands up and said: 'I am responsible.' Nobody contradicted her. The ATF and the FBI came under heavy media fire. Stephen Higgins, director of the ATF, was severely criticized and subsequently retired while on-site supervisors Philip Chojnacki and Chuck Sarabyn were dismissed but later reinstated at a lower rank. In response to the criticism, the ATF blamed the media for tipping off the Davidians about the raid, carefully forgetting that it had tipped off the media in the first place. Thanks to Janet Reno's honesty and willingness to take the flak, the heat on the FBI slowly subsided, particularly when fire investigators reported that the fatal fire had been started by the Davidians and not by FBI tanks knocking over lanterns. The clothing of the dead people showed evidence of lighter fuel and other accelerants, a clear indication that the blaze had been started deliberately.

But the FBI was not off the hook yet. A difference of opinion began to emerge among the various senior advisers, some of whom felt that a more softly-softly approach might have tempted the less fanatical Davidians to surrender long before 19 April. There was also a suggestion that impatience was the main reason the FBI pressed Janet Reno to end the stalemate. It was also claimed that the FBI knew that there was no current danger to the children in the compound from Koresh yet they led Reno to believe that the threat of abuse was ongoing. Were some advisers trying to back the new girl (she had only entered office once the siege was underway) into a corner so that she was only left with one possible decision? According to Justice Department reports and congressional testimony, Reno gave only a cursory reading to the three-inch-thick operations plan and back-up documentation about CS gas provided by the FBI two days before the assault on the compound. She told Congress: 'It's easy, in hindsight, to suggest the so-called surrender offer of April 14 was a missed opportunity, but we considered it carefully . . . We had hoped the Davidians might not react violently if we used gas in a slow, incremental manner . . . We will never know whether there was a better solution.'

Although acquitted of murder, eight Branch Davidians were convicted on charges ranging from voluntary manslaughter to weapons violations. The congressional hearings concluded that the Davidians killed themselves although argument still rages regarding accusations that the FBI initially refused to allow firefighters in to douse the flames. FBI photographer Farris Rockstool says: 'I'm left with the haunting opinion that many of the people were homicide victims. The assertion to me that the Branch Davidians committed mass suicide is the most irresponsible statement that can be attributed to the Waco incident.'

Janet Reno remained adamant that Koresh was responsible for the deaths of his followers. 'The fate of the Branch Davidians was in David Koresh's hands,' she told the hearings, 'and he chose death for the men and women who had entrusted their lives in him.'

Jeff Jamar, the FBI agent in charge of the government

operation at Waco, also maintained that the ultimate outcome of the siege was down to Koresh, although he accepted a degree of responsibility. 'I regret what happened', said Jamar. 'We consider it a monumental failure on our part, but it was a failure made certain by David Koresh.'

The Justice Department inquiry into Waco made a number of recommendations for the FBI to consider implementing. The question of fatigue should never be a prime consideration in resolving a situation and, to this end, it was suggested that the Bureau rotate its crisis management team and increase the size of its HRT squad. The inquiry also suggested better communications between the different elements of the crisis management team and the development of more effective anaesthetic gases. Just when it seemed that the ghost of Waco had finally been laid to rest, the FBI suddenly admitted in 1999 that they had used flammable tear gas during the Waco siege, shortly before the fatal fire broke out. Having always steadfastly denied that they had employed any weapons which could have started the fire, this U-turn provoked outrage and led to Janet Reno demanding an immediate inquiry. Seven years on, the truth as to precisely what happened at Waco seems to remain as elusive as ever.

The Law is an Ass

Police on a drugs raid smashed down the front door of a house and pinned a couple to the wall, only to discover that they had the wrong address. Hearing the commotion just before dawn on 14 October 1993, 51-year-old Brian Palliser thought he had been burgled and ran downstairs to challenge the intruders at his home in Gosport, Hampshire, UK. Instead he was confronted by a dozen police officers who dragged his wife Jean from bed and searched the house for 15 minutes. It was only then that the police realized that although they had got the right house number, they had got the wrong road! Their superintendent returned later to apologize to the couple.

*

When he decided to roast a turkey, Wisconsin police chief Richard Williams forgot that he had left his gun in the oven. As the turkey cooked, the gun went off, sending a bullet through the gas stove and into a bannister in the hall. Williams gave himself a one-day, unpaid suspension in May 1998 for violating his department's firearms policy.

*

The London Metropolitan Police were ordered to pay £7500 damages in 1993 to a nurse 'of impeccable character' who had been arrested and charged with being a prostitute. Patricia McNulty, 22, was returning home from a social engagement when she was stopped by police in the early hours of 7 June 1991. She was held in custody and appeared before Marylebone magistrates who 'forcefully' remarked that the charge could not be pursued because the woman was not 'a common prostitute'. No evidence against her was offered and she was discharged. Miss McNulty then sued the police for false imprisonment and malicious prosecution, seeking aggravated damages for 'the anxiety, distress and humiliation caused by this degrading treatment'.

*

After rescuing an injured cat, Gloucestershire policeman Phil Groom then contrived to kill it. The 37-year-old officer spotted the cat at the side of a road near Moreton-in-the-Marsh in January 1998 and put it in a box on top of his car. But he then proceeded to forget all about it and sped off with the box still on top of the car. After a few yards, the box fell off and under the wheels of a car following behind. The distraught officer confessed: 'I must have had my mind on something else.'

*

When former policewoman Clare Harrison was stopped by young PC Karl Horowitz at Stockton-on-Tees, County Durham, in October 1991 for not wearing a seat belt while driving her car, she flatly refused to reveal her age. Instead she told the constable that she was 'in the interesting age of somewhere between 25 and death'. Mrs Harrison, who had spent five years with the Durham force back in the 1950s, pleaded guilty to failing to state her date of birth to a police officer under section 164 of the Road Traffic Act and was fined £5 with £12 costs. On leaving Teesside magistrates court, she found a £25 fixed penalty ticket on her car for illegal parking.

*

In September 1991, Devon and Cornwall police broke up the farewell party of a man told he'd only got three months to live when they mistook it for an Acid House party.

*

A team of private detectives hired to gather evidence against a Yorkshire man spent four years and £50,000 monitoring and videoing the daily movements of a neighbour by mistake. Sent to record the activities of former advertising executive William Hood at his home in the village of Notton, near Wakefield, the cross-eyed private eyes instead focused on the house of retired schoolteacher Peter Arnott who lived around the corner. Mr Hood had been left partially brain-damaged after falling from a cage being raised on the forks of a side-loading truck while producing a brochure for Uponors, a Scandinavian firm which manufactures plastic pipes. When Mr Hood sued for damages, saying he was no longer able to work, Uponors' insurers hired the detectives to investigate his health. Whereas Mr Hood had to be cared for by his wife, Mr Arnott was quite sprightly as the private dicks discovered when secretly filming him labouring in his garden. They also followed him to the bank, on visits to friends and even photographed Mrs Arnott on shopping expeditions and at work. It was only when they presented the videos as evidence of Mr Hood's apparent good health that they were told they had been filming the wrong couple. One villager said: 'A van with blacked-out windows was parked outside and men were walking around with binoculars and cameras. They looked so suspicious that someone called the police, who told her they were private detectives. I can't see how anybody can be so incompetent.'

*

Called out to rescue an eagle owl from the top of a telegraph pole, officers from Northumbria scaled the 30ft high pole, only to find that the creature was a plastic decoy perched there by British Telecom to scare off unwanted nesting birds.

*

When a neighbour reported hearing gunshots from a flat in Selby, North Yorkshire, in 1998, armed police surrounded the building. The occupants emerged, red-faced, to explain that the 'shots' had been the sound of party-poppers as 19-year-old Katie Harris threw a surprise celebration for three friends. 'It was scary at first,' she said, 'but afterwards I couldn't stop laughing.' A police spokesman commented: 'It was an honest misunderstanding. You can't afford to take chances.'

*

Having been in the Nashville, Tennessee, police force for just three months, 23-year-old Joyce Allen and her partner, Officer Terry Coats, witnessed a robbery at Johnny's Sak-Ful drive-in market in 1981. While her partner walked towards the door of the store, Allen drew her gun, pointed it at the door and took cover. Moments later, the door opened and three men ran out. Officer Allen shot all three, killing one and wounding the other two. They were the store manager and two innocent bystanders respectively. The real robber was subsequently flushed out with tear gas after back-up had arrived. Miss Allen was dismissed from the force, not for killing the manager but for wounding the customers. Her police chief Joe

Casey explained that she hadn't violated any rules by killing the manager because she had reason to believe that he was the robber and he had not obeyed police orders to stop. However it was 'not reasonably certain' for her to believe that the other two were involved in the robbery.

*

A group of policemen who arrested a burglar on the roof of a bank in Rainham, Kent, had to be rescued by firefighters after they became stuck.

*

Following reports in March 1995 that a man had been seen with a shotgun outside a Kidderminster building society, police swarmed into the area and pinned a man down on the pavement. The man quietly explained that he had just collected the gun from the engravers nearby.

*

Two off-duty policemen leapt into action when they found a corpse at a country hotel, only to get the shock of their lives when he jumped to his feet and asked them what they thought they were doing. PCs Mick Cotterill and Grant Darbey, who were guests at a party at the Botleigh Grange Hotel near Southampton in 1998, had tried to revive the man by checking his airways and loosening his clothing, unaware that he was an actor taking part in a murder mystery weekend! A Hampshire police spokesman said: 'It was a bit of a surprise when the man made a full recovery so quickly in front of them.'

*

In June 1993, Oxford magistrates heard how two patrol officers with Thames Valley Police stopped a father and son for not wearing seat belts. An argument broke out, as a result of which the police called for considerable, and somewhat unnecessary reinforcements. As the defence lawyer pointed out: 'It should not have taken 21 officers, a helicopter and a heavily armed squad to question two men over a traffic offence.' All charges against the father and son were dismissed.

*

In May 1998, police were called to a bank robbery, only to discover a troupe of mime artists cashing a cheque. The group, called Squ-Wiph, had their faces brightly painted and were wearing dark suits to appear at a Brighton arts festival. Following the false alarm, police in the Sussex town asked the group to avoid banks while in costume.

*

Shortly after the First World War, King Amanullah of Afghanistan stayed at London's Ritz Hotel where he became fascinated by English traditions. The visit made such an impression on him that when he returned to his native country, he tried to pass a law requiring all of his male subjects to wear bowler hats. It was not a popular move and Amanullah was forced to abdicate.

*

On 26 August 1997, police swooped on the offices of Northampton Town Football Club following an anonymous tip-off that a cannabis plant was growing in the club reception area. The officers left clutching a sprig of plastic weeping fig.

*

Seeing three youths fleeing with his pushbike in February 1996, Dr Adrian Rogers, Conservative Party candidate for Exeter, dialled 999 and set off a full-scale hunt by Devon and Cornwall police. The force were accused of wasting taxpayers' money after using a helicopter and three patrol cars in the unsuccessful search for the missing bicycle.

*

Trained as detector dogs for drug raids, police dogs 'Laddie' and 'Boy' found their employment suddenly terminated following one such raid in the Midlands in 1967.

While being questioned, the two suspects patted and
stroked the dogs who eventually fell asleep. But when
the investigating officer moved to make an arrest, one
dog growled at him and the other jumped up and bit him
on the thigh.

*

As part of his 1966 campaign to keep the streets clean, Mayor
Heltor Rocha ordered that all mules passing through the
Brazilian town of Angra Dos Reis must wear nappies. The
directive prompted revolt from police and mule-owners alike.
Police Chief Euripides Da Silva promptly handed in his badge,
saying the rule was impossible to enforce, while Adriano
Siqueira, owner of 110 mules, lamented: 'I can't afford to
buy nappies for all my animals. Think of the size! And at least
three a day will be necessary.' Mayor Rocha was clearly out to
show that the ass is a law.

The Shooting Of Steven Waldorf:
A Case Of Mistaken Identity

Police shoot-outs happened in other capital cities, not London. And certainly not in the peaceful, affluent backwater of
Kensington. But in January 1983, at the height of rush hour,
officers pumped five bullets into the body of an innocent film
editor as he sat in a car stuck in a Friday evening traffic jam,
having wrongly identified him as a dangerous fugitive. As *The
Times* wrote: 'It was a trail of mistakes and coincidences that
went terribly wrong.'

The man Scotland Yard were looking for was David Martin, a gunman who had been arrested for a string of robberies
and for shooting a police constable but who had managed to
escape from a cell at London's Marlborough Street Court just
before Christmas 1982. Martin's girlfriend was freelance

model Sue Stephens and, with no sign of the prisoner, Det. Chief Supt. George Ness, who was in charge of the hunt for Martin, decided to concentrate on her in the hope that she was still seeing him. George Ness formed a squad of 21 officers, drawn from local detectives and officers of Scotland Yard's C11 (criminal intelligence) branch, to mount an intensive watch on Stephens and to follow her every move.

George Ness distributed a poster to police stations warning that Martin was highly dangerous and had to be assumed to be armed. Guns were issued to some officers and the team was told that Martin was violent and cunning and would not hesitate to use firearms. The men were further told that Martin had 'a pathological hatred for authority, particularly directed towards police officers, even more particularly those officers who had arrested him and dealt with him'.

Detective Constable Peter Finch had first-hand experience of Martin's capabilities. The previous September, he had arrested Martin after a desperate struggle in the corridor of his Marylebone flat. Martin was disguised as a woman and produced two guns with which he threatened DC Finch: 'I will have you. I will blow you away.' In the course of the tussle, Martin was shot in the neck by another officer. George Ness knew that Martin might try to carry out that threat if confronted again and so he told his men that if they were led to Martin, a challenge was to be avoided until specialist firearms officers arrived.

On 14 January, Det. Con. Finch and Det. Con. John Jardine were among the men who drew the standard police .38 Smith and Wesson revolvers. Jardine had been accredited to use guns in 1969 and Finch in 1981. Each had received refresher courses three times a year, but neither had drawn guns on operational duties. Indeed although at the time a total of 4476 Metropolitan Police officers were trained in the use of firearms, over a period of three years guns had been drawn on only 300 occasions with fewer than 50 rounds actually being fired, resulting in just six people being injured. By no stretch of the imagination could the Metropolitan Police be termed 'trigger-happy'.

Their guns holstered, the two men formed part of an elaborate police convoy detailed to follow Sue Stephens – a convoy which included a black taxi, a motor cycle and several cars. Officers followed Stephens from her Kilburn flat in a car driven by a friend, Lester Purdy. The latter was due to meet 26-year-old Steven Waldorf, with whom he was involved in a film company, with a view to hiring a car for use in a film. The three arrived at the car hire shop off Portobello Road in west London, closely observed by some of the police vehicles. One police radio message reported: 'We still have three targets, including Susie, waiting for a hire car.' At that point, none of the officers seemed to take much notice of Steven Waldorf even though, with his long fair hair and long nose, he bore a striking resemblance to David Martin. From listening in on Sue Stephens' telephone calls, the police were certain that Martin was to be in the yellow Mini at some stage that day. And as Lester Purdy drove west in a yellow Mini with Steven Waldorf in the front passenger seat and Sue Stephens in the back, it suddenly dawned on the police that the third person – Waldorf – might actually be David Martin. But they needed a positive identification. One radio report said: 'It is looking good, it may be our target. We can see his large nose, his hair, it is looking good.' Another officer, in the car closest to the Mini, was more cautious, using the words: 'We might, I stress might, have the wanted man.'

George Ness was in a car at the rear of the convoy when the Mini became stuck in heavy traffic in Pembroke Road near the junction with Earls Court Road. He had earlier ordered the car containing Det. Con. Finch not to get too far forward to make an identification but now, with the traffic at a standstill, he decided to send someone ahead on foot to take a closer look at the occupants of the Mini. Finch knew Martin better than most of the team and the police radio announced: 'Peter is going on foot.' As Finch crept up to the passenger door of the Mini, he would later testify that he 'was 100 per cent sure' it was Martin. 'I was looking through the glass and I saw a three-quarter profile of Martin. I saw his large nose, his hair and even his high cheekbones.' Moving alongside, DC Finch fired two shots into the near-side back tyre of the car and his remaining four bullets through the closed near-side window at the man he mistakenly thought was Martin. Believing that the gunfire was being returned, colleagues rushed to Finch's aid. A total of 14 bullets were fired, five of them hitting the unfortunate Steven Waldorf. It was only with Waldorf slumped across the seat, half in and half out of the car, that Finch realized that he and his fellow officers had shot the wrong man. No weapons were found in the Mini.

Steven Waldorf was rushed to hospital to be treated for gunshot wounds and a fractured skull. Miraculously, although suffering severe injuries including a damaged liver and almost dying from loss of blood, he survived.

The real David Martin was recaptured two weeks later after a dramatic chase along the London Underground and was subsequently sentenced to 25 years in prison, but Detective Constables Finch and Jardine were left facing a charge of attempting to murder Steven Waldorf.

It emerged that Waldorf was unlucky on three counts: he looked like Martin, he knew Martin's girlfriend, Sue Stephens, and he happened to be in the yellow Mini on the day when the police were expecting Martin to show. It was a dreadful chain of coincidence. As he recovered from his injuries, Waldorf told the *News of the World*: 'I can honestly say I've never met David Martin. The only link between us is his girlfriend, Sue Stephens.' Waldorf explained how he had met Stephens while on a blind date with Lester Purdy. 'Lester spotted two very pretty girls, real sweeties. They gave him the eye and invited him to their place. Lester asked me along and I finished up with Sue Stephens. I went to her flat about four times. I gather police had been watching it, and photographed me going in and out.' If it had struck any of the officers at that stage how similar Waldorf looked to Martin, the bloodbath could have been avoided.

Finch and Jardine, both 37, stood trial at the Old Bailey in October of that year. Both pleaded 'not guilty' to the charge of attempted murder. They also denied wounding Waldorf with intent to cause him bodily harm. The officers claimed their actions were justified because they honestly, though mistakenly, believed Waldorf to have been Martin and, thinking Martin would be armed, both men feared for their lives. The two officers had excellent records. The most recent internal assessment of DC Finch, who had joined the force in 1961 and had two commendations, said that he was 'a mature officer who thinks before acting in all circumstances'. And the appraisal of DC Jardine, a policeman for 18 years, reported that he was 'rarely flustered. Does not jump to conclusions'.

Attorney-General Sir Michael Havers, QC, outlined the events of 14 January in Pembroke Road. He said that, when ordering Det. Con. Finch to take a closer look at the Mini on foot, Det. Supt. Ness had stressed that Finch should not attempt to make an arrest unless it became absolutely necessary. The officer in the vehicle with Finch had expected him to walk along the street, casually pass the Mini, look into the passenger window and report back. But as Finch walked along the pavement, he drew his revolver. This, said Sir Michael, was quite contrary to all standing instructions. Finch claimed that he called out 'armed police' but Sir Michael said that nobody in the surrounding area or in the Mini heard any such warning. Finch fired two shots into the near-side back tyre to deflate it – even though the car was stationary in traffic – and then four more at Waldorf who was hit in the back.

Three cars behind the Mini, Det. Con. Deane heard firing. 'He went towards the Mini and saw Finch firing and glass flying in all directions,' continued Sir Michael. 'Although mistaken, he thought the firing was two-way and coming from inside the car as well. He was wrong, but one can understand how he made the mistake. He fired five shots towards the car – four of them went through the rear windscreen.' Det. Con. Deane had not been prosecuted because it was felt that he had made an honest mistake.

Explaining Det. Con. Jardine's part in the shooting, Sir Michael said: 'When Jardine reached the off-side window of the car, Waldorf had by then fallen across the driver's seat and was lying out of the open door with the upper part of his body and head on the tarmac of the road and the other part of his body on the front seat. Jardine, then at a distance of six to 12 ft, fired three shots at that man lying half in and half out of the car who had already been shot. He missed his head, two shots missed altogether and one hit him in the body. By the time he finished firing five bullets had entered different parts of Waldorf's body. There he was with five bullets in him, lying half out of the car, and Finch comes over to him and strikes him several times over the head with his empty pistol, fracturing his skull and a bone in one hand.' Witnesses had seen the pistol raised to head height before being brought down on the wounded Waldorf who was then brought out of the car and handcuffed face down in the road. Studying his face closely, Finch then realized that he had made a horrifying mistake, said Sir Michael.

The Attorney-General went on: 'It does not matter, in fact, whether it was Martin or Waldorf because there was no need, in the submission of the Crown, to take those actions at that stage – either to shoot him as Jardine did when he was half in and half out of the car, or to fracture his skull with a revolver, as Finch did. Whether Finch was standing or crouching in order to strike Waldorf hard at least twice, surely he must have been in a position to stop him getting a gun, even if he had a gun to go for. If you are pistol-whipping a man that closely, you must be in a position to restrain him.'

The prosecution also alleged that, after the shooting, Jardine had told investigating officers: 'I intended to totally incapacitate him and the only way to do that with a gun was to kill him.'

Against the backdrop of this 'Shoot to kill' claim, Steven Waldorf, looking pale and thin, his voice barely audible, recalled the moment his world caved in. He thought the first shots were a car backfiring, then he thought he had got caught up in cross-fire. Finally, 'it became pretty apparent I was the target. I was trying to think if I had any enemies. The car windows came in and the bullets kept coming through. I remember being hit.' He remembered trying to grab Lester Purdy's shoulder as his friend frantically escaped from the car, but did not have the strength to hold on. 'Bullets kept coming through. I tried to duck. I still imagined I had the strength to actually leave, but I did not have enough energy in my body. I don't know the words to describe the pain I was in. When I was hit over the head with a gun, I didn't even feel it.' But he did feel his hands being 'brutally ripped' up his back as police handcuffed him. Told by counsel for Det. Con. Finch that the officer 'deeply regrets his terrible mistake' and was asking him to accept his apologies, Waldorf made no reply.

The two other passengers in the Mini told of the confusion in the dark. They said they had no reason at first to believe that the attackers were police because they heard no warning and also the gunmen were casually dressed. Both thought they had somehow got caught up in terrorist activity. After clambering out of the car, Lester Purdy testified how he went back to see a man with a revolver in one hand dragging Steven Waldorf out of the car. 'He looked limp and I thought he was dead.'

Taking the stand after the judge had directed that the attempted murder charge against him be dropped, Det. Con. Finch told how, when the Mini got stuck in traffic and it was suggested that an officer who knew Martin should try and identify him, he got out of the unmarked police vehicle some 250 yards behind and, wearing a large blue anorak with his gun in his holster on his right hip, approached the Mini. 'After I got out of the car, I drew my revolver. I knew that if it was Martin in the car, he wouldn't hesitate to shoot me. I had to be prepared and I felt that this was, as the rules say, an occasion when I should draw my weapon. The anorak was very large and if I wanted to try to get it out, I would have had difficulty. I was not going to run along the street and start fumbling under the anorak at the last minute. I was holding the gun in my right hand straight down the side of my leg so I would not display it to the public.'

As the traffic moved forward, Finch increased his pace until he caught up with the Mini. Wearing a flat cap so as not to look like a policeman in case Martin identified him, Finch drew level with the passenger door. 'I was sure it was him, absolutely positive. I had made my identification as I had been told to. I was nervous and tense. My intention was to walk away or get away as soon as I could and tell other officers. I started to back off, I was going away and when I got towards the rear side of the Mini, I saw that the driver turned his head round to the left and was looking at me. He then turned it back and said something to the front passenger who then turned round in between the two front seats and reached towards the rear seat. I immediately dropped down on my haunches because I thought he was going for a gun.'

Although he admitted that he hadn't actually seen a gun in the car, or anything that looked like one, he pulled up his own gun into a position in front of him with arms outstretched. 'I feared for my life. I thought I was going to be shot from my previous experience with Martin. The only words I could get out were "armed police". It didn't come out very well at all. My voice faltered so it was not a loud shout. I saw his body in the rear near-side window still reaching. I raised my gun and I fired a pair of shots but these went into the tyre. It was because I was nervous that they did so. It was bad shooting, the gun was moving in my hand, I then raised myself into a higher position and moved forward towards the passenger door. I was still on the edge of the pavement. The shoulder area was the largest part which I saw and that was where I aimed. He was moving about a great deal, his head was bobbing and weaving. I think I fired two paired shots. I intended to shoot him in the upper arm. I think I noticed DC Deane at the rear of the Mini and he started to fire. This surprised me – I didn't think there was another armed officer on the street besides me.'

After DC Deane had finished shooting, Finch saw the slumped body hanging out of the front passenger seat. 'He was moving, he was coming out and I still thought I was vulnerable, me without any ammunition and DC Deane doing a reload. From my experience with Martin, even when he had been shot he was still a very dangerous man. He was still capable of getting a gun out when I arrested him. I thought that was going to happen this time.' Finch, who emphatically denied a suggestion by Sir Michael that he had embarked on a 'private enterprise mission from beginning to end', said that he felt 'absolutely terrible' when he realized his mistake. 'But,' he added, 'I believed I was doing the right thing at the time.'

The attempted murder charge still stood against Det. Con. Jardine, however. He recounted his version of the shooting of Steven Waldorf. 'Everything happened extremely fast. As soon as the firing started, DC Deane got out of the side of our van and ran up towards the Mini. I reacted slower than him and ran towards the Mini also. There were shots being fired the whole time. When I got to the Mini the rear window was shattered. I had the impression of DC Deane cowering down behind the Mini. I thought he was taking cover. I went to the off-side of the Mini where I saw the driver's door open and the man I now know to be Waldorf lying half out of the car. His hands were the thing I noticed immediately – they were making what I would call groping movements down his body. There was only one explanation. For what had gone on before, the man had to have a gun. It had to be somewhere. I decided to shoot him before I was shot. I brought the gun up in both hands and fired two shots towards him, I think probably at his head, but it was sense of direction shooting. I think I was probably going for his head because I had to stop him doing what he was doing.'

Summing up, Mr Justice Croom-Johnson said that once the jury accepted that the constables had made genuine mistakes, they must put themselves in the detectives' position, believing that David Martin was in the car. 'If you think in a moment of sudden and unexpected peril that person only did what he thought was necessarily honest and instinctive, then you would think it very strong evidence that only reasonable defensive action was taken.' Officers were entitled to shoot first in self-defence, added the judge.

The jury of eight women and four men took one and three-quarter hours to acquit both policemen of all charges. Although Geoffrey Dear, Assistant Commissioner of the Metropolitan Police, announced that they would be facing internal disciplinary measures, an inquiry recommended that no further charges be brought against Finch or Jardine. Their suspensions were lifted but neither they nor DC Deane would ever be allowed to carry guns again.

Steven Waldorf was not surprised by the verdict. 'I don't think I could actually ever forgive them, but I can't blame them. It's the system that's at fault, not them. When you think that they fired 14 bullets and only five hit me – and none of them killed me – that had to be luck. It was lucky the police were bad shots. At least I think it was luck – I don't know whether we're lucky or unlucky when the police are incompetent.' In March 1984, Waldorf received £120,000 in compensation from the Metropolitan Police.

In the wake of the Steven Waldorf shooting, the Home Office introduced new rules regarding the issue of weapons. Whereas previously in the Metropolitan Police area firearms could be issued by an inspector, the new directive stated that they must be authorized by an officer of commander rank or above. In provincial forces, the Home Office document specified that the chief constable, deputy chief constable or assistant chief constable must make the authorization. Additionally all officers issued with a firearm had to be 'strictly warned' that it was to be used only in cases of 'absolute necessity' to protect the public, themselves or colleagues as a last resort and as a means of defence. The changes also meant that armed police had to carry a card reminding them of the law concerning firearms and their use. The aim was to ensure that there would be no repeat of the bloody mayhem which shattered the peace of a west London street and left an innocent man fighting for his life.

Chapter 3

Criminal Negligence

Son of Sam: Trapped by a Parking Violation

Over a 12-month period between 1976 and 1977, the city of New York was gripped with fear of a shadowy assassin calling himself 'Son of Sam'. He preyed on young couples sitting in stationary cars during the early hours of Saturdays or Sundays, shooting dead six of them and wounding seven others. He left behind precious few clues, only to be finally undone when he received a parking ticket for leaving his car next to a fire hydrant. The ticket was traced to 24-year-old postal worker and former auxiliary policeman David Berkowitz. And it was this squat little man with a child-like face who turned out to be the terrifying Son of Sam.

Berkowitz was a paranoid schizophrenic who lived alone in the Yonkers district of the city in a room lit only by a bare bulb and where the sleeping accommodation amounted to nothing more than a mattress. The floor was strewn with empty milk cartons and on the wall he had scrawled messages such as, 'In this hole lives the Wicked King' and 'I kill for my Master'.

Berkowitz had felt rejected from the outset. Born illegitimate, he was put up for adoption by his mother. While other teenagers were out enjoying themselves with the opposite sex, Berkowitz led a solitary existence. He later complained that girls despised him and spat at him in the street. 'Girls call me ugly,' he wrote in a letter to his absentee father, 'and they bother me the most.' He vowed revenge.

Living in his squalid surroundings, Berkowitz became increasingly paranoid. He was kept awake night after night by a barking dog – a black Labrador belonging to a neighbour, Sam Carr. The dog was thought to be the origin of the 'Son of Sam' sobriquet. Berkowitz wrote Carr a series of anonymous letters and eventually resorted to shooting the dog, although not fatally. Berkowitz would also later claim that voices – including that of the dog – had been urging him to kill since 1974, but experts believed that he had invented his 'demons' in a bid to establish a defence of insanity.

Berkowitz embarked on his campaign of revenge against women on Christmas Eve 1975. Armed with a knife, he attacked two girls. The first screamed so loudly that he was forced to flee; the second suffered a punctured lung but survived. So he sought to arm himself with something which would eliminate the possibility of failure – a .44 Bulldog revolver.

On the night of 29 July 1976, two young women were sitting in the front of a car parked in the Bronx. Shortly after 1 a.m., Berkowitz walked up to the car, pulled a gun out of a brown paper bag and fired five shots. One woman was killed instantly but the other escaped with a thigh wound. On 23 October, Berkowitz struck again, this time outside a bar in Queens, wounding a man as he sat in his sports car talking to his girlfriend. A .44 bullet was found on the floor of the car. Then, in the early hours of 26 November, he approached two more girls as they were sitting in front of a house in Queens. He asked for directions, but before they had a chance to reply he pulled out his gun from the brown paper bag and started shooting wildly. A bullet lodged in the spine of one of the victims, paralysing her for life; the other girl recovered. Bullets retrieved from the front door of the house and a mailbox showed that the pair had been shot by the same gun used in the July killing.

The police were mystified as to the motive behind the shootings. There was no attempt at sexual assault or robbery. They concluded that they were dealing with the most terrifying killer of all – someone who picks victims at random and shoots them for the sheer hell of it.

The attacks continued into the New Year – always in the Bronx and Queens and invariably between 2.30 and 3 a.m. on a Sunday. On 30 January 1977, a young couple were kissing goodnight in a car when the calm was destroyed by the shattering of the windscreen. Shot by Berkowitz, the girl slumped into the arms of her boyfriend. A few hours later, she died in hospital. On 8 March, an Armenian student was shot in the face by Berkowitz at close range. The bullet shattered her front teeth and killed her instantly.

As women were warned not to travel alone at night in the city, there was a double killing on the morning of 17 April when Berkowitz opened fire on the occupants of a car parked in the Bronx. Until then, the police had no clue as to the killer's identity. Since he always struck at night and at great speed, descriptions from survivors were vague. But now one of the police officers at the murder scene found an envelope addressed to Captain Joseph Borrelli of the New York Police Department. It was written by the killer and chastised the NYPD for describing him as a woman-hater. 'I am not', he protested. 'But I am a monster. I am the Son of Sam. I am a little brat . . . I love to hunt, prowling the streets, looking for fair game . . . tasty meat . . . The weman (sic) of Queens are prettyist of all.' In the letter, a clear imitation of the Jack the Ripper correspondence, the killer claimed that, as a child, he had been brutally treated by his father who had later ordered him to go out on to the streets and kill people. Desperate for publicity, he also wrote to Jimmy Breslin, a journalist on New York's *Daily News*, but Breslin, who had written extensively about the killings, simply passed the letter on to the police.

On 26 June, another young couple were shot at almost point-blank range as they said goodnight in their car parked in Queens. Four shots shattered the windscreen but these victims were luckier than most – Berkowitz's aim had been below par and they escaped with relatively minor wounds. His bloodlust remained unabated but, with Queens and the Bronx swarming with police, he decided to try his luck further afield. He had no desire to be caught yet – his mission was far from accomplished. At 1.30 on the morning of Sunday 31 July, a 20-year old girl was sitting with a man in a parked car near Brooklyn beach when their windscreen suddenly exploded as Berkowitz unleashed four bullets. Both occupants were shot in the head. The woman was killed; the man was blinded for life.

But for the first time, Berkowitz had committed a serious blunder. While carrying out his murderous attack, he had parked his car illegally near a fire hydrant on Bay 16th Street. A woman out walking her dog had spotted two police officers sticking a parking ticket on what turned out to be Berkowitz's car and moments later, she had seen a man run to the car, jump in and drive off at speed. When she heard about the shootings, her suspicions were aroused and she informed the police. Only four parking tickets had been issued in the Bay area that morning and just one of those was for parking near a fire hydrant. The carbon copy of the ticket in the officer's notebook contained the registration number of the car and the Vehicle Licensing Department was able to supply the name and address of the owner – David Berkowitz of Pine Street, Yonkers.

Three days after the Brooklyn murder, detectives spotted a Ford Galaxie parked outside an apartment building in Pine Street. On the seat, they could see a .44 revolver (which turned out to be loaded) and a note written in the same style as the 'Son of Sam' letters. The police staked out the street and waited for the owner to return to the vehicle. At 10.15 that evening, Berkowitz went up to the car. Deputy Inspector Tim Dowd, the man in charge of the hunt, called out to him, 'Hello, David.' Berkowitz looked momentarily stunned before calmly replying: 'Inspector Dowd – you finally got me!'

The news that Berkowitz had been arrested came as a shock to the few people who knew him. Even though he had written anonymous letters to people he thought were persecuting him and had been reported to the police on more than one occasion as 'a nutcase', nobody suspected for a moment that he would turn out to be Son of Sam.

Berkowitz's attempt at proving that he was insane fell on deaf ears. He was declared fit to stand trial and pleaded guilty. He was sentenced to 365 years in prison. One of the most notorious killers of modern times had been brought to justice – all because he hadn't watched where he was parking his car.

Thomas Henry Allaway: A Spelling Mistake

After luring an innocent London girl to her death in Bournemouth, chauffeur Thomas Henry Allaway made strenuous efforts to cover his tracks. But in the end, he was let down by his poor spelling. And it was this repeated inability to spell certain words which, more than anything else, sent him to the gallows.

Irene May Wilkins was the daughter of a London lawyer and had served in the Women's Army Auxiliary Corps during the First World War. A pleasant young woman, she was looking for a post as a school cook and inserted the following advert in the *Morning Post*:

Lady Cook, 31, requires post in a school. Experienced in school with forty boarders. Disengaged. Salary £65. Miss Irene Wilkins, 21 Thirlmere Road, Streatham, SW16.

The advert appeared on the morning of Wednesday, 22 December 1921 and before noon of that day, Miss Wilkins received in reply a telegram from Bournemouth. It read:

Morning Post. Come immediately. 4.30 train Waterloo. Bournmouth Central. Car will meet train. Expence no object. Urgent. Wood. Beech House.

Disregarding the fact that the sender could not spell either 'Bournemouth' or 'expense' – she may have attributed the errors to the girl in the Post Office – Miss Wilkins wired back straight away to say that she would come down for an interview. Leaving Streatham at around 3 p.m., she caught the 4.30 express from Waterloo. Shortly after her departure, the telegram she had sent to Bournemouth was returned to Thirlmere Road since the Post Office said that the name and address given in Bournemouth did not exist. Her mother was puzzled, to say the least.

Early on the morning of Friday, 23 December, the body of Irene Wilkins was found in a field between Bournemouth and Christchurch. She had died from blows to the head, inflicted by a heavy instrument. She had put up a fierce struggle and, although her clothes were pulled up around her waist, she had not been raped. It seemed that the killer had been disturbed before he had the opportunity to assault her sexually. But the murderer had left behind an important clue in the form of a set of Dunlop Magnum car-tyre tracks in the lane near the body. From the extra deepness of the tread, it was clear that the car had stopped adjacent to where the body was found.

The police concluded that the driver of the car which had taken Miss Wilkins from Bournemouth Central station to the murder scene must have known the area well and so they ordered every chauffeur and owner-driver in the district to report for questioning. This sort of thing was feasible in the

1920s when there were still relatively few cars on the road. In particular, the police noted the drivers' movements between 7 p.m. and 9 p.m. on the evening of the 22nd (this had been established as the time of murder) and whether their vehicle was fitted with Dunlop Magnum tyres. Meanwhile a witness, Frank Humphris, came forward to say that he had seen Miss Wilkins arriving at Bournemouth Central on the evening in question and had watched her being driven off by a man dressed as a chauffeur. A second witness corroborated the story, adding that the car was a Mercedes.

It also emerged that, in addition to the telegram sent to Miss Wilkins, two others in the same handwriting had been despatched from the Bournemouth area in recent days with the intention of luring young women to the seaside resort. Both contained schoolboy spelling errors. In the first telegram, sent on 17 December, 'advertisement' was spelt 'advertisment', 'immediate' was spelt 'immidiate', 'if' was spelt 'iff' and once again 'Bournemouth' was written as 'Bournmouth' and 'expense' as 'expence'. In the second telegram, sent off on 20 December, the word 'pleasant' appeared as 'plesent' and, as a result of the unusual construction of the letter 'c', the word 'car' looked more like 'ear'. This trait was repeated in the third telegram – the one sent to Miss Wilkins – where, in addition, to the misspellings of 'Bournemouth' and 'expense', the sender had copied out the Streatham address as 'Thirlmear Road' instead of 'Thirlmere'. Fortunately the recipients of the first two telegrams had not been able to answer in person.

The three telegrams were vital clues and so, whenever a driver was interviewed in connection with his car tyres, he was also instructed to write down from dictation the triumvirate of telegrams. It was a laborious task but one which the police were certain would trap the killer. In the meantime, on 31 December, nine days after the murder, a case containing Miss Wilkins's references was found hidden in rhododendron bushes in Branksome Wood on the other side of Bournemouth. This reaffirmed the police view that they were looking for a local man.

As the screening of local drivers continued, Frank Humphris came forward again to report that he had seen the same car which had whisked Miss Wilkins away near the station on 4 January. This time he had scribbled down the registration number. It was that of a Mercedes, owned by a Mr and Mrs Sutton who employed as their chauffeur a former soldier by the name of Thomas Henry Allaway. The car was fitted with three Dunlop Magnum tyres and one Michelin. But what Allaway lacked in education, he clearly made up for in animal cunning because when he was subjected to the dictation test, he disguised his handwriting in such a way that it was vertical as opposed to the sloping hand of the telegrams. Faced with no match, a junior officer consigned the Allaway report to file and let him go.

But Superintendent Garrett, the officer in charge of the case, had already become suspicious of Allaway's behaviour and was pretty much convinced that he was the murderer. However, by April 1922, with no firm evidence, he resolved to go back through every document relating to the case and chanced upon the earlier report consigned to file. He was now more certain than ever that Allaway was his man but the only samples of Allaway's handwriting he had were from after the murder and bore no relation to the telegrams. What he needed was something from an earlier date.

On 20 April, Allaway, beginning to feel the heat, stole a cheque book from his employer, filled in several cheques, forged Mr Sutton's signature and with the proceeds – some £20 – fled to London and to Reading where he was finally arrested. In his pocket the police discovered betting slips in the same sloping handwriting as the telegrams. Away from Bournemouth, Allaway had dropped his guard and had not bothered disguising his writing. Allaway's wife thought he had been taken in for nothing more serious than forgery and willingly handed over earlier specimens of her husband's handwriting, including some postcards and a long letter written to her while he had been based in Germany. The letter was not only in the same slanting hand as the three telegrams but it also contained many of the characteristic spelling errors.

The case against Allaway was building up steadily. Mrs Sutton revealed that, on 29 December, Allaway had driven her to take tea with her sister who lived at Branksome Wood. It was nearby that Miss Wilkins's case had been found two days later. In addition, Mrs Sutton divulged that Allaway had often driven her through the district where the murder had taken place and was thus aware of its remote nature. And a tea salesman, who kept two vans in the same garage as the Mercedes, stated that at 9 a.m. on 24 December, straight after the police announced that they were looking for a vehicle with Dunlop Magnum tyres, Allaway changed a Dunlop Magnum tyre on a rear wheel of the Mercedes for a Michelin.

Allaway was placed in an identification parade and was picked out by a newsagent who had sold him a copy of the *Morning Post* on 22 December. Three Post Office girls were also called upon to identify him. Two failed to do so but the third picked him out immediately, both by his face and voice. She distinctly remembered querying the word 'car'. Frank Humphris also picked out Allaway without hesitation. The police even unearthed the connection with the fictitious 'Wood. Beech House' of the telegram sent to Miss Wilkins. Knowing how difficult it would be for someone who was illiterate to pluck an invented address out of thin air, the police sensed that Allaway would have chosen something with a vaguely familiar ring. Sure enough, they found that Mr Sutton's son lived at Beech Hurst, Beechwood Avenue and that Allaway had frequently driven his employer there.

Following the identification parade, Allaway was asked whether he wanted to make a statement. Hoping to throw the police off the scent once more, he opted to write it rather than dictate it, deliberately using the new upright style which he had obviously spent weeks perfecting. In fact, his first few words actually sloped backwards. If he had contented himself with a short account, he might have got away with it but as the statement wore on and he began to tire, the writing lapsed into the slanting hand of the three telegrams. Next, he was asked to take down the three telegrams again from dictation. When he had performed this task in January, he had scrawled his answers resting the paper on the mudguard of the Mercedes so that the writing looked nothing like his own. This time he displayed intense concentration to make sure that the writing remained vertical but he couldn't help himself when it came to his lousy spelling: 'pleasant' was 'plesent', 'expense' was 'expence' and 'Bournemouth' was 'Bournmouth'. The game was up.

Allaway stood trial for the murder of Irene Wilkins at Winchester in July 1922. He tried to deny that the long letter from Germany, signed 'your loving husband Tom', was in his handwriting, claiming that his wrist had been injured at the time and that he had persuaded a friend to write it for him. It was a futile gesture and the jury found him guilty. On the night before his execution, he finally admitted his guilt to the prison governor. It might all have been so different had he brushed up on his spelling.

Marlene Lehnberg: Not a Leg to Stand On

Surely the first rule when hiring a contract killer is to choose somebody who will not draw attention to themselves and can slip in and out of the vicinity quickly and unnoticed. So when

Marlene Lehnberg decided to have her lover's wife murdered, she was somewhat ill-advised in choosing as her hired assassin a man with an artificial leg!

Dubbed the 'Scissors Murder' by the popular press, the case caused a sensation in South Africa in March 1975. Crowds jostled outside the courthouse just to catch a glimpse of the two defendants – Lehnberg, a pretty 19-year-old white former Sunday school teacher and her hit man, Marthinus Choegoe, an impoverished coloured cripple. They were the oddest of odd couples. Even the stakes were bizarre. Almost without exception, the currency in contract killings is hard cash. It is the only language understood by all parties. But Lehnberg planned a different method of payment if Choegoe did away with Susanna Van der Linde: she promised him a radio, a car, sex – and a new artificial leg.

Marlene Lehnberg came from a respectable home in the highly desirable Constantia suburb of Cape Town where her parents were regular churchgoers. Remembered by friends as a quiet girl, she left home in 1972 at the age of 16 and began work as a receptionist in the orthopaedic workshop of Cape Town's Red Cross Hospital. There she was taken under the wing of 47-year-old father-of-three Christiaan Van der Linde, a technician in the orthopaedic department and seemingly a happily married man. At first the relationship between Lehnberg and Van der Linde was more 'father–daughter', but within a year it had developed into something stronger. She had become a young woman of quite stunning beauty, so much so that she was seriously considering a career as a model. Van der Linde, nearly three times her age, was naturally flattered by her attention and in April 1973 they embarked on an affair.

The lovers would meet virtually every weekday, at lunch and also after work when he would give her a lift back to the boarding-house where she was staying. He would then go home to his wife Susanna. Van der Linde took care to keep the two women in his life well apart. For that reason, he never saw Lehnberg at weekends. His wife never suspected a thing and for a year or so Van der Linde was able to enjoy the best of both worlds. However Lehnberg wanted to be more than just his bit on the side. She had fallen in love with him and begged him to leave his wife. In return, he fobbed her off with meaningless platitudes calculated to keep her interested until their next session of passion. Eventually it dawned on Lehnberg that the relationship wasn't going anywhere. In spite of his vague promises, Van der Linde – a powerful personality bordering on the arrogant – seemed to have no intention of leaving his wife. Lehnberg became frustrated at only being able to see her lover when it suited him and resolved to take matters into her own hands. She wanted him all to herself and realized that the only person in her way was Susanna Van der Linde.

In June 1974, using the name Marlene Pietersen, she wrote to 34-year-old Choegoe whom she had first met when he was a patient at the orthopaedic workshop. He had only one leg, having lost the other above the knee in an accident two years previously. An artificial leg had been fitted at the Red Cross Hospital. Choegoe lived in a slum area of Cape Town with the mother of his two young children. Being a cripple of mixed race in apartheid South Africa, his job prospects were, to say the least, slim. By contrast, Lehnberg, being white and beautiful, enjoyed a position of privilege and power. Just as Van der Linde seemed to exercise some form of control over her, she saw no reason why she should not exert similar influence over the hapless Choegoe. In her letter (typewritten to make detection more difficult), she wrote: 'Marthinus, if you are clever you can still earn good money.' She asked him to meet her at the workshop. Not in a position to turn down the prospect of any money-making scheme, Choegoe readily agreed to the rendezvous. He was captivated by her beauty and dutifully referred to her as 'Miss Marlene'. Describing his relationship with her and the power she held over him, he would subsequently testify: 'I felt bewitched'.

Not surprisingly, Lehnberg wasn't altogether convinced that Choegoe was up to the job of murdering Mrs Van der Linde so first she approached a young neighbour, Robbie Newman. She asked whether she could borrow his pistol to shoot Mrs Van der Linde and when he refused point-blank, she asked him whether he fancied shooting the woman instead. Newman told her she was mad. Fearing that having somebody bumped off wasn't as easy as it sounded, Lehnberg tried a different tack and attempted to worry Susanna Van der Linde into an early grave. In September 1974, she bombarded Mrs Van der Linde with a succession of telephone calls, each more explicit than the last. Lehnberg defiantly told her that she was having an affair with her husband but the wife dismissed her as some silly little girl out to cause trouble. In a fresh bid to force his hand, Lehnberg told Van der Linde that she was pregnant. Realizing that things were starting to get out of hand, he told his wife of the girl's claim. She told him to take no notice. When Van der Linde relayed this reply to Lehnberg, she said that she had miscarried over the weekend. Of course, she had never been pregnant in the first place.

Although Susanna was vowing to stand by her husband, Lehnberg was becoming a nuisance at work. Van der Linde had his position to consider and so he fixed Lehnberg up with a job with a different orthopaedic company, hoping that the relationship would cool. Lehnberg was devastated. Her letters to him became tinged with bitterness. In one she wrote: 'I gave up everything I had for you. Yet you won't give an inch. You would rather live for the rest of your life with a woman you do not love.'

Aware that Susanna Van der Linde was not going to fall to

pieces, Lehnberg reverted to her original plan of murder and set about grooming Choegoe for the task. Hiring a man with a pronounced limp and a marked tendency to fall over might not have seemed the smartest move in the world. And no one would have rated his chances too highly at an identification parade. To be cruelly honest, if Choegoe could hardly stand up in court, nor would his defence. However, Lehnberg, in that dominant way she had, convinced him that he was the ideal candidate as a hit man since he would be the last person in Cape Town that the police would suspect. Nobody would think he was physically capable of killing anyone single-handed. As will be seen, he wasn't.

Lehnberg arranged a meeting with him at Rondebosch Town Hall. She gave him the money for his bus fare and told him that she wanted him to do some work for her. She wanted him to kill a woman – she wanted him to 'haunt' the home of Susanna Van der Linde. As an incentive, she threw in her car and a radio which she had stolen from a neighbour. It was sufficient to persuade Choegoe to give it a go.

The Van der Lindes lived on the Boston Estate in the Cape Town suburb of Bellville. It was, of course, a white area and coloured visitors were rare and unwelcome. So Choegoe, particularly with his limp, stood out like a sore thumb. He first called at the house on the pretext of asking for change, but Mrs Van der Linde told him she had none and slammed the door in his face before he had time to draw breath. But the call did unnerve her and she went out and bought a dye gun as protection in case the spooky-looking stranger returned.

Lehnberg had given Choegoe her new work number and when he phoned to report his failure, she arranged another meeting for the following week at Rondebosch Town Hall. There she repeated that the woman had to be killed but this time came up with a more enticing reward. She promised him that 'they would make his leg better at the hospital if he killed

Mrs Van der Linde'. The offer of a new leg was certainly something to consider.

In a letter to Choegoe, after explaining that Mrs Van der Linde's son left for school early in the morning, Lehnberg urged: 'The date is now set for Tuesday 23rd. Wait 15 minutes and then go to work. Use a knife if it will be better or quicker but the job must be done. If you don't get it right, I'll wring your neck.'

If anything, Choegoe's second visit to Bellville was even less successful than the first. This time he didn't even get as far as knocking on the front door. Instead he was so scared that he just hobbled straight past the house.

Another failure brought another meeting with Lehnberg and another offer. Now she promised that if he carried out the killing, she would have sex with him. The prospect of getting his artificial leg over was extremely appealing but Lehnberg wasn't taking any chances. Having deduced that, left to his own devices, Choegoe was nothing short of a disaster as an assassin, she decided to give him a helping hand by driving him to Bellville herself the next day. So on 24 October, Choegoe, armed with a hammer he had brought from home, was dropped off by Lehnberg to set about his murderous business. He rang the doorbell but nobody answered. It was another abortive mission. Afterwards, the police found him wandering the streets three blocks from the Van der Linde residence and strongly advised him to make a swift exit from the neighbourhood and never to return. Choegoe took the hint and told Lehnberg that he was finished with the murder plan. But it wasn't that easy to escape from her wicked web.

It was now apparent to Lehnberg that as things stood Susanna Van der Linde was just about the safest person in the whole of Cape Town. Clearly Choegoe could not be relied upon to carry out the contract killing alone so Lehnberg realized she would have to tag along as his accomplice. On

28 October, she stole Robbie Newman's pistol and told her new boss that she was leaving for Johannesburg at midnight on 3 November – a clumsy attempt to establish an alibi for the morning of the 4th. Then on 1 November, Van der Linde finally got round to telling her that the affair was over. She was angry but remained convinced that if his wife was out of the way, he would come running back to her. So on the morning of 4 November, Lehnberg got into her white Ford Anglia and drove to Choegoe's ramshackle house. She arrived at around 7.30, taking Choegoe by surprise. As far as he was concerned, he had washed his hands of any involvement. But he had reckoned without Lehnberg's powers of persuasion. He later said: 'When she arrived at the house, she told me she was packed and on her way to Johannesburg.' He added that she wanted him to be a 'witness'. But on the way to Bellville, she handed him a gun loaded with five cartridges.

With the Van der Linde children departed for school, Lehnberg and Choegoe got out of the car and crossed the road to the house at about 9 a.m. Knowing that Mrs Van der Linde had already experienced one unwelcome encounter with Choegoe and would not in all probability open the door to him again, Lehnberg decided to ring the doorbell herself. The moment the front door was opened, Lehnberg flew at Mrs Van der Linde. They struggled through from the front step to the lounge where Lehnberg ended the contest by hitting her adversary hard on the jaw with the butt of the pistol. The savagery of the blow fractured Mrs Van der Linde's jaw and left her unconscious. Now that the victim was immobilized, Lehnberg told Choegoe to finish her off, reasoning that he would then take the rap for murder. He later testified: 'She told me to throttle the woman. When she was dead, she gave me the revolver and then told me to get the scissors, which were lying on a table near the telephone, and to stab the woman three times through the heart.' With Susanna Van der

Linde dead, Lehnberg set about further incriminating Choegoe by taking the deceased's dye gun and spraying green dye over his face and clothes.

Lehnberg thought she had been incredibly clever. Choegoe would soon be picked up but she calculated that there was nothing to link him to her. He didn't know her surname and all her letters to him had been typewritten. Needless to say, she would have been much better off hiring someone who couldn't be traced at all rather than a person who could not have been more obvious if he'd had 'hit man' stencilled on his forehead.

Mrs Van der Linde's body was discovered by her daughter shortly after 1 p.m. Predictably, it didn't take the police long to haul in Choegoe. A limping man had been seen in the district and when his house was searched, the police found the loaded gun which Lehnberg had told him to look after. He hadn't even been bright enough to dispose of it. They also found an envelope spattered with green dye. It had contained a letter from Lehnberg. Upon his arrest, Choegoe quickly confessed and implicated Lehnberg.

She pleaded not guilty, insisting that she hadn't been in the house on the morning of the murder. But evidence showed that a cripple such as Choegoe could not possibly have overpowered the victim alone, particularly since there had been a running fight between the front door and the lounge. The prosecution pointed out the reason that Lehnberg had felled Mrs Van der Linde was to incapacitate her so that Choegoe would be physically capable of finishing her off. Furthermore, Lehnberg's letters to Choegoe were traced back to her via the typewriter face and her macabre missive, imploring him to use a knife 'if you think it will be better or quicker, but the job must be done' was seen as definite proof of incitement and premeditation. Lehnberg wasn't so clever after all.

Lehnberg and Choegoe were both found guilty of murder and sentenced to death, the judge maintaining that there were no extenuating circumstances. But, amidst public outrage at the severity of the punishment, the case went to appeal where the court took a rather different view to the trial judge. It ruled that there were extenuating circumstances for both defendants, citing the source of the whole sorry affair as Christiaan Van der Linde who had cut a particularly unsympathetic figure in the witness box. Accordingly, the sentences were reduced to terms of imprisonment – 20 years for Lehnberg and 15 for Choegoe. This gave Marlene Lehnberg plenty of time to reflect on the folly of recruiting an assassin with only one leg.

Arthur Devereux: Widowed Before His Time

The tale of Arthur Devereux is an object lesson in how not to get away with murder. After going to enormous lengths to conceal not only the murders of his wife and children but also his implication in the killings, he was ultimately trapped by one word out of place.

Devereux met his future wife Beatrice at Hastings in 1896 at a time when he was working for a chemist in the town. They married two years later in Paddington, by which time he had found employment as a chemist's assistant in that area of west London. However, Devereux experienced difficulty in holding down a job for any length of time and this, plus the birth of a son, Stanley, put a strain on the family finances. Beatrice was an accomplished musician who could have earned enough to have supported the three of them but the arrival of twins Evelyn and Lawrence in 1903 came as a hammer blow. Whilst Devereux was very fond of Stanley, he never took to the twins and their birth meant that the family were reduced to living on the bread line. Beatrice became undernourished and depressed about the mysterious disappearance of her brother (who had bizarrely left his clothes on the beach in the West Country and hadn't been seen since) while Devereux struggled to cope emotionally as well as financially. He managed to make ends just about meet by selling a home-made toothache remedy but also resorted to drastic measures, forging false testimonials to obtain one job and another time posing as an American millionaire.

Such fantasies would have cut no ice with his arch enemy, his mother-in-law Mrs Gregory. To say that the two did not get on is like saying that the Boston Strangler wasn't a very nice man. Devereux had asked her to lend him some money and when she refused, he threatened to shoot her. He vowed that she would never darken the door of his home again and was said to have told one landlord that he'd blow her brains out if she ever called again. Mrs Gregory sensed that she was not welcome.

By December 1904, the Devereux family were in dire straits. Arthur's periods of unemployment were becoming more pro-longed, a situation which led to further friction with both his wife and mother-in-law. That month, the family moved into a top-floor flat in Harlesden, north-west London, under the assumed name of Egerton. Devereux informed the landlord that he only wanted the flat for six weeks, after which he was going to share a house with a friend. From this statement it would seem that Devereux had already decided to do away with the major drains on his meagre resources, but the fate of his wife and the twins was surely sealed on 2 January 1905 when he was released from his post as a chemist's assistant in Kilburn. This was through no fault of his own, but simply because the business had not proved as profitable as his employer had anticipated.

Mrs Devereux was last seen alive between 11 and 11.15 p.m. on the night of 28 January by her mother at Willesden railway station. On 31 January, Devereux told the milkman not to leave any more milk because his wife and the twins had gone away for a while. He told anybody else who enquired as to her whereabouts that she had been feeling unwell and had taken the twins to Plymouth to recuperate. He may have been able to fob the milkman and the neighbours off with any old story but his mother-in-law was another matter altogether. Although Mrs Gregory was not allowed to set foot in her daughter's house, Beatrice had always visited her on a regular basis. But now the visits had suddenly stopped. Mrs Gregory learned that a furniture van had called at the flat in Harlesden and that a large trunk had been deposited at the firm's warehouse in nearby Kensal Rise. Fearing the worst, she notified the police.

On 13 April, the police went to the warehouse. The owner revealed that a man called Arthur Devereux had contacted them on 7 February explaining that he had sold most of his belongings but needed a large box to store chemicals and books. The company gave Devereux a box and he took it away before returning it shortly afterwards. There had been nothing to arouse their suspicions until Mrs Gregory had appeared upon the scene. The trunk weighed some two hundredweight and was tightly bound with a strap, padlocked and double-sealed with red wax. It presented a formidable obstacle but after shaking it and not finding the vibration which would be associated with a contents of bottles and books, the police decided to open it. The inside was equally elaborate but it also contained the grim discovery Mrs Gregory had been dreading – the body of her daughter Beatrice and the 20-month-old twins, both still wearing their nightgowns.

Devereux had thoughtfully told the warehouse owner that he was leaving the area to work at a chemist's shop in Coventry and so it didn't take the police long to locate and arrest him.

At his trial in June, 34-year-old Devereux pleaded not guilty to murder. His story was that, on the morning of 28 January, he had argued with his wife who had been complaining about having to cope with all the family washing without her mother's help, this being a result of the directive forbidding Mrs Gregory to visit. Devereux said he had then gone out for the day with Stanley and had returned home late at night to find his wife and the twins dead in bed. He said there was a distinct smell of chloroform in the room. He usually kept this substance in his desk but it was missing. He guessed that she had administered chloroform to the children before taking her own life. Hiding the awful truth from Stanley – he told him they were all asleep – Devereux said that he had panicked because he was scared to face an inquest, mainly because he knew how much his mother-in-law detested him. And so, instead of getting in touch with the police, he had decided to conceal the bodies in the trunk. He then packed Stanley off to boarding school in Kenilworth, Warwickshire, and took the job in Coventry.

All too aware that hiding bodies was somewhat irrational behaviour, his lawyer tried to draw on the family history of behaving oddly. His father and grandfather had both attempted suicide and an aunt had thrown herself out of a window. Although the Devereux family were clearly one tree short of a forest, Arthur had been certified sane. The defence's hopes of suggesting otherwise had fallen on stony ground.

The prosecution maintained that Devereux, beset with money worries and after a particularly violent row, had persuaded his depressed wife to take a drink laced with morphine and then to feed it to the twins on the pretence that it was cough medicine. There was no evidence of chloroform. He had then acquired the trunk and had actually slept in the same room as the bodies – a thought greeted with revulsion by the jury. After mixing glue with boric acid to make the trunk airtight so that there would be no smell from the bodies,

Devereux had asked the removal men to put the trunk in storage. When it was being moved, he told the men: 'Don't tip it up.' He also told the firm that he didn't want Mrs Gregory to know that he was moving to Coventry. Neighbours reported seeing bonfires in the garden and hearing boxes being moved in the house. Witnesses also testified that he had sold two of his wife's framed music certificates and had sold his wife's clothes, claiming that they belonged to his sister. There was also a suggestion that he was having an affair.

However, what really clinched it for the prosecution was the fact that, answering the advert for a job on 13 January – 15 days before his wife's death – Arthur Devereux had described himself as a widower. This was not a wise move and it took the jury a mere ten minutes to find him guilty of murder. Perhaps the only consolation was that he didn't have much time to reflect on his folly for he was hanged at Pentonville Prison on 15 August.

Bungling Bandits

In 1978, Charles A. Meriweather broke into a house in Baltimore and threatened the woman occupant. Learning that she had little cash in the house, he ordered her to write a cheque instead. The woman asked him to whom she should make the cheque out and he replied: 'Charles A. Meriweather'. He was arrested a few hours later.

*

A would-be Texas grocery-store robber went to the trouble of disguising his face with a balaclava but forgot to remove from his breast pocket a laminated badge which bore his name, place of employment and position within the company – an oversight spotted by at least a dozen witnesses.

*

Wearing a pair of women's tights over his head and brandishing an imitation revolver, Irishman Eddie McAlea looked a menacing figure as he held up a Liverpool watchmaker. But shopkeeper Philip Barrett's fear quickly turned to bemusement when he noticed that the robber had forgotten to remove the cork from the barrel of the gun! Sensing that Mr Barrett was not about to hand anything over, McAlea cut his losses and fled, ripping off his mask as he did so. This was not a shrewd move since Mr Barrett immediately recognized him – he had been in the shop the previous day selling a watch. McAlea, who had only been released from prison six days earlier, was sentenced to another 30 months in jail. Mr Barrett said: 'At first I thought the robbery was the real thing but when I spotted the cork stuck in the barrel, I knew the fellow must be daft. It's the kind of story Irish jokes are made of.'

*

Not wishing to draw attention to himself, a bank robber in Portland, Oregon, handed the cashier a note ordering her to put all the money in a paper bag. She read the note, wrote on the bottom, 'I don't have a paper bag' and handed it back to the raider. His masterplan foiled, he fled empty-handed.

*

Staging a daring Post Office raid in Essex, three masked men burst into the shop waving shotguns, only to discover that it hadn't been a Post Office for 12 years. Instead it was nothing more than a general store and the gang's haul amounted to just £6. 'I think it was a bit of a disappointment to them,' commented the 76-year-old manageress.

*

Despite crashing his getaway car into a lamppost, a bandit in Denver, Colorado, still managed to escape on foot. But his luck ran out again when he got home as, while fumbling for his door key, he shot himself in the leg. The police found him holding his leg with one hand and his loot with the other.

*

Having been convicted for a previous break-in after leaving behind an imprint of his training shoe at the scene, 24-year-old Leroy Wynter decided to tread more carefully on his next robbery. Targeting a Wiltshire old people's home, he not only removed his shoes, but he also slipped off his socks and put them on his hands as gloves in order to avoid leaving any fingerprints. But the barefoot thief had reckoned without the fact that he would leave behind toe-prints, as individual as any fingerprint. He was jailed for two years.

*

Following a 1990 grocery shop raid, robber James Innis found himself hanging upside down from a fence, his trousers round his ankles, and with 20 New York cops waiting on the other side, pistols drawn. Together with accomplice Tyrone Thomas, Innis had stolen $207 from a grocery store on Seventh Avenue. A police patrol car saw the pair run off and gave chase. It was then that Innis tried to jump the fence, unaware that it led into the backyard of the 32nd Precinct station house in Harlem. Desk sergeant Joseph Rosado said: 'He was amazed the cops were there so quick. Not a bright guy!'

*

Finding his car had been broken into and his pager stolen, Bristol warehouse manager David Withers decided to leave a message on the missing pager, saying the owner had won £500 in a competition and giving a number to ring. Shortly afterwards, his mobile phone rang and the voice on the other end, belonging to builder Justin Clark, agreed to a meeting to collect his prize. When Clark turned up, the police arrested him for handling stolen property. Mr Withers said: 'I could not believe anybody would be that stupid, but obviously I came up against a total dimwit.'

*

In January 1998, a thief fled from the Yanmonoki Museum in central Japan with a 600-year-old Chinese platter dating from the Ming dynasty and worth an estimated £260,000. Making his escape, the thief dropped the priceless platter in the road, causing it to shatter into hundreds of pieces.

*

A 1975 raid on the Royal Bank of Scotland in Rothesay degenerated into farce when, on the way in, the three would-be raiders got stuck in the bank's revolving doors and had to be helped free by the staff. Undeterred, they returned a few minutes later and announced that it was a robbery. The staff thought it was a practical joke and refused to pay up. While one of the men vaulted the counter and twisted his ankle on landing, the other two made their escape, only to get trapped in the revolving doors again.

*

A would-be burglar at Sacramento, California, in 1984 got stuck in the chimney of the house he intended to rob. He was rescued by fire crews and arrested by police.

*

After breaking into a house in Swindon, Wiltshire, a burglar cheekily used the owner's phone to call his getaway driver. But his accomplice had dozed off and didn't get to the phone before it rang off. So he dialled 1471 and rang the number back. The call woke up the owner of the house who, realizing he was being burgled, called the police. The two men were swiftly arrested.

*

Stumbling across a pile of rusting metal, which they assumed was scrap, two Tyneside thieves loaded it on to their lorry. It was only after they were arrested that they learned it was a piece of modern art worth £34,000. The work, called *The Cone*, by internationally acclaimed sculptor Andy Gold-sworthy, was made up of circles of steel in the shape of a pine cone and had been allowed to rust so that it blended in with the scenery at Riverside Park, Gateshead. After Peter Widdrington and William Loder admitted theft, a spokesman for Gateshead Council revealed that the work had been rebuilt. He added: 'Some people just don't have an artistic bone in their body.'

*

A robbery which took place in Los Angeles in 1990 had seemingly been planned down to the last detail. The ten-strong gang, many of them armed, planned to storm the headquarters of a company which shipped cars across the United States. At first all went well as they kidnapped a security guard, selected nine cars and drove off in them towards the freeway. What they hadn't taken into account was the fact that each car had only a limited amount of petrol – less than a gallon to be precise. So as the gang made their audacious getaway, one by one their cars ran out of gas and spluttered to a halt, forcing the robbers to abandon their haul and complete their escape on foot.

*

Choosing to burgle a house bordering Watney Park Golf Club in Essex, two men were caught in the act by 24 off-duty policemen enjoying a golf day.

*

Bursting into a Milan bank, an Italian robber tripped over a doormat and went flying. As he did so, his mask slipped and his gun went off. Quickly regaining his composure, he hared towards the cashier, only to lose his footing again on the slippery floor, in the process of which he dropped his gun. Realizing that it was simply not his day, he abandoned the robbery and ran straight out of the bank into the arms of a waiting policeman who had just written him a ticket for parking his car illegally.

*

Planning to rob the home of an antiques dealer in 1933, a Parisian thief chose a novel form of disguise – a suit of armour. His reasoning was that it would terrify his victim into submission, but it merely had the effect of alerting the house-owner to his presence almost immediately. It also made it impossible for the would-be thief to escape, even after the police had been summoned. To add insult to injury, the burglar couldn't get the armour off when arrested and had to be fed through the visor for the next 24 hours.

*

Desperate to steal a car, 26-year-old Aundray Burns not only chose a police car, but also one with a policeman in it. In April 1991, Daniel Daly of the New York transit police was sitting in the passenger seat of his standard blue and white police car with rooftop lights while his partner, John Rankin, went into a shop to buy a new gun belt. Suddenly Burns jumped into the driver's seat, shouting, 'I gotta go, I gotta go' and tried to drive off. Alerted to the attempted theft, Officer Rankin rushed out of the shop and promptly arrested a cyclist who had gone to Officer Daly's aid. When the confusion was resolved, Burns was carted off to jail. Police spokesman Officer Al O'Leary said: 'What a town, eh? We've had subway trains taken for joy rides, buses stolen and found in other parts of the city, and patrol cars gone south for the winter, but this is the first time anyone has ever tried to take a patrol car with the officer in it!'

*

In 1996, an Italian burglar, unhappy about being freed from prison on condition that he lived with his mother-in-law, hit a police officer to ensure that he would be sent back to jail.

*

Having seized £4500 from the Co-operative Stores at Perivale, Middlesex, in 1978, two robbers ran to their getaway car. But the driver turned the ignition key the wrong way and jammed the lock. The pair then tried another car, but managed to repeat the feat. They were quickly arrested.

*

In 1984, a Washington robber armed with a sawn-off shotgun held up a Chinese laundry. To scare the owner into handing over the money, he decided to fire a blast into the floor but merely succeeded in shooting himself in the right foot. He was arrested in hospital.

*

In 1994, a Sunderland man had to be rescued by fire crews after using a manhole cover to smash a shop window, then stepping back and falling down the hole.

*

Trying to escape from police, a West German shoplifter jumped from an eight-feet wall and landed in the exercise yard of Düsseldorf Prison.

*

Deciding to help himself to a few items from the Barnsley branch of British Home Stores in 1979, a shoplifter was surprised to find himself apprehended by eight pairs of hands. The shop was holding a convention of store detectives at the time.

*

After robbing a store in Albuquerque, New Mexico, in 1980, the raider's trousers fell down as he made his escape. This caused him to drop his gun and most of the money. He was arrested by police and while protesting his innocence, his trousers fell down again.

*

A man planning to rob a Yorkshire village store reckoned he had left nothing to chance. Armed with a toy revolver, he had —

his motorcycle parked outside for a quick getaway and wore a full-face crash helmet to mask his face. However, he had forgotten that painted in inch-high letters around the helmet was his name. His arrest was swift.

*

In June 1984, Charlie Murphy went to the Safeway super-market on Fourth Street, Los Angeles, and filled out an application for a cheque-cashing ID card. He wrote his real name, his age (54), his Social Security number and his address in Long Beach. Twenty-five minutes later, he returned to the store, walked up to the same window where he had filled in the application form and demanded money, saying that he had got a gun in his pocket. At that point, nerves got the better of him and he fled empty-handed. Not surprisingly, the store manager remembered his face and that he had given his address, so he sent the police around to Murphy's home just two blocks from the store. The police remarked: 'He was not really one of our smarter attempted robbers.'

*

In 1972, a Mr J. Egan from London stole a barge on the River Thames but, to his surprise, was apprehended almost immediately. Alas, there had been a dock strike on and his was the only craft moving that day.

*

In 1998, a guard was caught smuggling a wad of money in his underpants out of a bank in Atlanta when a tiny security-dye capsule exploded, blowing a hole in his trousers.

*

Intent on stealing cash from a Southampton supermarket, a robber planned to hand the checkout girl £10 to pay for his groceries and when she opened the till, he would seize the contents. Sure enough, he handed her the £10, she opened the till and he grabbed the contents – all £4.37 of it. He then fled the supermarket, having lost £5.63 on the raid.

*

A bungling bank robber at Swansea, Massachusetts, fainted when the woman cashier he held up at gunpoint said she had no money. When he came to and made a bid to escape, he discovered that he had locked his getaway car with the keys inside.

*

Having broken into a house in Newcastle upon Tyne, a particularly dim burglar decided for a joke to take a photograph of his accomplice with his victim's camera. Forced to make a hasty exit, however, they dropped the camera and when the owner had the film developed three months later, there was a nice snapshot of one of the men carrying off her valuables. Both burglars were arrested within a matter of hours.

*

Three armed robbers, planning to raid a South Shields travel agents in July 1997, missed their intended target and burst into the optician's next door, waving a knife and an imitation sawn-off shotgun. Realizing they were in the wrong shop, they made a hasty exit and finally made it to the travel agent's. They demanded to know where the safe was but lost their nerve. Instead of a £30,000 haul in travellers' cheques, they ended up with just a whisky bottle containing foreign coins donated to charity. Their getaway car then ran out of petrol and they abandoned it, leaving behind vital clues which led to their arrest. The judge described it as 'not a very efficient robbery'.

*

Two Las Vegas robbers, thinking they'd come across a stash of casino gambling chips, ordered the driver of a lorry for the company 'Vegas Chips' to turn over his load at knifepoint. To their dismay, they found that the vehicle was full of potato crisps, not gambling counters.

*

Two teenagers who attacked a woman in Dalton, near Huddersfield, snatched her plastic shopping bag . . . which contained dog mess she had cleared up after her terrier.

Louis Voisin: Blodie Belgim

Louis Voisin, a French butcher working in London in the early years of the century, got it badly wrong. After murdering one of his mistresses, he tried to confuse the police by scrawling a note at the scene of the crime. But far from foxing them, the note with its blatant spelling errors – the sort which would also later sound the death knell for Thomas Henry Allaway – merely served to provide crucial evidence against him.

It was around 8.30 on the morning of 2 November 1917 that Thomas George Henry's road-sweeping duties took him to Regent Square, Bloomsbury, a quiet backwater in the heart of London to the south of St Pancras station. On the grass just inside the railings he noticed a bundle of sacking. Slipping his hand through the railings, he fumbled around the package and decided that it probably contained half a sheep. Quite why he jumped to this conclusion remains something of a mystery but perhaps in those days Londoners were in the habit of dumping dead sheep on their doorsteps. Evidently the possibility of having found a lump of mutilated mutton appealed to him – maybe he planned to sell it on to a butcher – because within a matter of seconds he had climbed over the 4ft 6in high railings and was undoing the string around the bundle and opening the sacking. But he discovered more than he had bargained for. The package turned out to have a second layer – a blood-stained sheet – beneath which, instead of a sheep, he found the torso and arms of a woman.

Henry recoiled in horror and blew the whistle which he had about his person to alert the police. However the initial shock quickly subsided and, before the police could arrive, his morbid curiosity had led him to open a second, smaller parcel nearby. This contained the legs. All that were needed for the set were the head and the hands.

There were two clues. The cotton sheet bore a red laundry mark II H and, on a piece of brown paper placed underneath the dead woman's vest, were written the words 'BLODIE BEL-GIM'. The writing was said to be of a 'distinctly foreign appearance'. Police experts estimated that the victim was around 30 years old and 5ft tall. She had given birth at some time in her life and was healthy. From the 'superior quality of her underclothing' it was also deduced that she had led a relatively comfortable existence. The police surgeon was particularly impressed by the expert manner in which the remains had been dissected. The body had not been mutilated or disfigured as might be expected from a sex murder, but had been taken apart purely for the purposes of transportation. This was not the work of a bungling amateur – the cuts were so precise as to indicate that the killer was a butcher. This theory was reinforced when examination of pieces of white fabric wrapped around the trunk and legs showed them to be the sort used by butchers to wrap meat.

The post-mortem established that cause of death was probably from a blow to the head, the impact of which had then drained the blood from the body. Acting on the 'BLODIE BELGIM' note, the police thought initially that the answer to the mystery lay among the community of Belgian refugees who lived in the vicinity of Regent Square. The feeling was that the killing might have been connected with national rivalries which had surfaced in the course of the First World War. *The Times* commented: 'There is a strong belief locally that the crime may have been committed by a German, his victim being a Belgian woman, and his motive hatred of the people who stood in his country's way.'

But it was the laundry mark which yielded the first breakthrough. It was traced to a French woman, Mme Emilienne Gerard, who lived in Munster Square near Regent's Park, about a mile from where the corpse had been found. She had been missing for three days and was of the same height and build as the victim. Furthermore, she had given birth to two children (one of whom had since died) and had fair hair which fitted the pathologist's profile of the dead woman, a conclusion arrived at from examination of the torso in the absence of any head. When neighbours were questioned about Mme Gerard, whose husband was away at the Front, one volunteered the information that her hands were badly disfigured by burns. So it appeared likely that the hands, along with the head, had been hacked off in an attempt to prevent the deceased from being identified. Another neighbour spoke of seeing Mme Gerard arguing violently with a middle-aged man on the corner of Munster Square. Both were talking in French.

When the police went to Mme Gerard's rooms, they found bloodstains in the kitchen and on the table an IOU for £50 signed by a Louis Voisin. There was also a picture of a man, who turned out to be Voisin. The police immediately set about finding M. Voisin. They didn't have to look far since he lived a mile or so away in Charlotte Street. The police arrived at 101 Charlotte Street to find Voisin entertaining a lady friend, Berthe Roche, in his basement rooms. The kitchen was splattered with blood. While the couple were taken in for questioning, a thorough search was conducted of the Charlotte Street address. One of Mme Gerard's earrings was found attached to a towel and, in the coal cellar, officers discovered the missing head and hands hidden in a cask of sawdust. The head was badly lacerated.

At the station, officers asked Voisin, through an interpreter, to write the words 'Bloody Belgium'. He made the same spelling errors as in the note found on the body. It was as good as a confession.

Delving into Voisin's background, the police learned that he was a stable-man by trade but did a spot of butchering work on the side. Mme Gerard had been employed as his house-keeper but the relationship had progressed beyond that. They became lovers and a letter to Mme Gerard from her husband indicated that he too suspected her of having an affair with Voisin. A PC Bendall, who knew the accused, had seen Voisin driving his horse and trap from the area of Regent Square towards Charlotte Street at 7.40 a.m. on the morning of 2 November. Voisin denied that it was him. The concierge at Charlotte Street came forward to reveal that she had seen Berthe Roche washing a blood-stained shirt on the morning of the 2nd. She was told that Voisin had clumsily killed a calf, causing blood to spurt all over the place. Meanwhile, the daughter of Mme Gerard's landlady told police that Voisin had informed her on the afternoon of Friday, 2 November that Mme Gerard had gone away to the country for two weeks.

At first, Voisin stuck to his story that Mme Gerard had gone away but then, as the evidence mounted, he changed tack, explaining how he had innocently stumbled across parts of the body while visiting her flat in Munster Square on Thursday, 1 November. 'When I arrived,' he said, 'the door was closed but not locked. The floor and carpet were full of blood. The head and hands were wrapped in a flannel jacket which is at my place now. They were on the kitchen table. That is all I could see. The rest of the body was not there. I was so astonished at such an affair that I did not know what to do. I go to Mme Gerard's every day. I thought a trap had been laid for me. I commenced to clean up the blood and my clothes became smeared.' He went on to describe how he later took the bundle containing the head and hands back to his house although he could offer no plausible explanation as to why he had done so, other than the fact that he was confused. He insisted that he had no reason to kill Mme Gerard but darkly added that she had started inviting undesirables back to her flat.

Not surprisingly, the forensic evidence did not back up Voisin's story. There was insufficient blood at the Munster Square address for Mme Gerard to have been killed there and what blood there was at Charlotte Street was human rather than animal.

Voisin maintained throughout that Berthe Roche had played no part in the proceedings, but the police thought otherwise. The pair were tried together for murder, the prosecution alleging that, during a Zeppelin raid on London on the night of 31 October, Mme Gerard had gone to Voisin's rooms, only to find him with Roche. There was a violent argument, as a result of which she was killed. Voisin then cut up and disposed of the body, leaving the 'Blodie Belgim' note in a vain bid to confuse the police. Instead it had precisely the opposite effect. The fact that Mme Gerard had received a succession of weak blows to the head suggested that they had been delivered by a woman rather than the muscular Voisin, but the judge ruled that there was insufficient evidence against Roche and instructed the jury to find her 'not guilty'.

However he ordered that she be remanded to be charged as an accessory after the fact.

She was subsequently sentenced to seven years' imprisonment, but was certified insane and died in 1919.

Louis Voisin was found guilty of murder and was hanged at Pentonville Prison on 2 March 1918.

The Brisbane Vampire: A Dropped Card

Tracey Wigginton was seriously weird. After being abandoned by her parents as a baby, she was raised by her grandparents, George and Avril Wigginton. But while Grandpa chased women, Grandma took it out on Tracey. As well as beating her, she turned her against men so that it was hardly surprising that the girl grew up to be a committed lesbian. However, it wasn't just her sexual preferences which singled her out from the crowd. She was 6ft tall, weighed 17 stone, was covered in tattoos and was heavily into sado-masochism. She also had a fascination with the occult and, in addition to watching horror videos, developed a taste for drinking blood which she collected from her friendly neighbourhood butcher. Tracey was a vampire.

In 1989, Tracey Wigginton was 24 and had left school seven years previously. She hung around Brisbane with her own gang who called themselves the Swampies. Besides Wigginton, the group, who all wore black clothes and heavy industrial boots, comprised Lisa Ptaschinski, Kim Jervis and Tracey Waugh, but no one was in any doubt that Wigginton was the leader. She exerted a powerful control over her disciples and claimed to be the Devil's wife. Some thought that even the Devil deserved a better partner.

Ptaschinski was her lover and, to prove her devotion, she would cut her wrist and allow Wigginton to suck the blood. This macabre practice may have gone some way to satisfying Wigginton's blood-lust, but it also made her crave more – to suck the blood of a stranger.

Haunting the city's gay bars, the fearsome foursome devised a plan to lure a total stranger into their evil web and kill him so that Wigginton could suck his blood. They decided that Ptaschinski and Waugh should pose as prostitutes and lure their victim into one of the city parks in the dead of night. In a secluded spot, Wigginton and Jervis would then kill him. After Wigginton had sipped his blood, they would then take the body to a cemetery, deposit it in a freshly dug grave and cover it with soil, ready to be concealed by a coffin when the funeral party arrived the following day. The plan seemed foolproof. It would be the perfect murder. And if they picked on some dead-beat, not only would there be no sign of a body but he probably wouldn't even be reported missing.

On the evening of 20 October 1989, the four women met at the seedy Club Lewmors. Wigginton and Jervis were armed with knives. About 11.30 p.m., they left the club, high on champagne, and, with Ptaschinski, who had stayed sober, at the wheel, started to tour the streets in Wigginton's green Holden sedan, searching out a suitable victim. On River Terrace, they spotted the man of their dreams – a middle-aged man by the name of Edward Baldock who had been out for a few beers with his mates and was now staggering home to his wife of 25 years. Seeing 47-year-old Baldock hopelessly hanging on to a lamp-post, the kinky quartet decided to move in for the kill.

They stopped and asked Baldock if he wanted a lift home. He was in no fit state to refuse and clambered into the back with Wigginton. Soon they were holding hands. Baldock thought his luck was in, especially when Wigginton instructed Ptaschinski to drive to Orleigh Park. She parked the car near the South Brisbane Sailing Club. It was dark and deserted, the ideal spot for what they had in mind. Edward Baldock's mind was elsewhere, encouraged by Wigginton asking him whether he wanted a good time. He readily agreed and the pair walked down to the water's edge and undressed. There, Wigginton, who had said she would kill her victim with her bare hands if necessary, sized him up but reckoned that even in his advanced stage of drunkenness, he was too strong for her to overpower single-handedly. She found some excuse to return to the car, leaving Baldock sitting there stark naked except for his socks.

Back at the car, Ptaschinski offered to help and took the second knife off Jervis. The two lovers sneaked up on the dazed Baldock. Wigginton wanted Ptaschinski to kill him but she couldn't go through with it. Wigginton was made of sterner stuff, however, and mercilessly plunged her knife into the poor man's neck and throat. She had attacked him with such ferocity that by the time she had finished, his head was only just hanging on to the rest of his body. The dastardly deed done, she fulfilled her ambition of drinking his blood.

For some reason, the women abandoned their plan to take the body to the cemetery but instead drove back to Jervis's flat, an appropriate setting for the occasion since it was a shrine to death. The focal point was a stolen headstone. Certain that nobody had seen them and that there would be no clues, they celebrated their night's work . . . until Wigginton suddenly realized that she had lost her bankers' card. The only explanation she could think of was that she must have dropped it while she was undressing in the park. Wigginton's cool evaporated as Ptaschinski drove her back to the park. If her card was found near the body, her days of freedom were surely numbered. They searched everywhere for the missing card, but to no avail. In the end, Wigginton came to the conclusion that she must have lost it somewhere else.

On their way back to Jervis's flat, they were stopped by a police patrol car and Ptaschinski was breathalysed. The test proved negative but in her haste to find the card, she had come out without her driving licence. The officers noted the details of the car.

Edward Baldock's naked body was discovered the next day by two women out for an early morning stroll. When the police arrived, they found Wigginton's bankers' card tucked inside the dead man's shoe. When further checks revealed that the green Holden stopped in the vicinity by the patrol car the previous night was also registered to Tracey Wigginton, they had a prime suspect. Questioned about how her card came to be found on the body of the deceased, Wigginton said that she and the girls had been playing around in the park earlier on the day of the murder and that she must have dropped it then. But there was still the matter of her car being stopped in the area at around the time of the killing.

Wigginton was arrested and came up with a new story. She told the police that when she went to the park in the evening, she had tripped over a dead body but had been too frightened to report it. It was as she fell over the corpse, she said, that her bankers' card must have fallen out. To add weight to her claim, she said that she and the other three had noticed a suspicious-looking couple hanging around the park.

Unfortunately for Wigginton, her three accomplices couldn't tough it out the way she could. Just as Ptaschinski hadn't been able to stab a harmless drunk, now her nerve went again and, wracked with guilt, she called into the nearest police station and told them everything. Until then, detectives had thought that Wigginton had killed Baldock as a result of a lovers' tiff. Only now did they learn the awful truth.

At her trial, Wigginton pleaded guilty to murder and was sentenced to life imprisonment. The other three pleaded not guilty, claiming that they were under Wigginton's spell and that they never thought for one moment that she was really going to go through with killing a total stranger. They thought it was just one of her weird jokes. Jervis was found guilty of manslaughter and received 18 years while Waugh was acquitted. Ptaschinski was not so lucky. Under cross-examination, she admitted that she had been fascinated by the 'thrilling and chilling' plan to murder a man and to drink his blood. Like her lover, she was found guilty of murder and sentenced to life imprisonment.

But just how had the incriminating bankers' card found its way into the murdered man's shoe? It was thought that in his drunken stupor Edward Baldock had seen the card lying on the ground after Wigginton had dropped it, assumed that it was his and tucked it inside his shoe for safe keeping. He hadn't proved such an easy victim after all.

Franz Müller: The Wrong Hat

German tailor Franz Müller thought he had committed the perfect crime. He had killed and robbed a passenger in the first-class compartment of a train. There were no witnesses and Müller had managed to flee not only the train but also the country. But in his haste to make his getaway from the compartment, he had mistakenly picked up the victim's hat, leaving his own behind in its place. For the police, it was almost as good as leaving a calling card.

Although still in its infancy, the railway network was an extremely popular and reliable mode of public transport in 1860s' Britain. The service had recovered from the PR blunder of running over the local MP at the opening of the Liverpool–Manchester railway in 1830 and, undeterred by such phenomena as leaves on the line in autumn, had gone on to earn a reputation for punctuality. So when 70-year-old Thomas Briggs, chief clerk of a City of London bank, had to cross from south of the Thames, where he had been visiting his niece, to his home in Hackney, the North London Railway was the obvious choice for the second part of his journey, especially as his residence in Clapton Square was close to Hackney Central station.

It was shortly after 8.30 on the evening of Saturday, 9 July 1864 that Mr Briggs said goodbye to his niece in Peckham and walked to the Old Kent Road to catch a horse-drawn omnibus towards the City of London. He alighted in King William Street and walked to Fenchurch Street where he boarded the steam train bound for Hackney. A smartly dressed man, as befitted his profession, he settled down in a first-class carriage with his back to the engine and waited patiently for the train to depart. At 9.50 p.m., it was, unusually, five minutes late leaving the Fenchurch Street terminus.

The train – in this instance a superior conveyance with no third-class compartments to cater for the lower orders – puffed its way through the smoky suburbs of north-east London. At Bow station, Mr Briggs spotted an acquaintance, a property owner by the name of Thomas Lee, standing on the platform. They exchanged pleasantries through the open window before Mr Lee moved further along the train to the second-class carriages. Mr Lee had noticed that there were two other men in the same compartment as Mr Briggs – one a thin, dark man and the other, who was sitting opposite Mr Briggs, was said to be 'a stoutish thick-set man with whiskers'.

The train left Bow at 10.01 p.m., its next stop being Hackney Wick four minutes later. As the train approached Hackney Wick, a lady in an adjoining compartment was alarmed to see her dress spattered with blood flying through the open window. But she heard no cries or commotion and thought little more of the incident except for how to get the stains out of her dress. At the same time, draper Thomas Withall, also seated in a first-class compartment next to that occupied by Mr Briggs, heard a strange noise – 'a horrid howling' – but assumed it was nothing more sinister than a dog.

When the train arrived at Hackney Wick, two young clerks, Henry Verney and Sydney Jones, who, coincidentally, worked at the same Lombard Street bank as Mr Briggs, climbed into an empty first-class carriage. As he sat down, Jones felt that the cushions were wet and sticky. He rubbed his hand over the upholstery and found it covered in blood. Further inspection showed blood on a window, a black leather bag and a silver-topped walking stick. Under the seat was a black beaver hat – crushed as if somebody had stood on it. The two clerks informed the guard whose hand-lamp revealed more blood on the door and door handle. Realizing that something was amiss, he locked the compartment and telegraphed the stationmaster at Chalk Farm who in turn notified the police.

The cause of the blood-stained compartment was quickly apparent. Twenty minutes after the ominous discovery, the driver of a train travelling in the opposite direction saw a dark mound on the track ahead, some half a mile south of Hackney Wick station. He brought the train to a halt within a few feet of the obstruction and discovered that the mound was a man's body. The man was badly battered, unconscious and bleeding profusely, but he was still just about alive. The injured man was carried to a tavern in nearby Wick Lane where Police Constable Duggan happened to be patrolling. Searching the man for clues to his identity, he found four sovereigns, 10s 6d in silver, some keys, a silver snuff box and some letters addressed to Thomas Briggs, Clapton Square, Hackney. A doctor then arrived and pronounced that the man had sustained a fractured skull, the result of two vicious blows to the head. Other head wounds were thought to have been caused by his fall from the train.

The police went to Clapton Square and Thomas Briggs's son formally identified the victim as his father. The son also recognized the walking stick and travelling bag, but definitely not the hat. He said that his father's hat was a specially made tall topper, purchased from Daniel Dignance, a high-class hatter in the City, and that he had been wearing it that morning when he had set off for Peckham. As for the black beaver hat, his father wouldn't have been seen dead in anything like that. The other missing item was Thomas Briggs's gold watch and chain, valued at around £12.

The following night, Thomas Briggs died. As far as the police could ascertain he had been attacked with his own walking stick, robbed of his watch and then thrown out of the train. The murder – the first on a British train – shocked the nation. It had been generally assumed that travelling in a first-class compartment was a safe form of transport but now women became apprehensive about journeying alone by train at night and well-to-do men took to hiding their watches from the view of suspicious-looking individuals. 'Who is safe?' wailed the *Daily Telegraph*. 'It would be impossible to imagine circumstances of greater apparent security than those which seemed to surround Mr Briggs. Well known – expected at home – travelling First Class for a mere step of a journey, on a line where stations occur every mile or so, and fringed with houses – if we can be murdered thus we may be slain in our pew at church, or assassinated at our dinner table.'

Descriptions of the missing hat, which bore Mr Briggs's name inside, and of the watch and chain, were printed in the newspapers and a reward of £300 was offered for information. The appeal quickly elicited a response. On 12 July Robert Death, who helped his brother John at their jeweller's shop in Cheapside, recounted how a young man had come in the previous morning asking for a valuation on a gold watch-chain, similar to the one in the papers. John Death had quoted him £3 10s and, although the man had appeared disappointed with this price, he asked for it to be exchanged for another chain of similar value. In fact, John Death had given the caller a gold chain worth £3 5s plus a 5s ring to make up the difference. The items were wrapped in a small cardboard box. All the Deaths could remember about the man was that he had a foreign accent, possibly German.

This development was also heavily publicized in the press

but the response was poor and it seemed that the trail had gone cold until, on 20 July, cab-driver Jonathan Matthews came forward with the vital piece in the jigsaw. Two days earlier, he had been reading a poster about the murder outside the Great Western Hotel at Paddington station and had recognized the distinctive name 'Death' as being on a small cardboard box with which his young daughter had been playing. He added that the box had been given to his daughter by a family friend, Franz Müller, a 25-year-old German tailor.

Mr Matthews was helpfulness itself. He not only provided the police with a description of Müller as well as his address and photograph, but also revealed that the description of the hat in the poster fitted one which Müller owned. Matthews knew this because he himself owned a beaver hat and Müller had admired it so much that he had asked whether Matthews could get one for him too. But there was bad news too. Matthews said that Müller was no longer in the country, having emigrated to America four days previously.

Nevertheless, the police sped round to Müller's last-known address – 16 Park Terrace, Old Ford, Bow – where he had lodged with a Mr and Mrs Blyth. It was little more than half a mile from the scene of the murder. Müller had been with the Blyths for seven weeks and they had found him to be a caring, considerate lodger. He had been talking about leaving for America for at least two weeks before the murder but it was not until the day after the attack on Mr Briggs that he excitedly told the Blyths that he had finally raised enough money to pay for the trip. Mr and Mrs Blyth said that Müller had sailed from London on the ship *Victoria* and further investigation revealed that he had paid for his third-class, or steerage, fare by pawning the gold chain he had acquired from the Deaths, along with a few other items. He had even written a cheery postcard to the Blyths, posted in Worthing. It read: 'On the sea, 16 July, in the morning. Dear Friends, I am glad to confess that I cannot have a better time as I have, for the sun shines and the wind blows fair, as it is at present moment everything will go well.'

Mrs Blyth remembered waiting up for Müller until 11 p.m. on the night of 9 July. When he had still not returned, she and her husband went to bed, allowing the lodger to use his key. At breakfast the next morning she noticed that he had a slight limp which he blamed on an ankle injury sustained while crossing the road. On the Monday evening he showed her and her husband a gold chain which he claimed to have bought from a man at the docks. Meanwhile Jonathan Matthews positively identified the crushed beaver hat found on the train as being Müller's, Mrs Matthews adding that Müller, not liking a flat brim had 'turned up the sides in the fashion worn by foreigners'.

Inspector Richard Tanner, the officer in charge of the case, had no doubt that Müller was the killer. Joined by two other detectives, plus Messrs Death and Matthews for the purposes of identification, he headed for New York on the steamship *City of Manchester*. The vessel's superior speed enabled the hunters to reach America two weeks before the hunted. When the *Victoria* eventually berthed at New York, it was met by a pilot boat containing the delegation from London. A startled Müller was picked out by Death and Matthews. Among his possessions were a gold watch and a cut-down hat which, having realized his mistake, Müller had altered to disguise its appearance. Müller was extradited back to England where he faced a hostile welcome from angry Londoners who did not much care for foreigners killing one of their own.

By the time his trial began at the Old Bailey in October 1864, Müller had already been named as the murderer by a coroner's jury and most newspapers. Much of the evidence at the trial concerned hats. At first the victim's son had been unsure as to whether the hat found in Müller's possession in

New York was his father's because it seemed shorter, but Mr Dignance, the hatter, confirmed that it was of the same type as had been made by the firm for Mr Briggs. The piece which had been removed, said Mr Dignance, was the section of the hat where the customer usually wrote his name. The witness pointed out that while the alterations to the hat had not been carried out by a hat-maker, the sewing was of a reasonably high standard, suggesting that it had been the work of some-one familiar with that particular skill. Müller, of course, was a tailor.

The defence did its best to discredit Matthews the cabman. Matthews had not exactly led a blameless life, having been jailed for theft at the age of 19, and the insinuation was that he had shopped Müller partly to get his hands on the £300 reward and partly to cover up his own role in the killing of Thomas Briggs. Matthews was initially unable to account for his movements on the night of the murder although he later claimed that he was at the cab stand at Paddington station between 7 p.m. and 11 p.m. And his insistence that he had not known about the murder until reading details on a poster on 18 July also seemed unlikely in view of the fact that his wife had been aware of it a week earlier.

The defence went on to note that there was no sign of any blood-stained clothing in Müller's room, the only exception being a rag which he used for polishing his shoes. It was also suggested that Müller, a relatively slight man, could not possibly have overpowered Mr Briggs – who was six inches taller and four stone heavier – and thrown him off the train in just three minutes, but this was surely reckoning without the age difference in the two men. At 70, Thomas Briggs was hardly in peak physical condition. Instead, thought the defence, the crime had been committed by two men – the same people seen by Thomas Lee in Mr Briggs's compartment a few minutes before the killing. Lee had been slow in coming forward, principally because he had been on his way to see a girl on the night of the murder and had wanted to keep the assignation from his wife. And when he was finally persuaded to give evidence, he had to admit that he was unable to identify Müller as one of the two men in the carriage.

This briefly appeared promising for the defence, but that was as good as it got. Attempts to establish an alibi for Müller were decidedly unimpressive, relying as they were on witnesses of dubious character. Perhaps the defence would have enjoyed better fortune if they had tried to prove that Müller was too stupid to have been the killer. After all, here was a man who, desperate for money, stole his victim's watch but failed to go through his pockets; inadvertently left his own hat at the scene of the crime and continued to wear the hat of the man whom he had killed; gave the jeweller's cardboard box to a friend's daughter instead of throwing it away; showed his new watch-chain to all and sundry; booked the passage to New York in his own name; and even told people which ship he was sailing on. It could be argued that these were hardly the actions of someone trying to cover up a crime of murder.

But the judge offered no help to Müller's cause, declaring that the prejudicial pre-trial publicity had actually been a good thing because it had helped to acquaint the jury with the facts of the case. The jury evidently decided that Müller had been stupid rather than wronged and took just 15 minutes to find him guilty. Various petitions were raised, including a personal plea to Queen Victoria from the King of Prussia, but these had no effect and Müller was hanged at Newgate before an enthusiastic crowd on 14 November 1864. His last words were: 'Ich habe es getan' – 'I did it'.

For all his incompetence, Franz Müller did create a fashion trend. The surgery he had carried out on Thomas Briggs's hat led to a craze in cut-down hats among young men. They were even known as 'Müller cut-downs'. It was a shame the man himself never got to see any of the royalties.

Six Careless Killers

After murdering his adopted aunt and uncle for their money, Ronald Harries went to great trouble to bury their bodies somewhere he thought they would never be found. He concocted a story to cover up their disappearance, however, not only was the fabricated yarn extremely flimsy, but a moment's panic led the police straight to the corpses.

It was on the evening of Friday 16 October 1953 that 63-year-old John Harries and his infirm wife Phoebe, who was nine years his junior, disappeared from Derlwyn Farm, Llangynin, in Carmarthenshire. They were last seen attending a Harvest Thanksgiving Service at the local Bryn Chapel. When neighbours noticed that John Harries's cows had not been milked, they became suspicious. He was an excellent farmer who would never neglect his duties. The police were informed and started to enquire as to the couple's whereabouts. Twenty-four-year-old Ronald Harries (a distant relative who had been adopted as a nephew by John Harries) said he had driven his aunt and uncle to Carmarthen railway station where they had boarded a train to London for a 'secret holiday', leaving him in charge of the farm. But the Harrieses were not prone to spur-of-the-moment decisions and besides an uncooked joint of meat was discovered in Phoebe Harries's oven, an unlikely state of affairs for someone about to go off on holiday. Ronald Harries had forgotten to check.

The local police suspected that Ronald Harries knew more about their disappearance than he was letting on and called in the services of Scotland Yard. Investigations into his background revealed that he was in financial difficulties. He had recently cashed a cheque for £909, which he said had been made out to him by his uncle, but on closer scrutiny it could be seen that the figure had been altered from £9.

Although the police were convinced that Ronald Harries had somehow done away with his aunt and uncle, without the bodies they had precious little evidence. So they decided to lay a trap for him. Ronald lived at nearby Cadno Farm and the police were certain that Mr and Mrs Harries were buried in the surrounding fields. Carefully they tied cotton threads across the gaps in the hedges all around Cadno Farm and then deliberately made a great deal of noise to alarm Ronald Harries. Terrified in case they had uncovered his secret, he panicked and crept out in the dead of night to inspect the graves. Finding them undisturbed, he breathed a huge sigh of relief and returned to the farm, blissfully unaware of the fact that he had provided the police with all the evidence they needed. At first light the next morning, officers traced where the thread was broken and it led them directly to John and Phoebe Harries, buried in a field of kale.

Despite his blunder, Ronald Harries tried to front it out. When informed that the bodies had been found, he expressed his sorrow but offered no admission of guilt. But when the murder weapon – a hammer – was discovered hidden in undergrowth near Cadno Farm and a witness testified to seeing Ronald rummaging through cupboards and drawers at his uncle's farm, it all pointed to Ronald Harries having killed his elderly relatives so that he could take over their farm. Tried at Carmarthen in March 1954, he was found guilty of murder and hanged at Swansea Prison. If his nerve hadn't failed him, he might just have got away with it.

*

Susan Smith was viewed by the God-fearing souls of Union, South Carolina, as the ideal mother. Once voted friendliest student in class at High School, the 23-year-old appeared to dote on her two young sons, Michael aged three, and Alexander, 14 months. The only blemish on her CV was a failed marriage, but even that wasn't seen as being her fault. When she filed for divorce on the grounds of her husband David's adultery, the judge came down on her side, awarding her custody of the children and ordering David Smith to pay maintenance. But on the night of 25 October 1994, Susan Smith committed the crime which would make her just about the most reviled woman in the United States.

She said that she had been driving the children in a sparsely populated area on the outskirts of Union when she had stopped at a red light. Suddenly a black man in his twenties had opened her passenger door, brandishing a gun. 'Shut up and drive,' he had told her, 'or I'll kill you.' Ten miles out of town, near the John D. Long lake, she said the gunman had ordered her out of the car. She had begged him to release the children, who were strapped into their seats in the back, but he had told her there wasn't time and had sped off, leaving Susan Smith screaming in the middle of the road: 'I love y'all.'

Smith first relayed snippets of her story to the occupant of a nearby house whom she called on for help. Later, through floods of tears, she was able to offer a description of the kidnapper to Sheriff Howard Wells. She said that he had been wearing a plaid jacket and a woollen hat and was breathless 'as though he had been running'.

The townsfolk joined forces to conduct a massive search for the missing children whose angelic faces were featured on newscasts across the nation. Smith herself, briefly reunited with husband David, went on TV to make an emotional appeal for the return of her sons. She broke down in tears as she said: 'Our lives have been torn apart by this tragic event. I can't express how much they are wanted back home.'

Few doubted that the tears were genuine. She appeared every inch the grieving mother, even though crimes like that just didn't happen in Union. Nevertheless there were dissenters. Some noticed her reluctance to look straight at the TV cameras while making her appeal and detectives were puzzled by her unwillingness to meet with experts on child abduction. One neighbour, 63-year-old Catherine Frost, said she saw through Smith straight away. 'I know because I lost two of my sons and I cried. And her tears weren't like mine.'

But there were more serious question marks against Smith's story, above all the fact that she wasn't familiar with how traffic lights operated in the area. It may sound trivial, but it was to lead to the unravelling of her web of lies. The red light at which she claimed her attacker had appeared was operated by approaching traffic and could only have been red if another vehicle was approaching or leaving the intersection. Yet Smith had insisted that there were no other cars around. It simply didn't add up. There were other baffling aspects to the case. She said that the gunman had appeared to be on the run from something or somewhere, yet no crimes or escapes had been reported in the area. Anyway, no carjacker would take children along for the ride – it would simply increase his chances of being caught. Also, no car had ever gone missing in Union County for more than a couple of days, yet, despite a nationwide search orchestrated by the FBI, Smith's vehicle seemed to have vanished off the face of the earth.

Still the people of Union continued to believe Smith's story even after it had been made public that she had failed two lie-detector tests, and when Catherine Frost dared to voice her suspicions on television, she was verbally abused. Smith made a second emotional TV appeal, sobbing that on the day of the kidnap, her son Michael had, for the first time, told her without prompting that he loved her. She also took the opportunity to dismiss rumours that she was a suspect. Holding one hand to her heart, she said: 'The Lord and myself both know the truth. I did not have anything to do with the abduction of my children.'

Outwardly the police said they believed her but at the same time they were working feverishly behind the scenes to crack her story. On 2 November, they searched Smith's home and removed a number of bags. Among the contents was a letter from the son of the owner of the textile mill where she worked as a secretary. They had clearly been lovers, but in the letter – dated 18 October, a week before the children disappeared – he had ended the relationship, saying that he didn't want the responsibility of taking on someone else's children. He wrote that he wanted to be with her but 'did not want any kids around'. At last, the police had their motive. Smith had taken her boyfriend's wish as her command. With the children out of the way, she would be able to rekindle the romance.

Smith was taken in for questioning and admitted that there was no black stranger – she had killed her children. She had strapped the boys into the car, driven to the lake, climbed out of the vehicle at the top of the boat ramp and rolled it down into the water with Michael and Alex trapped inside. The next day the police found the maroon Mazda and its hapless occupants at the bottom of the lake.

Appalled at how she had deceived them so wickedly, many, David Smith included, wanted Susan Smith to die for her crime. Her lawyers tried to depict the killings as a failed suicide attempt (Smith had said she had driven around for hours on the night of the murders, considering taking her own life) but the prosecution maintained that it was an act of cold-blooded murder, calculated to remove an obstacle to her love affair. She was found guilty of two counts of murder but escaped the death penalty, being sentenced instead to life imprisonment.

*

A simple word out of place cost Ethel Major her freedom and her life. One of four children of a Lincolnshire gamekeeper,

Ethel took up dress-making on leaving school but in 1915 she gave birth to an illegitimate daughter. In order to avoid the shame, Ethel's parents treated the baby girl as Ethel's sister. Three years later, Ethel married Arthur Major and the newly-weds lived with her parents. In 1919, they had their first child and, despite Arthur's income as a van driver, it was another ten years before they were able to flee the nest and find a place of their own.

Their move to the Lincolnshire village of Kirkby on Bain marked the beginning of the end for the Majors. The village tongues were soon wagging about Ethel's 'sister' Auriel and word got back to Arthur. Ethel had never told him the truth, so to discover after 16 years of marriage that his wife had an illegitimate daughter came as something of a shock, particularly since she steadfastly refused to divulge the name of the father. Their marriage went downhill fast and Ethel, who was known in the village as a strong-willed character, began to accuse Arthur of being a drunkard. He became increasingly violent towards her and when, in 1934, she discovered that he had been receiving letters from another woman, she decided to tell the world about her husband's appalling behaviour. He responded by arranging for an advertisement to be placed in the *Horncastle News*, announcing that he would no longer be responsible for his wife's debts. Quite a double act were the Majors.

The advert was scheduled to appear on 26 May 1934 but two days before that, Arthur Major died. He had first been taken ill on the 22nd, Ethel attributing his severe pains, twitching, foaming at the mouth and convulsions to some corned beef which he had eaten. At least that was what she told anybody who enquired as to her husband's well-being. Arthur himself thought she had been trying to poison him for some time and a workmate later remarked on seeing a bird drop dead shortly after taking a peck out of one of Arthur's sandwiches – so lovingly prepared by Ethel. However, the doctor diagnosed the cause of death as epilepsy. With Arthur still warm, the merry widow immediately cancelled the notice in the newspaper and arranged his funeral. Some mourners had already congregated at the house when the coroner dramatically stopped the proceedings. The problem was that the police had received an anonymous letter saying that a neighbour's dog had died after eating scraps of food thrown out by Ethel Major and, on exhumation, the dog's body had been found to contain strychnine. As a result, a post-mortem was carried out on Arthur Major and it showed that he too had died of strychnine poisoning.

If Ethel had been careless in putting out contaminated food for passing pets, she now committed the ultimate *faux pas*. Interviewed by the police, she said: 'I did not know my husband died of strychnine poisoning.' But the presence of strychnine was known only to the police and the medical experts. Told that strychnine had never been mentioned, she replied: 'Oh, I'm sorry. I must have made a mistake.'

The police did not think so but still could not work out how she had had access to the poison. Her father kept some strychnine in a locked box, but he had the only key, the other one having vanished some ten years earlier. It was the only piece of the jigsaw that was missing, so when a key fitting the box was found in Ethel's handbag she was charged with murder. She was tried at Lincoln Assizes where she was defended by the redoubtable Norman Birkett, who had never lost a murder case. No defence witnesses were called and Ethel Major herself did not take the stand. Even Birkett's powers of advocacy could not save the day and she was found guilty. Despite the jury's recommendation for mercy, she was hanged at Hull Prison on 19 December 1934.

*

Fifty-eight-year-old Vivian Messiter worked from a garage at Grove Street, Southampton, as an agent for an oil company.

He disappeared on 30 October 1928 and was not heard of again until the following January when his decomposed body, chewed by rats, was found behind some boxes in the locked garage. A puncture wound over the left eye suggested that the victim had been shot but the true cause of death turned out to be multiple fractures of the skull. Messiter had been battered to death with a heavy hammer.

A search of the dead man's lodgings unearthed a reply from a William F. Thomas to an advertisement asking for local agents. Thomas was known to the police and was already wanted in connection with fraud relating to a car theft in Manchester, but when officers went to his lodgings to haul him in for questioning, they discovered that he had fled the area. In his haste, however, he had left behind a series of valuable clues which revealed that his real name was William Henry Podmore.

The errant Podmore was tracked down to London. He admitted that he had worked as Messiter's assistant but denied having anything to do with his murder. The only crime that the police could pin on him was the Manchester fraud and for that he was duly sentenced to six months in prison.

In the meantime, officers had found a sales receipt book from which all the top pages had been torn out. This seemed highly suspicious. Podmore thought he had covered his tracks by removing the top copies but he had reckoned without the pressure of his pencil leaving indentations on the pages beneath. By using special photography, these were made legible and produced damning evidence against Podmore – the book recorded oil sales to non-existent people giving commissions to William F. Thomas, Podmore's alias. Podmore had been swindling Messiter.

Podmore was charged with murder in December 1929 and tried at Winchester Assizes. The prosecution claimed that Vivian Messiter had uncovered the scam of the bogus orders and had threatened to call the police, whereupon Podmore, with the fraud case already hanging over him, had bludgeoned him to death. Podmore then locked the garage, stole his victim's car and took his lady friend, who rejoiced in the name of 'Golden-Haired Lil' for a drive. A hammer found in the garage proved to be the murder weapon and an eyebrow hair on it linked it to the dead man. Found guilty, Podmore paid for his recklessness over the receipt book with his life.

*

During the Second World War, Leading Aircraftsman Arthur Heys was based at an RAF station near Beccles in Suffolk. Thirty-seven-year-old Heys was popular with his colleagues and, despite having a family back home in Colne, Lancashire, he had a reputation for eyeing up the girls.

On the evening of 8 November 1944, he went out to a dance with a group of fellow airmen but when it was time to return to camp, there was no sign of him. He eventually resurfaced shortly after midnight – at the women's quarters – whereupon the duty corporal ordered him back to his own billet. On his way back, he bumped into Winifred Mary Evans, a 27-year-old radio operator. Fuelled by alcohol, Heys was desperate for sex. After raping and suffocating her, he left her body in a ditch where it was discovered the following morning.

The police were fairly certain that the killer came from the base and at parade all the men were told to line up so that the duty corporal could pick out the man she had seen the previous night. Heys tried to hide in a different line but merely succeeded in drawing attention to himself and was quickly identified as the mystery airman. He told the police that he had been back in his quarters by 12.30 a.m. but his hut-mates put his time of arrival at up to an hour later. It was also noted that he had spent much of the morning after the murder cleaning his clothes – even to the point of skipping breakfast – but he hadn't been able to remove all the incriminating evidence, notably a hair on his overcoat which proved to be of the same type as Winifred Evans's. Nor had he been able to cover up the telltale scratches on his hands.

Charged with the murder, Heys managed one final act of stupidity. He sent an anonymous letter to the Commanding Officer of the base saying that Heys was innocent and that the letter-writer was the real culprit. It didn't take long to trace the letter back to Heys and since the missive contained details of the case known only to the police and the killer, it was tantamount to a confession. The police had all the evidence they needed and Heys's trial at Bury St Edmunds in January 1945 was little more than a formality. At the end of it, he was found guilty of the brutal murder of Winifred Evans and hanged at Norwich on 13 March 1945.

*

On 6 May 1927, a man arrived by taxi at the left-luggage office at London's Charing Cross station and deposited a large black trunk for safe-keeping. There seemed nothing untoward about the transaction until, over the coming days, the attendant was struck by the awful smell coming from the trunk. Eventually, five days later, he called in the police. When opened, the trunk was found to contain five brown paper parcels, wrapped with string. Each package contained a dismembered part of a woman's body.

Home Office pathologist Sir Bernard Spilsbury examined the remains and, piecing them together, came up with a short, plump woman of around 35. She had been dead for about a week and had died from asphyxia, although extensive bruising on the body indicated that she had been beaten unconscious before being suffocated.

The only clue the trunk yielded was a pair of knickers bearing the laundry mark P. HOLT. This was traced to a Chelsea family who stated that one of their previous employees must have stolen the garment. Furthermore, the description of the dead woman fitted a Mrs Rolls who had worked for the Holts. Mrs Rolls turned out to be Minnie Alice Bonati, a 36-year-old prostitute, and estranged wife of an Italian waiter. She had last been seen alive in Chelsea on 4 May. Mr Bonati formally identified the remains as being those of his wife.

In the meantime, the publicity attached to the case had brought another lead. The trunk was recognized by a second-hand dealer from Brixton who remembered selling it to a smart-looking gentleman of military bearing, a description which tallied with that given by the left-luggage attendant at Charing Cross. A shoe-shine boy then turned up with a left-luggage ticket which he had seen dropped out of a taxi window and this information led the police to the taxi driver himself who recalled taking a man with a trunk from 86 Rochester Row to Charing Cross station on 6 May.

Further investigation of the offices at 86 Rochester Row (which were conveniently opposite the police station) showed that one of the occupants – a John Robinson – had not been seen for several days. He was finally tracked down in Kennington and brought back to Scotland Yard to stand in an identity parade. Thirty-six-year-old Robinson, estranged from a wife whom he had married bigamously, denied all knowledge of Minnie Bonati, let alone of her murder. And the case against him looked alarmingly thin when neither the taxi driver, the left-luggage attendant or the second-hand dealer were able to pick him out at the parade. There seemed absolutely nothing to link him to the deceased.

Nor did his third-floor office look promising. There appeared no obvious sign of a struggle. But in his haste to cover up the murder and clean up the office, Robinson had overlooked one tiny thing. In dismembering the corpse, removing it without being detected and obliterating all traces of blood, he had neglected to empty the waste basket properly. And there, caught in the wicker work of the basket, was a blood-stained match. It was the only item in the office which gave any indication that the murder had taken place there but it was sufficient to shake Robinson's resolve. From insisting that he had never met Minnie Bonati, he suddenly changed his story. He said that Bonati had propositioned him at Victoria railway station. He had returned with her to the office where she had become abusive and started demanding money. He claimed she attacked him, and that in the ensuing struggle she fell and knocked herself unconscious on a coal bucket. Robinson said that in a panic he had rushed out of the building and was as surprised as anyone to return the following morning and find her body lying there in the very spot where she had fallen. Realizing that she was dead, he bought a knife, cut up the corpse and loaded it into the trunk. The only thing he denied was that he had killed her in the first place.

But at his Old Bailey trial, the jury did not believe Robinson's story that Minnie Bonati's death had been accidental. He was found guilty and hanged at Pentonville on 12 August 1927, convicted by a single bloody match.

Bart Caritativo: The Flawed Forgery

In the 1940s, there was a fashion among the wealthier families in California to employ Filipino male servants. One such houseboy was Bart Caritativo who worked in a large home in the north San Francisco suburb of Stinson Beach. He also undertook chauffering duties, in the course of which he became friendly with the housekeeper at the house next door, a lady by the name of Camille Malmgren. The latter had achieved every housekeeper's dream of marrying her rich boss and when he died, he left her his fortune. Instead of hoovering on a daily basis, she was now left to contemplate life as a wealthy widow in her forties.

Legal Blunders

Caritativo remained on good terms with Camille, especially when she discovered that he shared her literary ambitions. Ironically, it was his poor literacy which would eventually prove his downfall.

With so much money to her name, Camille was highly eligible and in 1949 she married again, this time to Englishman Joseph Banks. Her new husband was a heavy drinker, however, and on more than one occasion she felt compelled to book him into a clinic to seek treatment for his alcoholism. Throughout this traumatic period, Caritativo provided a shoulder to cry on. Banks did not appear to resent the Filipino's close relationship with his wife and the two men got on well, but then in 1954 Camille decided that she could no longer tolerate her husband's drinking and the couple were divorced. Nevertheless the former Mr and Mrs Banks still saw each other on a regular basis and Camille continued to live in the Stinson Beach house until suddenly, in September 1954, she thought that it was time to sell up and live abroad.

On 17 September, real estate agent Hilda Grunert called on Camille to discuss the sale of the house. She found Joseph Banks sprawled in the living room, surrounded by empty liquor bottles, and in the bedroom lay the body of Camille. Her skull had been split open by savage blows to the head. At first glance, Hilda Grunert had thought that Banks was simply drunk but closer investigation showed that he was clutching the handle of a large knife which was embedded in his stomach. It was a double tragedy.

Everything pointed to the fact that Banks, in an alcoholic rage, had killed his ex-wife and then taken his own life. But when police officers started to search the house, they soon came up with evidence which suggested a different sequence of events. On a table they found a note, purportedly from Banks, in which he appeared to confess to the carnage. It read: 'I am responsible to what you see and find.' The police also found what seemed to be Camille's will, leaving everything to Caritativo. However both documents – one supposedly written by Banks, the other by Camille – were remarkably similar. The writing may have been disguised, but both were grammatically poor and contained basic spelling errors. Suspicion fell on Caritativo, especially when he was subjected to a handwriting test which revealed many of the same defects present in the note and the will.

He was charged with double murder and tried in January 1955. A doctor testified that Banks had been too drunk to have stabbed himself and with the evidence that the will was forged, things looked black for the Filipino. In a last-ditch attempt to save his skin, Caritativo sacked his lawyer and told the court: 'I have lost the trust to my attorneys.' This simple phrase sealed his fate since he misused the word 'to' in the same way as in Banks's so-called suicide note. The jury had seen him score a spectacular own goal and did not take long to find him guilty. He was executed at San Quentin on 24 October 1958 and three years later the prison psychiatrist said that Caritativo had confessed prior to his death.

Chapter 4

Security Leaks

Group 4: A Licence to Escape

On 5 April 1993, as part of its ongoing privatization plans, the British government awarded the contract for the escort of prisoners to and from courts in Derbyshire, Nottinghamshire, Lincolnshire, Humberside and North and South Yorkshire to the security firm Group 4. The Prison Officers' Association, whose members, along with the police, had previously been responsible for escort duties, warned that Group 4 might not have the necessary expertise. And, over the first two weeks, this proved an uncannily accurate prediction as Group 4 contrived to lose no fewer than eight prisoners. In the House of Commons, Shadow Home Secretary Tony Blair likened the company's antics to an Ealing comedy. Meanwhile the prisoners had never had it so good. For some, a trip to court was as good as a passport to freedom.

It quickly became apparent that Group 4 were ill-prepared for the magnitude of the job. Within hours of taking over escort duties, they had lost their first prisoner when Christopher Hatch, a 21-year-old on remand for theft, public order and criminal damage charges, vaulted from the dock and ran out of Hull magistrates' court. On the same day in Leicester, around a dozen prisoners refused to get into a Group 4 security vehicle containing cells for the 300-yard journey to court. As a result, no prisoners had arrived at either the city's magistrates' court or crown court some two hours after the day's hearings were due to start. After three hours, the prisoners were finally talked round but it was a far from auspicious start for the new service. The Prison Officers' Association, with more than a hint of 'I told you so', described the day's events as 'deeply embarrassing for Group 4' but the security firm's director Michael Hirst – former Chief Constable of Leicestershire – did his best to put on a brave face. 'Inevitably there are going to be teething troubles,' he admitted, but predicted that the new system would be running smoothly within a week.

Two days later, Group 4 managers were summoned to a meeting with the head of the prison service after a prisoner in Spalding escaped by forcing open the hatch in the vehicle taking him to court. A third prisoner fled on 8 April, kicking open the window of a Group 4 van in Derby on his way to a remand centre.

As the privatization of the job came under fire, design faults in the vans were blamed for the escapes and plans were announced to put bars on the windows. The talks with Group 4 bosses were brought forward after it emerged that a fourth prisoner had escaped during that hapless first week. A 20-year-old, on remand for burglary charges, simply walked out of Mansfield magistrates' court. A police officer remarked: 'To have him released in this way is, to say the least, disappointing.' However, Group 4 weren't taking the blame for this one. The defendant had been due to appear later in the day at the same court on another matter and Group 4 attributed his sharp exit to a procedural error by court officials. Nevertheless, with Group 4 becoming something of a national joke, it was more unwelcome publicity, both for the company and the government.

A fifth prisoner made his bid for freedom on 15 April when a 17-year-old youth on theft charges fled the dock at Ilkeston magistrates' court where Group 4 staff were acting as custody officers. And in Nottingham, court hearings had to be postponed because Group 4 vans transporting prisoners got lost in the city's one-way system! This was too much for the opposition and in parliament Tony Blair told Home Secretary Kenneth Clarke: 'It's about time you took a grip on your own department and the prison escort service with some regard to the public safety, rather than like something out of an Ealing comedy.'

As Group 4's duties spread further afield, the tales of woe continued. In Newcastle upon Tyne, firefighters had to cut through the side of a Group 4 security van to release two men trapped inside. The driver had collapsed at the wheel, leaving his colleagues stranded in the back. More seriously, Humberside prisoner Ernest Hogg collapsed and died in a Group 4 security van while on remand. He had been drinking heavily and died from brain damage caused by inhaling his own vomit. These accidents brought renewed calls for modifications to be made to Group 4 vans. In a bid to stem the flow of escapes, Group 4 announced plans to introduce nylon ankle straps as leg shackles for prisoners in extreme cases. The move was criticized in some quarters and Group 4 felt the need to hire PR companies in an attempt to improve the company's image. At the same time, news leaked out that, owing to pressure of work over the Easter period, Group 4 had been forced to use administrative staff, including women typists, to drive prisoners to and from court . . .

Gradually Group 4 got their house in order but there were still a few hiccups along the way to keep us entertained. A prisoner in Pudsey, West Yorkshire, was taken to five different courts before finally arriving at the correct one five hours late and in July, a court heard how a prisoner at the Wolds remand centre on Humberside, which was run by Group 4, escaped by dressing up in his girlfriend's clothes. When his girlfriend Amanda Kirk came to visit, 24-year-old Craig Renshaw borrowed her hat and earrings and slipped into the dress she had been wearing. He then simply sauntered out of the remand centre past unconcerned Group 4 prison officers. Since she had been wearing leggings beneath her dress, she too was able to leave. Renshaw's defence counsel said: 'He was astonished that he was able to walk out of the centre dressed as a woman without being confronted.' Still, Renshaw was recaptured two days later when he curiously decided to return to the Wolds posing as a prison visitor.

In the same month, a Group 4 security officer tried to hand a prisoner over to a museum instead of to the crown court next door. Staff at the Harris Museum and Art Gallery in Preston were stunned when a custody officer turned up and asked: 'What do we do with him?' John Regan, the museum's development officer, said: 'They just turned up at the front door. The staff had to laugh. They suggested the prisoner might like to tour our new sculpture exhibition!' On the same day, Group 4 lost £500 when a bag of £1 coins fell from the back of one of its vans in London. It had not been a good day for the firm – but no worse than most others over that eventful three months.

Great Escapes

In August 1996, a prisoner at Parkhurst Prison on the Isle of Wight spent two days colouring his body yellow with a highlighter pen to feign jaundice, hoping to escape during a transfer to hospital. The plan was foiled when the inmate, serving six years for attempted robbery, was seen colouring his face when a guard looked through the cell-door inspection hatch during the night.

*

On one night in July 1978, no fewer than 124 prisoners escaped simultaneously from the supposedly top-security Alcoente

Prison, near Lisbon. Failing to notice that 220 knives and yards of electric cable had vanished, that prisoners had amassed a pile of spades, chisels and electric drills, or that numerous posters had suddenly sprung up around the prison (to hide the gaping holes in the walls), the ever-vigilant guards only heard about the mass breakout when one of the few remaining prisoners told them. With hindsight, perhaps it had not been a wise move to include in the prison cinema programme *The Great Escape*.

*

After fleeing Kirkham Open Prison, near Blackpool, in September 1994, car thief David Johnston hitched a lift near the M6 and told the driver: 'I hope you don't mind, but I'm an escaped prisoner.' The driver replied: 'Not if you don't mind that I'm a prison officer!' Johnston was soon back behind bars, cursing his luck. In fact, the prison officer was his third lift since absconding – his second had been with a police patrol officer who kindly drove him 15 miles on the motorway.

*

In December 1991, 26-year-old Jean Paul Barrett, serving a 33-year prison sentence for forgery and fraud, escaped from Tucson jail by having a forged release order faxed to the prison authorities.

*

Clyde Foster, who had been on the FBI's wanted list for a year since escaping from jail, was tracked down in December 1978 when he was found working as a custody officer in the Washington law courts. His job, which necessitated regular court appearances, was to vouch for the conduct of prisoners being granted parole. Ironically for one on the run himself, he had helped secure the release of countless prisoners over that 12-month period. Although Foster had changed his name, he was exposed when he unluckily found himself in court with a detective who had arrested him in 1976 as the ringleader of a car fraud and who thought he was still serving a five-year sentence at Petersburg, Virginia.

*

A Romanian who wanted to sample life in the United States set about achieving his aim by stowing away in a cargo container of a ship bound for New York. When the ship eventually docked, he slipped ashore from his hiding place in eager anticipation of experiencing the Big Apple. But as he gazed out at his new homeland, he was puzzled that there wasn't a skyscraper in sight . . . nor a yellow taxi . . . nor the Statue of Liberty. It was only when he was picked up by docks police that he learned that the ship's first port of call was not New York but Felixstowe.

*

Authorities at Manchester Prison were left red-faced in 1998 when they were forced to change the locks on all the cells after discovering that an official video showed close-ups of keys. The educational video, intended to be shown to inmates, had been made in 1994 and placed in storage. But when an officer decided to check the contents, he was horrified at what he saw and raised the alarm. As a result, the locks on all 700 cells were changed at a cost of over £80,000. A prison source explained: 'The video shows a prison chaplain doing the rounds. He gets to one door and in the process of unlocking it, the whole bunch of keys is seen dangling down in stark, zoom-lens close-up. Every single key in the bunch was on display. There are many prisoners here who can memorize a key just from looking at it once, let alone watching a video tape close-up. It is all very, very embarrassing that an internal prison video should assist would-be escapers.'

*

After six months of digging a secret tunnel from Saltillo Prison, Mexico, 75 convicts made their bid for freedom one day in April 1976, only to find that the tunnel emerged in the

nearby courtroom where many of them had been sentenced.
The stunned judges quickly sent them back to jail.

*

A man who escaped from Stanford Hill Prison, Kent, in
December 1990 was eventually recaptured after being found
asleep in a house he'd burgled in Andover, Hampshire.

*

In December 1984, Scott Robinson, a 23-year-old lorry driver
serving 11 months in San Jos Prison, California, for stealing
video games, boasted to a cell-mate how he had managed to
break into the prison's computer code and change his date of
release so that he could see in the New Year at home with his
children. But while bragging, he was overheard by a guard
who promptly put a halt to his scheme. A worried Santa Clara
County sheriff's office immediately launched an investigation
to see whether Robinson's generosity had secured the release
of any other prisoners.

*

No helicopters or high-performance motorbikes were needed
to spring Michael Mufford from the Gainesville Work Camp,
Florida, in 1994. Mufford, serving time for burglary and theft,
simply escaped by riding a lawn mower into nearby woods.

*

An armoured van lost $1.2 million in cash in February 1981
when its back door flew open in Philadelphia and two bags
containing the money fell out. The occupants of a car following behind could hardly believe their luck. The car screeched
to a halt and two men were seen jumping out of the car and
grabbing the bags before driving off laughing.

*

Determined to combat the theft of miniature bottles of whisky
from one of their aircraft in 1978, Pan-Am security guards set
a trap for the culprit. They wired up a cuckoo clock inside the
drinks cabinet. In the event of the cabinet door being opened,

the clock would stop, thus revealing the precise time of theft. The guards didn't tell the plane's crew of the trap – in case one of them was responsible for the missing booze – but the scheme backfired dramatically when a stewardess heard the ticking inside the cabinet and thought it was a bomb. She immediately told the pilot who carried out an emergency landing at Berlin where 80 passengers left the Boeing 727 in a hurry. Pan-Am admitted that it had been an unnecessarily expensive security exercise. The miniature bottles cost just 17p each whereas the cost of the emergency landing came to £6500.

*

After spending months digging a tunnel to take them out of their Brazilian prison, two escapees finally made their bid for freedom in 1994. Emerging in the street outside, they flagged down a passing car. Alas, the driver was a prison guard who promptly returned them whence they came.

*

A prisoner who tried to escape from Norwich Prison in March 1991 by squeezing through the bars of a first-floor toilet window had to be rescued by firefighters when he got stuck.

*

A plumber, a welder and an electrician serving time in a maximum security prison in the United States almost managed to build a helicopter because staff 'didn't see the significance' of the various parts scattered around the jail. The inmates' route to freedom was only lacking a big rotor blade when the creation was discovered at Nevada State Prison in May 1982.

Chapter 5

Bungled Executions

John Lee: The Man They Could Not Hang

After being convicted of the brutal murder of his employer, 20-year-old footman John Lee acquired legendary status when he went on to survive three attempts to hang him. He became known as 'The Man They Could Not Hang'.

Lee worked for 86-year-old Emma Keyse, a wealthy spinster who lived in a thatched cottage at Babbacombe, just outside Torquay. Miss Keyse, who had once been a maid to Queen Victoria, lived a blameless life and expected her servants to attend daily prayers. Lee, the son of a yeoman farmer from Abbotskerswell, near Newton Abbot, had first entered her service some five years earlier but had left to join the Royal Navy. After leaving the Navy through ill health, he was sentenced to six months' hard labour for stealing silver from his then employer, Colonel Brownlow of Torquay. It was the only blot on Lee's copybook and Miss Keyse, who had always found him to be trustworthy, agreed to take him back. But he soon became disenchanted with his low pay, especially when Miss Keyse professed herself dissatisfied with his work and reduced his weekly wages from two shillings and sixpence to two shillings.

In the early hours of 15 November 1884, Emma Keyse was found dead in the dining room. Her throat had been cut and her head battered with a heavy instrument. It was a particularly ferocious attack on an elderly lady. The killer had then used paraffin to start five separate fires in the house in an attempt to burn the body and it was the smell of burning which awoke the servants.

With no sign of a forced entry and no attempt at robbery, suspicion fell upon members of the household. A bloodstained knife and a hatchet were both found in a drawer in the pantry where Lee slept. An oil can kept in one of the pantry cupboards was also spattered with blood. A coat and pair of trousers which Lee had worn on the night of the murder were stained with blood and smelt strongly of paraffin. And one of his socks not only reeked of paraffin but also had human hair attached to it – hair which was found to match that of the deceased.

Lee was in a tight corner. He claimed that he had been asleep on the morning of the murder until hearing the cries of the other servants. As for the blood on his clothing, he maintained that he had cut his arm while smashing a window in order to let out the smoke. The police did not believe his story for one minute and he was charged with murder.

Lee's trial began at Exeter on 2 February 1885. It lasted just three days and, despite attempts by the defence to suggest that the cook's lover was somehow responsible for the murder of Miss Keyse, it took the jury a mere 40 minutes to return a guilty verdict. In passing the death sentence, Mr Justice Manisty described the crime as one of the most cruel and barbarous murders ever committed and warned Lee that he could expect no mercy. He also remarked upon Lee's calm and collected behaviour in the dock, hinting at what a cold individual it must have taken to slay the old woman in such a horrific fashion. In reply, Lee said: 'The reason, my lord, why I am so calm and collected is because I trust in my Lord, and He knows I am innocent.'

The remark was dismissed as sheer bravado and Lee was taken back to Exeter Prison in preparation for his execution, which was due to take place on Monday, 23 February. In the condemned cell, Lee continued to baffle all around him by his apparent indifference to his fate. The *Western Morning News* reported: 'When visited by his mother and other relatives his demeanour was by no means indicative of a man who realized, much less dreaded, the approach of death by hanging. While persistently asserting his innocence he assumed a cheerfulness, and even a jauntiness of manner, which to his friends was not less painful than surprising. In bidding his last farewell he betrayed not the slightest emotion – not even when his grief-stricken mother finally embraced him and reluctantly withdrew from his cell.'

On the Friday before the date of execution, James Berry, the new public executioner, travelled from his home in Bradford to Bristol and then, on the following morning, completed his journey to Exeter. He arrived at the prison at noon on the Saturday and proceeded to inspect the execution site, which was an old coach-house, usually home to the prison van. There were two trapdoors in the floor, covering a pit some 11 ft deep. The rope would be attached to an iron rod which in turn hung from an iron beam. When pulled, a lever would draw back the bolts which held the trapdoors in place so that they fell against the walls of the pit. Berry tested the apparatus twice and was satisfied that it was in good working order, although he did suggest that thicker doors with stronger ironwork be used in future. The governor agreed to look into the matter.

On the eve of his execution, Lee had a peculiar dream in which he was on the scaffold, waiting to be hanged, but the drop failed to work. He dreamed that three times they tried to hang him, but each attempt was unsuccessful. Lee relayed the details of his dream to the warders in his cell the following morning but nobody paid any attention . . . until later.

Executioner Berry was up at 6.30 that morning and an hour later he made his way to the coach-house where he tied a length of rope to the overhead rod and put the finishing touches to his preparations. He didn't bother testing the trapdoors again as they had appeared to be in perfect working order.

Shortly before 8 a.m., Lee was led out to face the music, to the accompaniment of the toll of the prison bell. Ten reporters watched as the condemned man remained as impassive as ever even when his legs were strapped together. The *Western Morning News* described the scene: 'As Lee walked into the building and . . . placed himself on the fatal planks, there was no faltering or sign of fear. He cast a glance at the rope above him, as if to assure himself that its fastenings were perfectly secured, and then inaudibly muttered something to Berry as the latter functionary adjusted the noose around the culprit's neck. There was even a dash of bravado in the unhappy man's demeanour as he glanced at the ghastly paraphernalia of death. A white cap was, in the usual manner, placed over the head and face of the convict.'

Berry asked Lee whether he had anything to say, but Lee said no. As the chaplain concluded his service, the hangman pulled the lever operating the trapdoors but, just as Lee had dreamed the night before, the doors failed to open. Berry jerked the lever back and forth in a desperate attempt to spring the doors into action but they would not be moved. So the noose and the cap were removed from Lee's head and he was moved forward of the doors while an axe, a saw and a plane were brought in to carry out emergency repairs. A few minutes later, the apparatus was tested and worked perfectly. Once again Lee's legs were pinioned and the rope and cap put in place. The lever was pulled but the result was the same as before – the trapdoors failed to open.

Berry and the prison officials were now in a state of panic. They had no idea as to a solution but were determined to give it another try. And so, while Lee was led to one side, the apparatus was tested once more. Onlookers felt considerable sympathy for the prisoner's protracted ordeal but Lee himself was content to watch the hasty amendments. A minute or so later, he was brought forward for a third time but the bolt still refused to yield and the doors remained firmly in place. At this, Berry stamped on them furiously but they held firm.

Some reports indicate that a fourth unsuccessful attempt was made to hang John Lee on that highly charged morning but the general consensus of opinion was that the mission was aborted after three tries. That was because the chaplain, the Reverend John Pitkin, decided he had seen enough. He said later: 'A great noise was heard, which sounded like the falling of the drop. But to my horror, when I turned my eyes to the scaffold, I saw the poor convict standing upon the drop as I had seen him twice before. I refused to stay any longer.'

Without the chaplain there could be no hanging and Lee was escorted back to his cell where he told the Revd Pitkin about his dream. As word spread about Lee's miraculous escape, the Home Secretary, Sir William Harcourt, was informed of the morning's mishaps. That afternoon, he decreed that Lee's sentence be commuted to penal servitude for life. Although it was a popular decision with many of the public, who thought that Lee had suffered enough on the scaffold, it did not go down well with the family of the deceased. Unaccountably, Lee revealed in a letter to his sister, written before the Home Secretary's decision was announced, that he was still hoping to be hanged. Presumably, he eventually became reconciled to his salvation.

For his part, James Berry was mystified and somewhat embarrassed by the turn of events, particularly as the apparatus had worked perfectly well, not only in the days leading up to the planned execution but also in the tests between the failures. In his opinion, his earlier misgivings about the ironwork catches on the trapdoors and the thinness of the doors themselves had been shown to be justified. He reiterated that he felt the wooden doors should have been three or four times heavier with ironwork to match, 'so that when a man of Lee's weight was placed upon the doors the iron catches would not have become locked, as I feel sure they did on this occasion, but would respond readily'. However the more widely held view was that heavy rain the night before had caused the trapdoors to swell. Although the coach-house had a roof, it may have leaked, resulting in the flooding of the stone floor. And Lee's weight would have been sufficient to compress and wedge the doors, but not enough to open them. Others, including Lee himself, felt that his let-off was the work of God. Lee stated: 'It was the Lord's hand which would not let the law take away my life.'

John Lee served 22 years in Portland Prison, Dorset – a considerable time for a life sentence. This was partly because of the severity of his crime and also because he had allegedly made repeated threats against his half-sister who had given evidence against him at his trial. When he was finally released, on 17 December 1907, he returned to Devon and had his intriguing life story published by *Lloyd's Weekly News*. Not long afterwards, the story reappeared in book form with the title *The Man They Could Not Hang*.

The proceeds from the sale of the book enabled Lee to live comfortably for a time and in 1908 he married Jessie Bulleid, a nurse at Newton Abbot Workhouse. They subsequently moved to London – where Lee worked as a barman – but in 1912 the marriage foundered amidst rumours that Lee had run off to Australia with another woman. His later life is shrouded in mystery but it is thought that he ended up settling in the United States and that he died in Milwaukee in 1933, aged 68. The failure of the hangman's trapdoor had given him a bonus of 48 years.

Will Purvis: A Curious Case of Justice

The hangman's inability to execute Mississippi farmer's son Will Purvis proved to be a blessing in disguise, not only for Purvis but for the American justice system as a whole. For 23 years, another man's deathbed confession affirmed that Purvis had been innocent of the murder for which he had been convicted and had been meant to die on the gallows. It was a lucky escape all round.

In the early 1890s, racial tension was running high in southern Mississippi. Black labourers were being persecuted by a gang of vigilantes known as the White Caps who professed to be upholding the forces of law and order. The White Caps was a secret organization and among its members in 1893 was 20-year-old Will Purvis who lived at Devils Bend, just outside the town of Columbia. One of his first missions was to assist in the flogging of Sam Waller, a farmhand who worked for brothers Will and Jim Buckley. Although Will Buckley was himself a member of the White Caps, he was appalled at the violence inflicted upon his employee and announced that he was going to see the perpetrators brought to justice. To this end, the Buckleys and Sam Waller rode into Columbia to give evidence before a grand jury, but making their way back on 22 June they were ambushed and Will Buckley was shot dead.

Jim Buckley identified Purvis as one of the gang and claimed that he had fired the fatal shot. Purvis insisted that he had been at home – five miles away – at the time of the shooting and had witnesses to prove it. The evidence against him may have appeared weak but it was sufficient for Will Purvis to be charged with murder.

His trial in Columbia took place against a backdrop of fear. Whilst local residents weren't too concerned about the occasional black man being the victim of violence, the killing of a white man was a different matter altogether. It was felt that the White Caps had overstepped the mark and that someone – namely Purvis – should pay the price. Meanwhile the authorities were worried in case White Cap sympathizers tried to spring the defendant from jail. Consequently security at the courthouse was tight. The state militia guarded the building although curiously spectators were allowed to take guns into court, the reason given being so that they could protect themselves in the event of a pitched battle. The outcome was a foregone conclusion. A scapegoat was needed and so it came as little surprise when Purvis was found guilty of the murder of Will Buckley and sentenced to death. Again he maintained that he was innocent and angrily yelled at the 12 jurors: 'I'll live to see the last one of you die!' His lawyers launched an appeal but this too proved unsuccessful and the date of execution was set for 7 February 1894.

A crowd of 3000 turned up to watch Will Purvis hang. Shortly before noon, he was led, ashen-faced, to the heavily guarded scaffold erected outside the courthouse in Columbia. Asked by Sheriff Irving Magee whether he had any last words, Purvis briefly addressed the assembled throng to repeat his innocence. He added that there were people present who could save his neck if they wanted to. The plea fell on deaf ears. Already bound by the wrists and ankles and with the rope firmly in position around his neck, the final touch was added in the form of the ominous black cap being placed over his head. Sheriff Magee picked up a hatchet and severed the stay rope which was holding the trapdoor in position. The door sprang open and Purvis plunged through it. But the knot on the noose had come undone as it took his weight and the noose had slipped over his head. The outcome was that, although Purvis landed with a mighty thump, he was far from dead.

For a few seconds he lay on the ground, dazed. When he

regained his composure, Magee and his three deputies lifted Purvis back up the steps of the scaffold so that they could try again, but the crowd would have none of it. Taking their lead from the Reverend James G. Sibley, pastor of the Columbia Methodist Church, they declared that they had just witnessed a miracle, a clear sign that Purvis was innocent after all. They demanded that he be spared, leaving Sheriff Magee with no option but to postpone the execution and take Purvis back to his cell while awaiting fresh instructions from the District Attorney.

Since the Sheriff had failed to carry out the sentence as required by the court of law, the defendant had to be re-sentenced before the same court where he had originally been tried. Magee himself had begun to have doubts as to Purvis's guilt but State Governor John M. Stone was not for turning. Purvis was thus sentenced to death once again but three more unsuccessful appeals to the Supreme Court earned a stay of execution. Even so, it would surely be nothing more than temporary.

The date for his second execution was finally set for 12 December 1895, but a few days beforehand he was sprung from jail by friends. He stayed on the run for three months, a price on his head, before surrendering to the authorities on 12 March 1896, still protesting his innocence. The new State Governor, Anselm J. McLaurin, agreed to look into the case and commuted the sentence to life imprisonment. And then, on 19 December 1898, bowing to public opinion, he granted Will Purvis a pardon.

Free at last, Purvis returned to work on his father's farm. In 1899 he married the daughter of a Baptist minister and bought a farm of his own. He went on to father 11 children.

Then, in 1917, a 60-year-old farmer by the name of Joseph Beard confessed on his deathbed that he had been part of the gang which had murdered Will Buckley. He named Louis

Thornhill, who was already dead, as the actual killer. Beard's task had apparently been to shoot Jim Buckley but, after seeing Thornhill gun down the other brother, Beard's nerve failed him. Three years later, the innocent Will Purvis was awarded $5000 in compensation.

Purvis eventually died on 13 October 1938 at the age of 66 . . . three days after the death of the last juror at his trial. He had been as good as his word.

Margaret Dickson: The Woman Who Rose from the Dead

Margaret Dickson must surely go down in history as the only murderer to be married a month after she was hanged!

Separated from her husband, Dickson left her two children behind in Musselburgh, east of Edinburgh, and set out to visit two aunts living in Newcastle upon Tyne. By early 1723, she had reached the village of Maxwellheugh, just south of Kelso, and had accepted an offer of work from the Bell family. She decided to stay a while but the sojourn turned sour when, according to Dickson, one of her employer's drunken sons, William Bell, forced himself on her while she was asleep. The body of the resultant baby was found in the nearby River Tweed on 9 December 1723 by William Bell's brother. Margaret Dickson claimed the child had been stillborn and that she had kept it in her bed for some eight days, but since she had concealed her pregnancy her case was not very plausible and she was charged with murder.

Although there was no real evidence that the infant had been murdered, Dickson was presumed guilty for not having summoned help when the baby was born and for disposing of the body in such a callous manner. Found guilty, she was sentenced to death and hanged in Edinburgh on 2 September 1724 before a crowd of thousands. She was left hanging for approximately half an hour, during which time the hangman tugged her legs to make sure that she was definitely dead. Satisfied that she was, he had her cut down and placed in a coffin.

However, that was by no means the end of Margaret Dickson. The coffin was placed on a cart by Dickson's friends in readiness for its journey to Musselburgh but on the way out of the city a gang of surgeons' apprentices tried to hijack the corpse for dissection. A scuffle broke out. The apprentices were put to flight but the coffin was slightly damaged and air had got into it.

The friends of Margaret Dickson continued on their way until the cortège had reached the village of Peppermill. The cart was left unattended in the road while the thirsty travellers stopped for refreshment. In their absence, two passers-by studied the coffin out of curiosity and were amazed to hear a noise coming from inside it. The friends were alerted and implored to open the coffin. On doing so, they saw that Dickson's limbs were twitching. One of her veins was then opened and she groaned, 'Oh dear! Oh dear!' . . . as well she might. She was moved to a nearby hillside, where the blood began to return to her lips and cheeks, before being taken on to Musselburgh. She was still alive on reaching her destination and over the next few days her condition continued to improve to such an extent that she was well enough to attend church on 6 September, the Sunday after she was hanged.

Hardly surprisingly, Margaret Dickson became a local celebrity. The crowds flocked to see the woman who had risen from the dead, including her former husband. And a month later, it was reported that the couple had remarried. The authorities made no attempt to re-arrest her since, under Scottish law, her sentence had been carried out once she was cut down from the gallows. For her part, Dickson was so grateful for her salvation that she vowed to spend one day each week for the rest of her life fasting and praying. So what had caused her remarkable recovery? Some said it was the air being allowed into the coffin or the sudden jolt from the fracas; others thought it was an act of God, sparing her life for a crime she didn't commit.

Albert Fish: Short-circuited the Electric Chair

Albert Fish was one of the century's most repulsive murderers. There was scarcely a perversion in which he did not actively participate, indulging himself freely in sado-masochism, murder and ultimately cannibalism. He even looked forward to his execution, telling reporters: 'What a thrill that will be if I have to die in the electric chair. It will be the supreme thrill – the only one I haven't tried.' And he certainly got his money's worth since all of the needles which he had inserted into his body over the years caused a short circuit on the first attempt. As a result, a second surge of 3000 volts had to be pumped into his body. Albert Fish died a happy man.

Fish laid much of the blame for his twisted behaviour on his miserable childhood. Born in 1870, he was raised in a Washington, DC, orphanage where he and the other children were subjected to terrible cruelty. He would later remark: 'I saw so many boys whipped it ruined my mind.' He married at the age of 28 and for a while led a respectable existence as a house decorator. However, in 1917 he discovered that his wife was having an affair and this seemed to push him over the edge. A father of six, he took to serving his children raw meat and wandering out in the middle of the night, stark naked, to howl at the moon. He also constructed a paddle studded with nails and encouraged his children and their friends to lash his bare buttocks with the fearsome implement until they drew blood. If nobody else was around, he would content himself with self-flagellation and also enjoyed burning himself with white hot pokers and irons. But his favourite pastime was injecting himself with needles. When he was finally arrested, doctors found no fewer than 29 needles in his body, mostly in the genital area.

Word got around about Fish's warped mind and he was examined at Bellevue Asylum, New York, but released as a non-violent masochist who only sought to inflict pain upon himself. In all, he was arrested eight times on a range of charges from larceny to sending obscene letters and actually served three months in jail for his part in a mail swindle. Yet nobody realized that he was also arguably the most dangerous man in the United States – certainly where children were concerned.

By his own admission, he had molested over 400 children in a 20-year period and had murdered at least three before committing the killing which was to lead to his demise. Using the alias Frank Howard, Fish had ingratiated himself with the Budd family of Manhattan. To the Budds, he appeared nothing more than a harmless old gentleman who liked to pop round with presents for their children, so when he asked Mrs Budd whether he could take 12-year-old Grace to a children's party, she saw no problem. It was the last time the Budds would see their daughter alive.

Instead of escorting Grace to the party, Fish took her by train to his empty cottage in White Plains, Westchester County, New York. Between them on the seat was a box in which Fish kept what he later described as his 'implements of hell' – a butcher's knife, a cleaver and a saw. As they stepped off the train, Fish realised that he had forgotten the box and sent Grace back to fetch it. Once inside the cottage, Fish took all his clothes off. The girl was horrified but Fish silenced her by strangling her and carving up her body. Over the next nine days, he ate strips of Grace Budd's flesh, cooked with vegetables. These meals kept him in a constant state of sexual arousal.

With no body discovered and no clues as to her disappearance, for six years the Budds prayed that one day their daughter would come home safe and well. Then, in 1934, Fish suddenly wrote to them and confessed to having murdered Grace. The Budds informed the police who headed straight for Fish's cottage. But they were too late to prevent him claiming another child victim. He had snatched five-year-old France McDonel from outside his Long Island home, taken him to the cottage and strangled him. When they came face to face with him, the Budds identified Fish as 'Frank Howard'. The area around the cottage was dug up and buried there were the bits of Grace Budd that Fish hadn't already eaten.

When Fish was tried in White Plains in March 1934, his horrific confessions were read out in court. The defence argued that he was insane but the prosecution produced a team of psychiatrists who testified that he was perfectly responsible for his actions. Fish himself stated that he was 'queer' rather than insane and insisted that he didn't really understand himself.

Found guilty of the callous murder of Grace Budd, Fish was sentenced to death, an event he gleefully anticipated. On 16 January 1936, he marched enthusiastically into the execution chamber at Sing Sing and even helped officials attach the electrodes to his legs. As additional electrodes were attached to his head, Fish grinned merrily, savouring every minute. A flick of the switch then sent 3000 volts surging through his body, but the presence of so many needles meant that the first charge did not finish him off. Instead, a blue cloud of smoke rose from his head as Fish let out an evil laugh. It needed a second surge to put Albert Fish where he belonged.

Willie Francis: Second Time Unlucky

On the morning of 8 November 1944, Andrew Thomas, a 54-year-old drugstore owner, was found dead at his home in St Martinville, Louisiana. He had been shot once in the head and four times in the body and, from the fact that his pockets had been rifled, robbery seemed the obvious motive. It seemed that the killer had got away with it until nine months later, 16-year-old Willie Francis, a former employee at the store, was picked up in Port Arthur, Texas, on an unconnected charge of robbery and assault. Under interrogation, Francis also confessed to the St Martinville murder, saying that he had decided to kill Andrew Thomas after being rebuked by him for sloppy work. He had waited for Thomas to arrive home one night and then gunned him down, making off with the victim's watch and a wallet containing $4. Francis said he later sold the watch.

It may have taken the police a while to catch up with Francis but it didn't take long for him to be brought to trial. A month after being arrested, he stood sullenly in the dock at St Martinville and listened as the judge sentenced him to death. Normally a 16-year-old might have expected some mercy but Francis appeared a particularly cold-blooded individual. The killing was clearly premeditated and he had shown no remorse whatsoever for it.

The execution date was set for 3 May 1946 and Francis, by now 17, was strapped into the electric chair ready to meet his fate. The switch was thrown but it was immediately apparent that the equipment was faulty. Far from frying, Francis was still very much alive. 'Take it off,' he shouted from under the hood. 'I'm smothering.'

The current was switched off, the straps were removed and while Francis was taken back to jail, the chair was taken away for testing. It had been working perfectly when it was tested shortly before the bungled execution but now experts reckoned that a wire had come loose. The poor connection had earned Francis a six-day reprieve. Back in jail, he told warders that when the switch was thrown he had felt a current of electricity which 'tickled him a bit, but did not hurt much.' In any case, he said, he wasn't worried about dying because he knew the Lord was with him.

So was Bertrand DeBlanc, a St Martinville attorney who conducted a campaign to win Francis a permanent stay of execution. DeBlanc maintained that Francis had already been electrocuted, albeit unsuccessfully, and therefore could not legally go to the chair again. When this argument foundered, he pleaded for clemency on the grounds that Francis had been spared by an act of God. The State Pardon Board dismissed this appeal too.

If nothing else, DeBlanc's round of appeals bought Francis more time and finally an agreement by the US Supreme Court to review the case in October. The appeal stated that Francis had already been subjected to 'the most gruelling experience known to man' and should not have to undertake it a second time.

But the Supreme Court reiterated the earlier ruling that it would not be unconstitutional for the same punishment to be carried out again, requiring DeBlanc to come up with some new ideas . . . and fast. With time running out, he made a fresh appeal to the State Pardon Board in April 1947 in which he claimed that the real reason Francis had survived the electric chair was because 'the executioner and other persons connected with the carrying out of the execution' had been 'so drunk that it was impossible for them to have known what they were doing'. Although DeBlanc was able to present evidence to support this allegation of professional misconduct, the Pardon Board would not be swayed and once more rejected the appeal.

The matter was taken to the Supreme Court, the petition describing events at the ill-fated execution. 'The scene was a disgraceful and inhuman exhibition, that as soon as the switch controlling the current was taken off, the drunken executioner cursed Francis and told him he would be back to finish electrocuting him, and if the electricity did not kill him, he would kill him with a rock.' Whilst expressing concern about the allegations, the Supreme Court felt unable to overturn the previous judgments.

Willie Francis had remained philosophical about his prospects. Right from the outset, he had fully expected to die and wasn't going to lose any sleep over it now. Indeed, he seemed to be keen to get it over with and actually instructed DeBlanc not to make any last-minute appeals. Shortly before noon on 9 May 1947, Francis, now 18, was once more strapped into the electric chair. Asked whether he had anything to say, he answered: 'Nothing at all.' The executioner threw the switch and this time there was no hitch. The electric chair did its job, sending Willie Francis to an early grave.

Capital Calamities

Convicted of murdering an engineer in Florida in 1901, JB Brown was standing on the gallows with the rope around his neck when it was discovered that the death warrant bore the name of the foreman of the jury instead of Brown. The last-minute reprieve proved a fortunate blunder for all concerned. For after Brown's sentence was commuted to life imprisonment, another man confessed to the murder in 1913, allowing Brown to be set free.

*

Due to be put to death for his part in a plan to assassinate King Louis XIII of France in 1626, Count Henri de Chalais endured a particularly painful and prolonged experience at the hands of a stand-in executioner. With the regular executioner nowhere to be found, the task of beheading the nobleman by sword was given to an inexperienced assistant who didn't succeed in severing the head until the 29th stroke. Indeed, after as many as 20 strokes, the count was still clinging to life.

*

Following his unsuccessful attempt to snatch the English crown, James, Duke of Monmouth, bastard son of Charles II, was beheaded in 1685 . . . although it took five blows from the axe before head and shoulders finally parted company. It was only after the execution that the Keeper of the King's Pictures discovered that there existed no official portrait of Monmouth. So the decapitated head was stitched back on and the dead Monmouth placed in a chair to have his portrait painted by German-born artist Sir Godfrey Kneller.

*

It took three attempts over a period of nearly 10 minutes to electrocute John Evans in Alabama's Holman Prison in April 1983. The first 30-second shock of 1900 volts burned off one of the straps on his left leg but doctors said that his heart was still beating. So the process was repeated. The second attempt also failed to have the desired effect, despite witnesses reporting that they could see smoke rising from the electrodes on his head. As Evans was prepared to receive the third half-minute surge, his lawyer appealed in vain for clemency from Governor George Wallace. It later emerged that Evans had suffered both fourth and second-degree burns while he was still alive.

*

Emperor Menlek II of Abyssinia was so impressed by stories telling of the efficiency of the electric chair that in 1890 he ordered three from New York – despite the fact that Abyssinia had no electricity! The fact did not seem to connect in the emperor's mind and it was not until the consignment arrived that he realized they wouldn't work. He threw out two of the chairs and used the third as his throne.

Joseph Samuels: Survived Three Hangings

A habitual criminal from the age of 14, Joseph Samuels led something of a charmed life, defying the hangman's rope on no fewer than three occasions. Ironically having cheated so many attempts to execute him, he drowned at sea shortly afterwards.

Samuels first fell foul of the law in 1795 when he was found guilty at the Old Bailey of stealing from a house and sentenced to seven years' transportation. By the time he was finally transported to Australia it was 1801 which, in view of the fact that he had already served six years in an English jail, meant that his sentence was almost completed. He was duly freed but landed in more trouble in 1803 after meeting up with an unsavoury character by the name of Isaac Simmons. A fellow convict, Simmons had surprisingly managed to find a niche as a special constable in Sydney, but his behaviour remained far from exemplary and some of his colleagues suspected him of theft.

On the evening of 25 August 1803, the Sydney home of a woman called Mary Breeze was broken into and several articles were stolen, including a writing-desk containing cash. The crime was reported to Constable Joseph Luker who immediately suspected Simmons and his cronies. Constable Luker told Mary Breeze that he planned to catch the culprits red-handed that night in the scrubland around the back of the house where he expected them to be shifting the stolen goods. However, the following morning Luker's body was found near a track. He had been repeatedly and savagely stabbed in the head before being finished by a fearsome blow from his own cutlass, the force of which left the guard of the weapon embedded in his skull. It was an atrocious attack.

The stolen writing desk, smeared in blood, was found some 300 yards from the body. Its contents had been removed. Also found near the body was the wheel of a barrow and when this was traced to a nearby address, a number of men were arrested, among them Joseph Samuels and Isaac Simmons . . . but only after the latter had been a pallbearer at Constable Luker's funeral. Samuels protested his innocence, saying that he had been at Simmons's house at the time of the theft, but a witness identified him as having been near Mary Breeze's home.

In a bid to secure immunity from prosecution, Samuels decided to come clean about the robbery and stated that it was his work and that of a man named John Russell. He denied all knowledge of the murder. But the police did not believe Samuels's claim that another defendant, Richard Jackson, was entirely innocent and when Jackson too confessed to the robbery, Samuels's hopes of evading prosecution were dashed. Samuels alone was found guilty of robbery and sentenced to death.

The execution was due to take place on 26 September. On the gallows, Samuels declared that while sharing a cell with Simmons, the special constable had confessed to killing Joseph Luker, a charge on which Simmons had already been acquitted in court. Simmons was among the spectators that day.

It was to have been a double execution but the second man earned a last-minute reprieve. Samuels didn't think he would be so lucky as the hangman tied the noose around his neck but, against all the odds, the rope snapped and the prisoner fell to the ground in a state of semi-consciousness. Stunned by this unexpected development, a group of men rushed to fetch Samuels for a second attempt. A new rope was used but no sooner had he been left hanging there than the rope unravelled so that his legs touched the ground. After two failures, many spectators were in favour of abandoning the execution altogether, believing that Samuels had been spared by God, but the authorities were determined to carry out the sentence. Once more Samuels, by now unconscious, was hoisted up to the gallows, a third new rope around his neck. But this proved no stronger than the first two and, unable to take his weight, it broke, sending Samuels crashing to the ground again.

In the face of a hostile crowd clamouring for Samuels's release, the execution was postponed and Samuels was granted a reprieve. Shortly afterwards, his sentence was reduced to a term of imprisonment which he served at Newcastle, further up the coast.

He never learned his lesson, however, and in 1805 was flogged for his part in a burglary. He then escaped from custody and spent several months on the run. On 1 April 1806, Samuels and seven other escaped convicts fled Newcastle in a boat, aiming for a safer haven. But on their second night at sea, a terrible storm hit the area and, although the government sent a rescue ship, there was no sign of any survivors. Samuels may have been able to defeat the hangman, but Mother Nature had proved a tougher adversary.

Chapter 6

Misguided Prosecutions

'Boring' Ken Barlow: A Pyrrhic Victory

The character of *Coronation Street*'s Ken Barlow has long been one of television's great enigmas. Although married three times (his first wife Val fell foul of a faulty hairdryer plug; his second, Janet, committed suicide; and the third marriage, to Deirdre, ended in divorce after acrimonious affairs on both sides), he has always been perceived as essentially boring – a dull crossword and slippers man, the nearest thing in the street to an intellectual. The description has always irked William Roache, the actor who has played Ken Barlow in Britain's longest-running soap opera since the very first episode in 1960. As the only survivor from the original cast, Roache has naturally become quite attached to Ken but, like most actors, he is also eager to distance himself from certain aspects of his screen character's personality. So when, in November 1990, the *Sun* newspaper ran a story by freelance journalist Ken Irwin which, among other things, accused William Roache of being as boring as his screen persona, Roache sued for libel.

Ken Irwin had earned his place in *Coronation Street* folklore back in December 1960 with that opening episode, of which he wrote: 'The programme is doomed with its dreary signature tune and grim scene of a row of terraced houses and smoking chimneys.' Despite the inaccuracy of this particular prediction, Irwin had gone on to enjoy a long and distinguished career with the Mirror Group of newspapers and was widely regarded as one of Fleet Street's most respected journalists. The article in the *Sun* claimed that William Roache was 'universally nicknamed BKB – Boring Ken Barlow' and also alleged that he was as smug and self-satisfied as Ken Barlow, that he was hated by his fellow cast members, regarded as a joke by the programme's producers and that he had been lucky not to have been written out of the series on several occasions. Not unreasonably, Roache was furious, saying that he was 'devastated and humiliated' by the article.

In suing Ken Irwin, Kelvin MacKenzie, editor of the *Sun*, and its publishers, News Group Newspapers Ltd, for libel, Roache engaged the services of leading solicitors Peter Carter-Ruck and Partners. At the age 77, Carter-Ruck was a veteran in his field, a man known as the scourge of the press for his success in libel cases against newspapers. The case against the *Sun* came to court in November 1991, but not before the newspaper had made a formal offer to settle the matter for £50,000 damages. The actor rejected the offer. It was a decision which would return to haunt him.

The case at the High Court in London lasted five days. Among the witnesses were five fellow members of the *Coronation Street* cast who took the stand to refute the allegations against their colleague. Betty Driver (alias barmaid Betty Turpin) told the jury that Bill Roache was 'the least boring person I've ever met in my life' while Bill Waddington, who played cantankerous war veteran Percy Sugden, said: 'Can I put Bill Roache into one word? He is a gentleman.' The testimony of the cast prompted considerable confusion as fact and fiction frequently became blurred. One witness, actress Amanda Barrie, who played café owner Alma Sedgewick, described how she had had an affair with Mike Baldwin but was now having one with Ken Barlow. 'I mean Alma is, not me,' she added after a pause. The remark was met with uneasy laughter. William Roache himself had to correct counsel for the *Sun* twice for addressing him as Ken Barlow and, after telling the jury of his anger when he confronted the man who had seduced his wife, Deirdre, felt compelled to explain: 'No, I'm sorry. That was what Ken Barlow did, not me.' He went on to defend Ken, insisting that Barlow wasn't really boring, just 'a sad and tragic figure'.

Charles Gray, QC, acting for Roache, explained that just because his client was a soap opera star did not mean he had 'the hide of a rhinoceros'. Mr Gray said that the article in the *Sun* 'conveyed the suggestion that Mr Roache is a thoroughly unpleasant individual and that he is worthless in the job into which he has put so much over the past 30 years'. It had, he claimed, caused great distress to the actor and his family. Mr Gray said that the newspaper maintained that the article was fair comment but he pointed out that it was apparently based on information from sources which its author, Ken Irwin, was unable to name. Summing up, Mr Gray said that the *Sun* should have 'put up or shut up'. They could have defended their corner or gracefully admitted that they had done Mr Roache a 'serious injury', he added, before concluding that they had done neither. In fact, the *Sun* had apologized for saying that Bill Roache was hated by the rest of the cast.

David Eady, QC, for the defendants, insisted that the article was a matter of comment on Mr Roache and was based on Mr Irwin's long-standing association with the programme. He added that the jury should keep a sense of proportion when considering what the case was about. Was being described as 'boring' the most heinous slur imaginable? 'Most of us,' he said, 'if accused of being boring, smug or self-satisfied, might not like it, but few of us would sue.'

After two and a half hours' deliberation, the jury awarded damages of £50,000 – precisely the sum which the 59-year-old actor had turned down. Normally, when a libel jury's award does not exceed the amount 'paid into court' by the defendant, the costs of the case from that point onwards are paid by the plaintiff. Had Roache been awarded £50,001, the *Sun* would have had to pay his costs as well as its own but the jury's announcement left him facing an estimated legal bill of £125,000. Thus the news of the sum awarded was greeted with dismay in the Roache camp. His second wife Sara, herself a former actress, burst into tears while he sat stony-faced, scarcely able to believe what he was hearing. Mrs Roache continued sobbing, her husband gripping her tightly by the hand, as counsel argued over who should pay the costs of the case.

To the relief of the Roaches and to the surprise of many, Mr Justice Waterhouse ruled that News Group Newspapers should foot the bill. The judge also granted an order forbidding the defendants from repeating the libels. He said he was awarding costs against News Group Newspapers because William Roache would have had to come to court anyway for the order to be made. Regarding the order, the judge ruled that Roache had a 'well-founded apprehension' that the *Sun* might repeat the libels. The judge said he was influenced by the way in which the newspaper had reported an earlier stage in the trial when it had repeated allegations about Roache's youthful romances, even though they had not been read out in court.

Outside the court, William Roache and his wife were besieged by well-wishers. In a faltering voice, Roache declared: 'We have won. Sara and myself have been to hell and back, quite honestly, and I don't think it is right that one should have to go through what we have been through to justify our good name. And it has been justified. The support from the public has been unbelievable. These newspapers should not be able to get away with it.'

Tom Crone, legal manager of News Group Newspapers, immediately announced that they would appeal against the award of costs. He said: 'We offered Bill Roache £50,000 and an apology a month ago, but his side told us to write out a cheque for £200,000 or forget it. We were not prepared to do that.' The battle was far from over.

A year later, in November 1992, the tables were turned in the most dramatic fashion when the Court of Appeal overturned the ruling on costs by the trial judge and held William Roache liable for all the legal costs of the case, including those of the trial, which had been incurred after 7 October 1991, the date of the payment into court by the *Sun*. Not only would the sum swallow up his £50,000 damages but he would also be left with an outstanding bill of around £70,000, a crippling blow even for someone with annual earnings of £160,000.

Allowing the newspaper's appeal, the Master of the Rolls, Sir Thomas Bingham, sitting with Lords Justices Stuart-Smith and Simon Brown, said that William Roache's decision to go ahead with the case 'can only, in my view, have been because he wanted to win a larger sum from the jury than the defendants had offered'. Whilst the trial judge had accepted that Roache had been obliged to pursue the case in order to obtain an injunction banning further publication of the libel, Sir Thomas said there was no evidence that Roache feared that there might be a republication. He said that the *Sun*'s offer to settle had been proof that the newspaper did not want to fight the action and added that if Roache had accepted the settlement offer, he would have recovered his costs and been entitled to a public statement roundly vindicating him. Also, an undertaking would undoubtedly have been made not to republish the libel.

Lord Justice Stuart-Smith was particularly damning in his choice of phrase. In his judgment, he said that the power to make a 'payment into court' as a pre-trial offer of settlement was 'a most useful weapon in the hands of a defendant faced with a greedy plaintiff who is making unreasonable demands for damages'. The Court of Appeal concluded that it was obvious from correspondence between the solicitors that the case had gone to trial only because Roache had wanted a sum 'very greatly in excess' of what the paper felt was justified. The popular press were quick to latch on to these remarks under headlines such as '"GREED" OF KEN OF THE STREET'.

A jubilant Tom Crone said afterwards: 'Bill Roache practised the gospel of greed and now he has to pay the price. He has learned the first lesson of libel, which is that if you don't like losing, don't play the game. He could have had £50,000 and a full apology. All we wanted was an honourable settlement but he chose to go after fool's gold and now he has lost a fortune.'

Roache was not in court but issued a statement through Peter Carter-Ruck saying that he was 'deeply disappointed' by the decision which highlighted once more 'the unfair burden which falls upon the private litigant'. It was a black day for the actor.

In view of his experiences to date, one might have thought that William Roache would have had enough of libel cases for one lifetime. But no. In the spring of 1998, it was announced that he was suing his former solicitors, Peter Carter-Ruck and Partners, for negligence over the firm's handling of his ill-fated libel case against the *Sun*. This action seemed rather at odds with an appreciative letter which Roache had apparently written to Carter-Ruck after the original trial in which he thanked the solicitor for all he had done.

The next chapter in the saga of Ken Barlow was heard in the High Court in Manchester in June 1998. William Roache was suing Peter Carter-Ruck and Partners over the rejection of the *Sun*'s initial offer of £50,000. Roache claimed that the firm should have warned him in detail about the risks of pressing on with the case once the newspaper had made its offer. He said that he had turned down the offer to settle the libel claim out of court because he had not been informed in detail of the danger of ending up paying a massive bill for costs. Roache told the judge, Mr Justice Newman: 'Had I known the possibility of getting very little more and the tremendous risks involved, I most certainly would have taken the £50,000 paid into court.' His counsel, Peter Griffiths, added: 'The advice he received fell short of the advice he should have been given by a solicitor with special libel expertise.'

However, Thomas Shields, QC, a member of Roache's legal team during the libel trial, maintained that the possibility of taking the £50,000 had been discussed. He told the court: 'I will always remember the discussion. I think Mrs Roache said to Mr Roache that he was a gambler in golf and that he goes for his shots. I think he might have exchanged words or looks with his wife and said he was going to go for it.'

At the end of the seven-day trial, Mr Justice Newman rejected William Roache's claim of negligent advice. In his judgement, he said that Mr Roache's decision to continue had been dictated by hopes of achieving a higher sum. He said the actor had been told by his lawyers that he had a 60–40 chance of getting more than the £50,000. 'He considered he had a 60 per cent chance of a much greater award and he went ahead because he was prepared to take a 40 per cent risk of losing £50,000 in order to take the chance of recovering very much more. At the material time, the unpredictability of the level of awards from juries was great and the likelihood of an award far in excess of that which a libel lawyer may consider to be reasonable was always a prospect. He took the view that £50,000 was not reasonable. He did not go on because he was greedy, nor did he go on against the advice of his legal team. Quite naturally, he felt the publishers should be hurt by an award. The plaintiff was very unlucky.'

This was scant consolation to William Roache who now faced the prospect of a bill for an additional £80,000 on top of the previous £125,000. Ironically he had been filming an episode of *Coronation Street* a few hundred yards away at Granada Television studios when the judgement came through. He later spoke of his disappointment that his 'eight-year nightmare' had resulted in an enormous financial burden. That burden became so great that in April 1999 he declared himself bankrupt. People can still say what they like about Ken Barlow, but, after everything that he has been through, nobody could ever claim that William Roache's life was boring.

Tommy Docherty: A Trial Of Two Halves

Tommy Docherty was one of the most colourful characters in British soccer. As a wing-half with Preston North End and Arsenal, he won 25 Scottish international caps between 1952 and 1959 before turning his hand to club management. Known to all as 'The Doc', he revitalized Chelsea in the 1960s, creating a young team that was exciting to watch. Docherty earned a reputation for sharp one-liners but his outspoken nature did not endear him to all club chairmen and, following short stays at Rotherham United, Queens Park Rangers and Aston Villa, he arrived at Old Trafford in 1972, attempting to breathe new life into the ailing giant of Manchester United.

United's problem was that too many of their stars were past their sell-by date. So Docherty built a brave new side, composed of willing youngsters, and led them to successive FA Cup finals in 1976 and 1977. But Docherty had made enemies along the way, particularly among the players he had ruthlessly, if necessarily, discarded. One such player, Scottish international winger Willie Morgan, would cause Docherty many a sleepless night over a four-year period as a libel case backfired and saw Docherty himself on trial for perjury.

Willie Morgan was seen by many as the natural successor to the errant George Best. He had the same long hair and a degree of Best's wing wizardry. What he didn't appear to have was Best's fondness for birds and booze. In recognition of his talents and stability, Morgan had been made captain of Manchester United by Docherty but then, in the summer of 1974, Morgan suffered a serious eye injury while playing tennis. His form suffered, he was dropped, relieved of the captaincy a year later and transferred soon afterwards to Burnley for £30,000 before moving on to Bolton Wanderers. By then, Docherty was grooming Morgan's replacement, Steve Coppell.

In June 1977, Morgan appeared as a guest on the Granada Television football programme *Kick Off*. He didn't mince his words when discussing Docherty. 'When he goes, I think the rejoicing in Manchester will be like winning the Cup again, and when that happens it will be a good club again.' Lest any viewer be in doubt as to his feelings on the matter, Morgan added that Docherty was 'about the worst manager' he had ever played under.

At that time, Docherty was going through a particularly sticky patch in what was always a turbulent career. A scandal was just breaking over his affair with Mary Brown, wife of the club physiotherapist Laurie Brown – the event, which, more than any other, precipitated Docherty's departure from Old Trafford a few months later. Docherty was incensed by Morgan's comments but didn't intend taking any action on the grounds that since he was used to dishing out criticism, he had to be prepared to take it as well. However, his legal advisers told him that he could launch a successful libel action against the player and the television company so, against his better instincts, he pressed ahead.

The libel action against Willie Morgan and Granada Television reached the High Court in November 1978, by which time the 50-year-old Docherty was manager of Derby County. No wonder he used to say he'd had more clubs than Jack Nicklaus!

Peter Bowsher, QC, for Docherty, claimed that the programme had damaged Docherty's reputation as a skilled and fair-dealing manager and that on it, Morgan 'had written Mr Docherty off as a manager'. He went on: 'Mr Morgan left Manchester United with a very deep-seated grudge against the plaintiff. Within two months he had given an interview to a Sunday newspaper attacking Mr Docherty. His malice towards the plaintiff simply festered.' Of Docherty, Mr Bowsher said: 'He is not averse to strong criticism, so long as it is fair.'

Morgan had prepared his defence thoroughly. As one observer noted: 'The result was an overwhelming arsenal of offensive weaponry which succeeded in making plaintiff Docherty look like the defendant.' Morgan and his lawyers came up with 29 counts of alleged impropriety and paraded a line-up of star witnesses in former Manchester United players Alex Stepney, Lou Macari, Ted MacDougall, Paddy Crerand and Denis Law. Docherty had crossed a lot of people in his time and now they were coming back to haunt him.

Among the allegations put forward to prove that Docherty was not a good manager was that he had accepted £1,000 from Southern Leaguers Dunstable to induce George Best, who was then in dispute with United, to play for the Bedfordshire team. Docherty strenuously denied this. On a more personal level, the defence claimed that Docherty 'sang a dirty ditty' about Morgan in February 1975 at the annual Catholic sportsmen's dinner in Manchester – an occasion attended by priests, nuns and a bishop. It was also claimed that Docherty had said he was 'going to sort Morgan out' and that Morgan would be 'on his way before the end of the season'. Morgan was indeed relieved of the club captaincy at the end of that season.

Taking the stand, Docherty said that he had been 'very

upset' by Morgan's comments. 'I felt it was the remark of a bitter person,' he continued. 'I think the record I had at Manchester United was a good one.' He added that he was still greeted warmly at the club. Docherty attended court with Mary Brown and the pair had to listen to the rehashing of their romance for the benefit of the jury and the tabloids. Docherty was also asked about the free transfer granted to United and Scotland legend Denis Law in 1972. He testified that Law had known that he was to be transferred and hadn't been at all disturbed by the prospect. In fact, said Docherty, the free transfer was like a 'golden handshake'.

On the third day of the trial, John Wilmers, QC, for the defence, cross-examined Docherty about the transfer of Law. Wilmers said that at the end of the season Docherty had told Law that he would be on the transfer list. Docherty agreed that this was true.

Wilmers: 'Law protested and you agreed to take him off the list?'

Docherty: 'Yes.'

Wilmers: 'But the next day, when Law had travelled to Scotland to visit his sick mother, he heard on television that he was on the list?'

Docherty admitted that he had given the news to the media.

Wilmers: 'No decent, competent manager would dream of treating a man like Law that way?'

Docherty: 'It was the wrong thing to do . . . it was very wrong.'

Docherty admitted knowing that Law's mother was ill and agreed that it wasn't a nice thing to do in the circumstances.

Wilmers suggested that Docherty gave a different version of events to a newspaper and said that Docherty's earlier testimony in court about the Denis Law transfer bore little resemblance to the truth. 'You told a pack of lies to the jury about this, didn't you?'

Docherty: 'Yes, it turned out that way.'

Wilmers: 'You are simply not to be trusted when you say something, whether in the papers or on oath?'

Battered into submission, Docherty mumbled that he did not agree with that assessment, but it was too late. His case was damaged beyond repair and, after a brief adjournment, he announced that he was dropping the libel action.

Willie Morgan was ecstatic, telling reporters: 'I am delighted that Mr Docherty has, by his withdrawal, accepted that what I said was justified.' Docherty was left with his reputation in shreds, a bill for £30,000 and, most serious of all, a second trial, this time for perjury.

The second trial took place in October 1981. In the interim, Docherty had gone for more rides on the managerial merry-go-round, from Derby to Queens Park Rangers (for the second time), to Australia with Sydney Olympics and then to Preston where he had enjoyed such a distinguished playing career. Typically, he lasted only five months as manager. He had also endured another brush with the law while in charge of Queens Park Rangers. In bed at the Kensington Hilton Hotel one morning, he answered a knock on the door to be confronted by two police officers from Derby. He was arrested and taken straight up to Derby where he was subjected to interrogation concerning alleged irregularities over players who had been transferred to America while he had been manager at Derby County. Docherty explained that there was nothing improper about the transfers and he was duly released. But it was a hassle he could have done without.

For his perjury trial, Docherty had graduated to the Old Bailey – the Wembley of the legal profession. He was charged on two counts – his testimony about the Law transfer and secondly that he falsely swore that he didn't know of a term in an agreement relating to the transfer of striker Ted MacDougall under which United would pay the player's former club, Bournemouth, an additional £25,000 when MacDougall scored 20 goals . . . until United were sued for breach of contract. In outlining its case, the prosecution said Docherty had told 'deliberate lies' on oath at the High Court to persuade the jury that he was a faithful employee who served the best interests of Manchester United.

Denis Law told the court how shocked he had been at being given a free transfer. 'I had been at Manchester United for 11 years and certainly wanted to finish there. The thought of a free transfer never entered my head.'

Then it was Docherty's turn. He said that he had felt that Law could no longer do a job for the club in the top division and asked the board for permission to give him a free transfer. Docherty said that club chairman Sir Matt Busby thought that he (Docherty) was making a mistake, but the rest of the board agreed with Docherty and the decision was taken to give Law a 'free'. He denied knowing anything about the clause in MacDougall's contract.

Regarding his High Court testimony, Docherty maintained that he had not deliberately lied at the first trial but had become 'hopelessly confused' by the intense cross-examination to which he had been subjected. He said he had been bullied and intimidated while giving evidence. 'At that time I was in such a mess I did not know what was happening.' All his years of press conferences and television interviews had failed to prepare him for the witness box which he found to be 'the loneliest place in the world'. Richard du Cann, QC, defending him, told the jury that Docherty had been 'psychologically crippled' during the libel proceedings and had been so 'knocked about' by the defence counsel that he would have agreed to almost anything. Some of the questions put to him, said Mr du Cann, were totally unfair.

The jury sided with Docherty and unanimously acquitted

him on both counts. Relieved that the ordeal was over, he quipped: 'I've been in more courts than Bjorn Borg.'

Docherty later admitted that 'suing Morgan was the biggest mistake of my life'. Some might say that he had quite an extensive portfolio to choose from. In the aftermath of the trials, the after-dinner stories began doing the rounds. Willie Morgan revealed that during the first trial his barrister had asked him to tug on his gown every time Docherty lied in the witness box. After half an hour, the barrister apparently ordered Morgan to stop because the gown was being tugged so frequently that it was losing its shape. In different circumstances, it was the sort of story Tommy Docherty would have enjoyed telling.

Gillian Taylforth: Caught by a Sucker Punch

In 1992, Gillian Taylforth was one of the best-known faces on British television. For seven years, she had played Kathy Beale – a woman more sinned against than sinning – in the BBC's top-rated soap opera, *EastEnders*. In return for a salary of £80,000 a year, she had turned Kathy Beale into one of the show's few sympathetic characters – a rape victim twice over and someone trapped in a loveless marriage with an ungrateful son. However, the dramas of Albert Square paled into insignificance when Taylforth brought an unsuccessful libel case against the *Sun* newspaper. At the end of it, her reputation lay in tatters, her name was a byword for crude jokes and she was saddled with a legal bill of £500,000. Apart from the *Sun,* the only other winner was Range Rover whose vehicles, it emerged, were spacious enough to accommodate the sort of off-the-road activity not usually referred to in the handbook.

Gillian Taylforth's off-screen life was almost as colourful as Kathy Beale's. Her lover was business consultant Geoff

Knights, a man who was no stranger to the police. With his liking for fast cars and fast women, Knights was a flash wheeler-dealer who had convictions dating back to 1969 for burglary, criminal damage and assault. It was a volatile relationship and one which came to a head – so to speak – on 20 June 1992 when the *Sun*, under the headline 'TV KATHY'S SEX ROMP FURY', ran a story which claimed that Taylforth and Knights had been caught by police in a compromising position while their Range Rover was parked in a slip road off the A1 at Boreham Wood in Hertfordshire. The story said that a police officer had stumbled upon Taylforth giving Knights oral sex in the front of the vehicle and stated that Knights had been cautioned for an indecent act. Taylforth's version of events was that the pair had been returning from Royal Ascot where Knights had consumed as many as five bottles of champagne. As a result, she said, he was feeling a bit queasy and so, when she pulled off onto the slip road, she bent over to rub his stomach. And that, she insisted, was what the police officer saw.

That would have been the end of it had Taylforth not taken umbrage at the *Sun* story. Maybe she confused her screen role with reality and became so used to playing the wronged woman that she decided to defend her good name against what she perceived as a vicious slur on her character. Perhaps she was afraid that the adverse publicity would see her sacked from *EastEnders,* but in the past soap stars had committed more grievous sins than a minor sexual indiscretion and survived. And as it turned out, even after she had lost the case, she remained with *EastEnders* for a further three and a half years before eventually leaving of her own accord. Or maybe it wasn't actually Taylforth's idea to sue the *Sun*. Although the party line was that she was doing it 'for my good name', rumours persisted that Knights was the driving force, acting against what he saw as police persecution.

Certainly he had reason to be puzzled as to how such a trivial incident at a small police station came to make its way into the country's biggest-selling national newspaper three days later.

Then again, there was the money. Victorious libel cases against newspapers could mean big bucks. In 1987, Jeffrey Archer had picked up £500,000 from the *Daily Star* while the following year actress Koo Stark had been awarded £300,000 against the *People* and Elton John had settled for £1,000,000 against the *Sun*. In the light of these awards, there seems little doubt that some celebrities, angry at press intrusion, saw the set-up as a gravy-train – a chance to make a nice little killing and teach the tabloids a lesson at the same time. The cautionary tale of William Roache was regarded as nothing more than an unfortunate blip. Whatever her motives in bringing the case, Taylforth did not appear to entertain the awful possibility of defeat. She was convinced that she would emerge victorious and with her reputation restored, although in truth it had only ever been damaged to *Sun* readers. The rest of the nation knew nothing about the incident . . . but they soon would. A story which should have been quietly consigned to the cuttings files was to become the talk of breakfast tables up and down the land. The resultant, self-inflicted publicity would make Gillian Taylforth a laughing stock.

The case was heard at the High Court in London in January 1994. the *Sun* could afford to hire one of the best barristers money could buy – George Carman, QC, a man who specialized in libel cases and who was renowned for his fearless cross-examination. A fellow QC once described him as the 'past master of the wink wink, nudge nudge' and another colleague remarked: 'He does not hesitate to go for the jugular.' In every respect, George Carman was a formidable foe. For her part, Taylforth forked out some £75,000 to secure the services of Michael Beloff, QC.

Thirty-eight-year-old Taylforth, who was suing for 'serious, scurrilous and unwarranted attacks against our characters and reputations', set out to convince the jury that she was nothing other than a demure mother of high moral integrity. Accompanied by her family and dressed in a smart suit, she looked every inch the part. She testified that on the day in question, Knights had suffered a pancreatic attack after drinking too much champagne. When she pulled the vehicle over on to the slip road, he undid his belt and trouser zip to relieve the pressure on his stomach caused by the attack. She insisted that she was merely rubbing his stomach to ease the pain and bridled at the very suggestion that she and her lover had been involved in any sexual pastime. 'How could anyone think I would stop on the A1 to have oral sex with cars and all the traffic going by?' she demanded indignantly.

After reading the story, she said she felt 'utter disgust. It's cheap and makes me feel really sick to my stomach. I felt absolutely ashamed and yet I had done nothing wrong. I felt people were looking at me and laughing.' She went on to speak of her distress when hearing a DJ joking about the matter on radio and how she had been taunted by small boys in the street asking for 'a blow job'.

Michael Beloff tried to pour scorn on the police version. He told the jury: 'I hope I am not being indelicate when I say that you don't need any expert to tell you that when you are feeling sick, you don't want sex. It isn't that you have had too much to drink and you are developing brewers' droop. Shakespeare put it rather better in *Macbeth*, saying that drink "provokes the desire but it takes away the performance". It's not even that the man's mind is willing but the flesh is weak – it's more basic than that. You simply cannot get an erection when you are about to throw up.' He then began the task of attempting to discredit the police evidence and suggested that 49-year-old Police Constable Terry Talbot, the officer who had stumbled across the couple, 'was utterly mistaken. He had put two and

two together and regrettably made five.' Beloff suggested that
after PC Talbot had summoned reinforcements because Mr
Knights had become angry and was being sick on the grass
verge, it was too late for him to back down. He claimed that
the officer had invented the whole story because he knew that
cautioning a well-known actress would make him the centre of
attention. He accused PC Talbot of 'revelling in the limelight'.

But the officer, who had received two commendations for
bravery in the line of duty, was made of stern stuff. He told the
court how he had approached the parked car and had seen
Taylforth's head moving slowly up and down over Knights'
lap. 'The gentleman was sitting in the near-side seat with his
eyes closed. I tapped on the window. I saw for a fleeting
moment that he was holding his erect penis with his right hand
and trying to replace that in his trousers.'

Despite counsel's most strenuous efforts to force him to
admit that he was somehow mistaken or was deliberately
lying, PC Talbot would not be swayed. As for Knights's
physical condition at the time, the officer remarked: 'Someone
who is hurt or ill does not normally want to fight with
policemen.' This view was supported by Professor John
Farndon, an expert in pancreatitis, who said that anyone
who was suffering a pancreatic attack would want to rest,
not shout at policemen. The Professor added that Knights'
description of the attack was not consistent with pancreatitis.

PC Talbot did admit to one mistake – but only on having
been too easy on the couple. Instead of letting them off with a
caution, he confessed that, by rights, he should have arrested
them. His superior, Inspector Francis Monoghan, echoed
these sentiments. 'The actress should have been arrested along
with Mr Knights for outraging public decency and using
abusive language.'

As in the past, the police were proving a veritable thorn in
Knights's flesh. When the court heard that, on the fateful

evening, Knights had actually signed a police caution admitting the sexual offence, for once he was almost lost for words. His only explanation was that he had drunk so much champagne that he hadn't known what he was signing. The police alleged that while Taylforth had been allowed to drive home to care for baby Jessica, Knights had turned abusive and had said: 'Take your uniforms off and I will f— fight you outside.' The police stated that Knights eventually calmed down and agreed to accept a caution over the sex act. They claimed he had remarked: 'You know how it is – we had a good day at the races and just got carried away!' Knights vehemently denied using those words.

Taylforth said of the caution: 'We didn't understand it meant admitting the offence. We thought it was just a slap on the wrist for using abusive language to the police.'

But the efforts to portray Knights and Taylforth as respectable citizens were starting to crumble. In addition to his previous run-ins with the police, it was alleged that in 1993, Knights had punched an *EastEnders* scriptwriter during a brawl after claims that the married man was having an affair with Taylforth. These accusations, although denied, did nothing to help the couple's case.

The British public, however, were lapping up every minute. With its heady combination of emotion, drama and sleaze, it was better than any television soap opera. There were certainly more laughs than in *EastEnders*. At one point, the judge, Mr Justice Drake, agreed to two reconstructions of the incident in the court car park. First, the jury watched intently as Taylforth and Knights placed themselves in the front of a Range Rover. Taylforth was forced to admit that oral sex in the front seat of a Range Rover was a gymnastic possibility. Their places were then taken by two *Sun* journalists re-enacting the police version of events, directed by PC Talbot. Both hacks emerged with smiles on their faces.

The tabloids took to running Gillian Taylforth jokes and comedians incorporated the case into their acts. Bernard Manning, not known for his coyness, came out with: 'Gillian Taylforth asked this scouser if he wanted a blow job. He replied, "Not if it affects my Giro cheque." ' It finally began to dawn on Taylforth what a dreadful mistake she had made in pursuing the case to court. Her private life had become horribly public. Small wonder that midway through the trial she told friends that she wished she had never started libel proceedings.

The strain was beginning to tell on Taylforth, principally because the *Sun* had produced a perfectly timed knockout blow – a video which destroyed what was left of her reputation. With the trial already in progress, the *Sun* had received a phone call from a man identified only as 'Herbie', claiming that he had in his possession a video which would vindicate the newspaper entirely. No money changed hands and the judge, satisfied that 'nothing improper' had taken place in the securing of the video, gave permission for it to be screened in court. Taylforth's counsel tried to block the screening although it appears that the actress herself had no idea as to its contents. She is unlikely ever to forget them.

The video had been made during a private lunchtime party with showbiz colleagues in April 1988 to celebrate the 20th anniversary of the Anna Scher Theatre in Islington, North London. The session had started in the theatre and continued at a wine bar. It had not been intended for public consumption but now, simply because Taylforth had decided to sue the *Sun*, it was played out in all its lurid detail before a hushed court-room and relayed to the rest of Britain via the national press. The video could not have been more damning. It showed Taylforth simulating oral sex at the party, both with a wine bottle and a large German sausage, accompanied by the words: 'I'd like to state I give good head. I give very good head.' The video faded as she started to unbutton her blouse at the wine bar.

Suddenly the manufactured image of the woman who found the thought of oral sex in a public slip road so abhorrent was exposed as a fake. The veneer of respectability was wiped away. She protested that the video was just a 'joke', adding: 'I was very drunk. It was a private video. If someone had said it was for public use, I would not have done it.' But George Carman didn't see the funny side and described her behaviour as 'pretty disgusting'. Taylforth reiterated: 'Had I been sober, it would not have happened . . . It's not very nice, no.'

Carman then launched a scathing attack on her. 'The tacky and cheap video,' he told the jury, 'exposed her performance in the witness box as a sham. She is not quite the demure lady.' He went on: 'Miss Taylforth's daughter Jessica has been waved in and out of the script as if she is the president of the Mothers' Union. That is not the whole picture. The reality is that there is another side that has been carefully concealed from you. It is not a shameful side. It is a coarser side. Drunk or otherwise, with friends or otherwise, Gillian Taylforth was behaving in a way that one hopes the majority of women in this country would never behave. And she was doing that because in drink she can be given to a certain coarseness in sexual matters, of a kind some of us might not find particularly pleasing, and something she didn't seem to be ashamed about in any way.' Adding that the sex act in the vehicle was probably a jape, a dare from one partner to the other, he returned to the contents of the video and concluded: 'The words "I give good head" could well turn out to be her epitaph.'

The jury took over five hours to reach a majority verdict. When the foreman announced that the jury had found in favour of the defence – namely the *Sun* – Taylforth's sister Janice reacted angrily, snapping at a police sergeant who had given evidence: 'Satisfied, are you?' Taylforth herself went to pieces. On hearing that she and Knights were responsible for the legal fees – estimated to be around £500,000 – she collapsed and was whisked away to hospital in an ambulance.

Later, when the enormity of the verdict had sunk in, she told reporters: 'I was in deep shock when the verdict came in. I just couldn't breathe. Finding the money to pay these costs will be a serious struggle. It's not going to be easy. My whole character has changed – my faith in human nature has gone. I have always been an open and honest person, but I have come out of this a different woman – a very, very cynical person. The video was a joke, taken by someone who was a friend from the age of 17, someone I trusted. I don't know who gave or sold that video, but I feel I can't trust anybody now. I am emotionally drained. If I had known then what I know now, I don't think I could have gone through the ordeal of the case. But at the end of the day it is all about clearing your name and that is what Geoff and I tried to do.'

The *Sun* was naturally overjoyed, calling it a victory for common sense and noting that 'the jury was clearly not prepared to accept that four police officers were lying under oath'.

Gillian Taylforth had paid the price for gambling on taking on the combined might of the press and the police. Libel cases are risky ventures at the best of times but when two people had as many skeletons in their cupboard as Taylforth and Knights, they were doomed to failure.

Wasting the Court's Time

When Californian gambler Toshi Van Blitter ran up debts of $350,000 playing blackjack in 1985, she filed a suit to have her debts cancelled, claiming that the casino had been negligent in failing to inform her that she was a lousy player and in not suggesting that she attend classes on how to play blackjack. Her claim was rejected by two federal courts.

*

When a barley crop was destroyed in 1521, the French authorities decided to prosecute a gang of rats for wilful damage. The rats were defended by lawyer Bartholomew Chassene who, when his clients failed to appear in court to answer the charges, claimed that they had been intimidated by 'evilly disposed cats' belonging to the prosecution. He demanded a cash undertaking that the cats would not attack the rats on their way to court and when the prosecution refused to guarantee the rats' safety, the case was dismissed.

*

Two years previously, there had been a similar case at Stelvio in northern Italy where crop damage had resulted in a warrant being issued for a number of moles. The moles were required 'to show cause for their conduct by pleading their exigencies and distress'. The moles, too, failed to appear in court and were sentenced to exile in their absence. In its mercy, the court promised them safe conduct 'and an additional respite of 14 days to all those which are with young'.

*

After restaurant hostess Maria Dillon broke off her engagement to Chicago lawyer Frank Zaffere in 1992, he sued her for everything he had spent on courting her. Adding up the cost of a car, a fur coat, a ring, a typewriter, plus the champagne he had bought to toast their future happiness, he arrived at a total of $40,310.48. He finally saw sense and dropped the lawsuit three months later.

*

In December 1990, a British judge attacked the waste of £13,500 of public money in bringing a man to trial over a 2p bill. The defendant, Londoner Keith Gonaz, had intended to fill his car with £10 of petrol but accidentally put in another 2p worth. He refused to pay the extra, pointed a rolled-up umbrella at the cashier, made a machine-gun noise and drove off. The cashier pressed the panic button, thereby alerting the police, and Gonaz was arrested a few minutes later. He was subsequently charged with possessing an imitation firearm (the umbrella!) and with threatening behaviour. Judge Bruce Laughland ordered a not guilty verdict on the first charge and the jury found Gonaz not guilty of threatening behaviour. The judge said of the two-day trial: 'Each court costs at least £25 a minute to run, not including counsel and solicitors' fees. Pursuing this matter and holding a trial by jury was an unjustified waste of public time and money.'

*

In 1996, a Los Angeles lawyer brought proceedings on behalf of his co-plaintiff, his pet poodle, claiming that its constitutional rights had been violated by a restaurant which had ordered it to leave. The claim was dismissed.

*

Also in 1996, an Israeli woman sued Danny Rup, the country's leading TV weather forecaster, in the Haifa Small Claims Court because of an inaccurate weather forecast which, she alleged, caused her to catch flu by dressing without warm clothes.

*

Discovering Scotsman Tom Lane lying in a broken shop window, police officers on the Isle of Wight arrested him and charged him with breaking and entering. But Ryde magistrates threw the case out when they heard how 36-year-old Mr Lane had really been acting out of a sense of public spirit. He told the court he had been on his way home in the early hours of New Year's Day 1970, having celebrated Hogmanay in the traditional Scottish fashion. 'I heard a crash of glass from the shop. I saw two men running away and spotted what I thought was another man in the window. I crawled through the hole in the glass and leaped on him.' As they tussled, Mr Lane realized that the 'intruder' was a shop window tailor's dummy. He said he was so convulsed with laughter that he was still lying there when the police arrived.

*

In 1993, a New York appeals court rejected a claim brought by housewife Edna Hobbs against a company which marketed a kitchen gadget called The Clapper. The complainant said that, in trying to switch on the appliance, she had clapped her hands until they bled. The judge ruled that she hadn't adjusted the sensitivity controls properly.

*

Although one was a Swedish car and the other a jar of Indian pickle made in Bolton, motor manufacturers Saab reckoned that calling a new range of spicy chutneys Memsaab could cause confusion. So the international car giants embarked on an expensive two-year battle against the tiny House of Raja firm to try and ban Memsaab pickles from the shelves. But in 1997 Saab were forced to back down after the Trade Marks Registry ruled that the House of Raja could use the name Memsaab – an Indian term of respect for a European married woman. House of Raja marketing manager Sital Raja said: 'This ordeal has brought our business to a halt and put a huge strain on the family. It has cost us about £8000. There were times when we thought we would have to change the name. It was like the big fish trying to eat the little fish.' Saab commented: 'We tried to settle it amicably but we didn't find any common interest.'

*

In September 1995, a judge ordered a report to be sent to the Home Office after a trial costing £10,000 at Carlisle Crown Court ended in the conviction of a man who had denied stealing bacon and cheese worth £6.

*

A man who shot himself in the arm to drain snake poison from his bloodstream was fined £2 at Taree, Australia, for carrying a firearm on a Sunday. Charles Peters of Coolongalook was bitten while lying near a log one day in 1969. As he had no knife, he held his rifle to his arm and shot himself to make the bite bleed. He tied string around the arm as a tourniquet before fainting. Peters was found by passing hikers and taken to hospital where he was interviewed the same day by a detective and charged.

*

Back in 1725, English highwaymen Joseph Williams and John Everitt fell out over the proceeds of their robberies. Williams successfully sued Everitt for £200 but Everitt, afraid of ending up in a debtors' prison, instructed attorney William Wreathock to start an action for the account to be settled between the two villains in the Court of Exchequer. Everitt's lawyers fully expected that Williams would settle out of court to avoid being exposed as a criminal but instead he held firm. The outcome was that Everitt's attorneys were each fined £50 for wasting the court's time and Jonathan Collins, who had acted as counsel for Everitt, was ordered to pay the costs of the case himself. The feuding robbers soon had weightier things on their mind. For Williams was hanged in 1727 and Everitt in 1830, both after committing further offences of highway robbery.

*

A California spelling bee contest provoked a bizarre lawsuit in 1987. The beaten finalist's father sued the event sponsor, the Ventura County *Star-Free Press,* claiming mental distress, and seeking $2 million in damages. A superior state court judge and a state court of appeals dismissed the suit, stating that the major reason the complainant's son had lost the spelling bee was not because the contest was badly run but because he had misspelled 'iridescent'.

*

A Norfolk pensioner waged an eight-month legal battle costing him £745, simply because he was convinced that his gas bill was 1p too high. Although British Gas agreed to waive the bill and offered him £10 for his trouble, retired bus driver Philip Flinders was determined to take the matter to court. And he remained unrepentant even after a county court judge ruled that British Gas had no case to answer. 'At least I have succeeded in getting an explanation,' he said.

*

Stood up on a date by waitress Alyn Chesselet in the spring of 1978, San Jos accountant Tom Horsley decided to seek financial reimbursement for his wasted 100-mile journey. At the San Francisco Small Claims Court, he filed a suit against Miss Chesselet on the grounds that she had 'broken an oral contract to have dinner and see the musical *The Wiz*'. He told the court that he intended to claim payment for the two-hour round trip at an accountant's minimum rate of £4.70 an hour plus 9.4p a mile in car expenses. Together with the sum spent on serving the court papers, this came to a total of £21. When the court got in touch with Miss Chesselet, she said that Mr Horsley was 'nuts'.

*

In June 1998, three young men were cleared at the Old Bailey of stealing two cans of lager worth £1.80 after a trial costing the taxpayer an estimated £131,000. The trial collapsed after two and a half days when the judge ruled there was insufficient evidence to proceed. The prosecution had alleged that the three students were in a convenience store in Ealing Broadway when the cans of Stella Artois lager vanished from a fridge. One of the accused was said to have slid them into his pocket while his companions shielded him. When they left, a cashier called the police. Stopped nearby, the trio denied the theft. Originally heard at Ealing Magistrates Court, the case was passed to Isleworth Crown Court after the defendants elected for trial by jury. Then, because there were insufficient cases at the Old Bailey, this minor offence was transferred there to Court 17, normally the venue for trials involving murder, armed robbery or multimillion-pound fraud. The jurors watched security video footage, said to back up the prosecution claims, but the three were freed after the judge said that the case could not proceed after live evidence was contradicted by the video footage. As the Crown Prosecution Service came under fire for pursuing the case to the highest criminal court in the land, a leading QC remarked: 'It's a wicked waste of public money and would be laughable if it were not so costly. To trawl a trivial matter like this through the courts with the taxpayer forking out from his pocket is an absolute nonsense.'

Jeffrey Archer: A Sting In The Tail

Jeffrey Archer had always been a chancer, one of life's great survivors. Lady Thatcher called him 'the extrovert's extrovert', John Major likened him to the Unsinkable Molly Brown of *Titanic* fame, but others found his exuberance and brashness less attractive. Consequently, throughout his political career, the millionaire author had been viewed with deep suspicion by certain members of his beloved Conservative Party who saw him as a liability, a man who could not be trusted. At times these whispering campaigns became positively deafening but no matter how deep in the mire he appeared to be, he repeatedly managed to come up smelling of roses.

Never was this more apparent than in 1987 when, after being forced to resign as deputy chairman of the Conservatives following allegations in the *Daily Star* that he had enjoyed sex with a prostitute, he bounced back and won a record £500,000 in libel damages from the newspaper. His honour was restored. Then in 1994 he was involved in a row after buying shares in Anglia Television, a company of which his wife Mary was a director. Days later the company announced a takeover bid and Archer sold the shares at a tidy £77,000 profit. He strongly denied the allegations of insider trading and was duly cleared of any impropriety, his only concession being to apologize to the loyal Mary for any embarrassment he may have caused her. Once again, the Archer bandwagon steamrollered on relentlessly. By November 1999 he had risen to Lord Archer of Weston-super-Mare and had been selected as Conservative candidate to be mayor of London, but just when he seemed within touching distance of his finest hour, his past finally caught up with him. Following further newspaper revelations, Archer admitted having asked a friend to lie for him before the 1987 libel trial. Suddenly his cosy world came crashing down. He resigned from the mayoral race and was faced with the triple threat of expulsion from the Conservative Party, possible criminal charges and a massive financial bill. His career and reputation lay in shreds.

Educated at Wellington School, Somerset, and Brasenose College, Oxford, where he distinguished himself as an athlete and entrepreneur (he signed up the Beatles for a charity concert), Archer became Tory MP for Louth, Lincolnshire, in 1969 at the tender age of 29. However, his meteoric rise to fame received a setback a few years later when, acting on a dud tip, he invested £427,000 in a Canadian company called Aquablast and was forced to sell his Daimler car and his Chelsea home as he was plunged towards bankruptcy. His financial difficulties led him to pull out of the 1974 election, but in typical Archer fashion he fought back by writing his first novel – *Not A Penny More, Not A Penny Less* – in just ten weeks. The book became a bestseller and Archer was on his way again.

His sheer enthusiasm made him the darling of the Tory blue-rinse ladies and he was rewarded with the deputy chairmanship of the party. However, on Sunday 26 October 1986, following an elaborate 'sting', the *News of the World* published a front page story under the headline TORY BOSS ARCHER PAYS OFF VICE GIRL, claiming that Archer had paid Monica Coghlan, a 35-year-old Lancashire prostitute who used the working name 'Debbie', the sum of £2000 to go abroad. The money – wrapped in a brown envelope in bundles of £50 notes – had been handed to Coghlan by an Archer aide, Michael Stacpoole, two days previously on platform three at London's Victoria Station. Trapped on tape, Archer admitted arranging for the money to be handed over to Coghlan but denied having met her in Shepherd Market, the Mayfair red-light district nestling just around the corner from the sumptuous hotels of Park Lane and Piccadilly. Indeed he steadfastly maintained that he had never met Monica Coghlan and that he had merely paid her to go abroad in order to avoid any possible scandal.

Archer immediately resigned as Conservative deputy chairman. In a statement he said: 'Some weeks ago, I received a telephone call from a woman who gave the name of Debbie. She told me that she was a prostitute and that a "client" of hers was letting it be known that we had met in Shepherd Market and had had an association. I told her that this was absolutely false and that to my knowledge we had never met. I subsequently received further telephone calls from her to the effect that the press were pursuing her as a result of disclosures to them by their "client" and that she did not know how to avoid the press. Foolishly, I allowed myself to fall into what I can only call a trap in which a newspaper, in my view, played a reprehensible part. In the belief that this woman genuinely wanted to be out of the way of the press and realising that for my part any publicity of this kind would be extremely harmful to me and for which a libel action would be no adequate remedy, I offered to pay her money so that she could go abroad for a short period. For that lack of judgement, and that alone, I have tendered my resignation.'

While the nation struggled to come to terms with a leading public figure handing over £2000 to someone he had never met (satirists referred to £2000 as 'an Archer'), the *Daily Star* went a step further, alleging that Archer and Monica Coghlan had sex at a seedy London hotel on the night of 9 September. Archer decided to sue.

The case against the *Daily Star* was heard in July 1987 and was labelled 'the libel trial of the decade'. Beforehand the newspaper realized that it had mixed up the dates and changed the night of the alleged liaison to 8 September. It claimed that Archer had approached Coghlan, a prostitute specializing in 'kinky sex', around midnight in Shepherd Market but before he could fetch his car to pick her up, she had met one of her regular clients – a solicitor – who took her to the Albion Hotel in Victoria. The *Star* said that Archer followed them and was recognized by the solicitor who decided to expose him to the press. According to the *Star,* Coghlan and Archer, who is said to have told her he was a car salesman, had sex in room 6a on the second floor, Archer allegedly paying £50 plus another £20 so that he could 'take his time'.

Archer maintained that on the evening of the 8th, he had gone to his favourite restaurant, Le Caprice off Regent Street, with the editor of his books. When the editor and his wife left at around 10.30pm, Archer said he stayed on to talk to Terence Baker, his film and TV agent, who was in the bar, before driving him home to South London around 12.45am. Archer testified that he then returned to his flat on the Albert Embankment and went to bed alone. Archer reiterated how, two weeks later, he had received a call from 'Debbie' who said she was being hounded by a client who had recognized Archer at the hotel and wanted to sell her story. Unbeknown to

Archer, the call was being taped by the *News of the World*. On the tape, Archer sounded bewildered and surprised. 'I was worried obviously,' he told the court, 'that anyone could be going round telling lies. I was a worried man, a nervous man, knowing I had never met this girl, knowing I had never had any association with her and yet that appeared what the story would be.' He added that he felt 'sympathy' for Coghlan and paid her money to go abroad, although he admitted that he had been an 'utter fool' to do so. The *Star* said that Archer had paid the money because he was guilty.

Monica Coghlan described her encounter at the Albion with Archer as brief, between 10 and 15 minutes. 'Nothing much was said because it was over so quickly,' she said. 'He kept repeating that I was lovely and commented on my nipples.' She readily identified him in court. 'I had no difficulty seeing his face. I was lying on top of him the whole time.' She proved an emotional witness, at one point rounding on Archer and shouting: 'He's a liar and he knows it. He's even putting his wife through it.'

Mary Archer was to prove a key witness. By turns aggressive and tearful, she told the court that the very thought of her husband having sex with a prostitute was preposterous. 'Anyone who knows Jeffrey would know that far from him accosting a prostitute, if one accosted him, he would run several miles.' She also poured scorn on Coghlan's testimony that the skin on Archer's back was rough and spotty. 'Jeffrey has an excellent skin,' said Mary. 'He has no spots or blemishes anywhere.' In the end she had to be helped from the witness box, sobbing inconsolably.

The scene left a profound impression on the judge, Mr Justice Caulfield, who, in his summing-up, questioned whether Archer would have paid for the sexual services of another woman while married to the 'fragrant' Mary. He told the jury they had to choose between Archer's word and that of a prostitute who had used 'guile and cunning'. 'You may think his history', said the judge, 'is worthy and healthy and sporting. What is always a great attribute of the British is their admiration, besides their enjoyment, of good sports like cricket and athletics. And Jeffrey Archer was President of the Oxford University Athletic Club and ran for his country. Is he in need of cold, unloving, rubber-insulated sex in a seedy hotel, round about a quarter to one on a Tuesday morning after an evening at The Caprice with his editor?'

The jury of eight men and four women evidently thought not. After four hours of deliberation, they decided that Archer's character was as unblemished as his back and awarded him £500,000 in damages, at the time the highest sum paid out in a British libel action. As the jurors left the court, Archer shook hands with and thanked each one. The last juror replied: 'It was a pleasure.'

And so Jeffrey Archer was vindicated, apparently guilty of nothing more than an error of judgment. Yet still there were doubters. Adam Raphael, then political editor of the *Observer*, had testified that on the day the *News of the World* first printed its story about Archer and Coghlan, Archer had told him that he had met Coghlan. A second journalist told a similar story. And Terence Baker's evidence regarding Archer's alibi had seemed confused. Nevertheless, in October 1987 the *News of the World* settled with Archer and agreed to pay £50,000 to the charity of his choice.

Fast forward to 1999, by which time Archer had spent two years orchestrating his campaign to be mayor of London, in the course of which he had visited all 74 constituencies with his customary boundless enthusiasm. In October he had defeated Steven Norris in a ballot to choose the Tory candidate, but his victory conference descended into farce when his biographer Michael Crick pursued him from the room shouting questions about shadowy aspects of his past. From his electoral platform, Archer had declared that 'openness' and 'freedom of information' were what London needed, but it is doubtful whether he had in mind the issue of the *News of the World* dated 21 November 1999. In it, Ted Francis, TV producer and erstwhile Archer friend, came forward after nearly 13 years of silence to reveal that, in January 1987, Archer had persuaded him to write a letter to Archer's lawyers falsely stating that they had dinner together at the Sambuca restaurant, off Sloane Square, Chelsea, on the night of 9 September 1986, and that Archer had even changed his diary to record such a meeting. This had given Archer an alibi for the time when the *Daily Star* claimed he was with Monica Coghlan although in the end it was not needed because the *Star* later amended the date to the 8th. Ted Francis had not even been called to give evidence at the trial.

The new disclosures did not prove that Archer had sex with Monica Coghlan, but they did show him to be a liar, a man with something to hide, a man who was prepared to get others to cover up and lie for him. He was utterly discredited. Archer couldn't wriggle out of this one. His incriminating conversations with Francis had been taped and published in the *News of the World*. His bogus alibi was blown to pieces.

In what was virtually an action replay of 1986, Archer immediately withdrew from the race to be mayor of London. In a statement he said: 'Thirteen years ago, I asked a friend, Ted Francis, to cover for me by saying that we were having dinner together on the evening of 9 September 1986 when in fact I was having dinner with a close female friend at a restaurant in Chelsea . . . I am saddened that years later Ted Francis has decided to profit from selling his story to the *News of the World*. The dinner was not relevant to the trial, and did not form any part of the evidence. Of course I should not have asked Ted to cover for me, even though it was beyond question that I was in the restaurant that night. I was simply trying to protect the person I was with.'

Speculation was rife as to the identity of Archer's mystery female companion. It was widely assumed to have been his former personal assistant, Andrina Colquhoun, an ex-debutante who had been given a BMW convertible as a leaving present by Archer. It was thought that Archer had been desperate to avoid dragging her into the libel battle, if only to head off allegations that they were having an affair. If nothing else, Ms Colquhoun was a fateful dinner companion for she was also booked to dine with Lord Lucan in 1974 on the night the missing Earl murdered his children's nanny Sandra Rivett.

Apart from the £20,000 he received from the *News of the World*, why did Ted Francis suddenly decide to tell all? He claimed that it was because he was horrified at the prospect of someone like Archer becoming mayor of London, with all the power which that position held, but there was also a secondary motivation – revenge. In 1987 Archer had put money into Francis's project to make a TV series based on Enid Blyton stories. Francis thought it was an investment, not a loan, and was horrified when, three years later at one of Archer's famous champagne and shepherd's pie parties, the author raised the matter publicly. Francis said: 'I was chatting to an actress when Jeffrey sidled up to us and said to her in a very loud voice, "You want to watch this man, you know. I lent him £20,000 once and I'm still waiting to get the money back." She was dreadfully embarrassed and I was deeply hurt. He humiliated me in front of my peers in the industry and I didn't understand why.'

Asked why he thought he had been asked to lie for Archer back in 1987, Francis believed it had been to save the novelist's marriage. Francis told Talk Radio: 'Jeffrey said to me: "What were you doing on September 9 last year?" I said I didn't know. He said, "Could we have been having dinner? I want you to say we had dinner. I was having dinner with someone else on that night and I can prove it, but it would embarrass me with Mary." Because I knew that he and Andrina were close, I connected it automatically with that and I knew or I guessed there had been strains put on his marriage by his relationship with Andrina. I did him a favour as a friend because I thought he was going to get in trouble with his wife.'

As further skeletons threatened to emerge from the closet, close scrutiny was placed on the evidence of Terence Baker, the man who had provided Archer with his crucial alibi. Baker had died in 1991 but an acquaintance told the *Daily Star*'s lawyers that the film agent had once confessed that he had lied in order to protect his old friend. Moreover, journalist Adam Raphael claimed to have seen a diary showing that Archer planned to dine with Baker at the Sambuca restaurant on 9 September 1986. At the trial, Archer had testified that he had bumped into Baker at another restaurant, Le Caprice, on the previous evening. Without Baker's evidence, Archer had no alibi for the time he was alleged to have been with Monica Coghlan.

The *Daily Star* swiftly attempted to recover the £500,000 damages and £700,000 in costs which it had been forced to pay after the 1987 trial. Adding on interest, the newspaper cheekily sent Archer a bill for over £3 million and gave him two days in which to pay. When no cheque was forthcoming, the *Star* launched a formal appeal against the original verdict. The basis was that had it been known that Archer had asked a friend to provide a false alibi, it would have destroyed his credibility in the eyes of the jury and affected the outcome or the amount of damages awarded. Furthermore, the knowledge that Archer was with another woman – as he now claimed – might have influenced the jury when considering allegations of womanizing.

To add to his troubles, Archer also had to consider the possibility of being charged by the police with conspiring to pervert the course of justice.

The case still has a large number of grey areas. Many questions remain unanswered and indeed the whole truth may never be known. Was Jeffrey Archer an innocent victim whose sole folly had been to hand over £2000 to a woman he had never met? Or did he have sex with Monica Coghlan, as she still insists 13 years on? Or, as Michael Stacpoole now alleges, was Archer trying to cover up for a long-standing affair with Andrina Colquhoun? The only certainty is that, as it turned out, Archer had no need to ask Ted Francis to lie for him. The *Star* had got the wrong night. His evidence was never required. As one barrister put it: 'Archer over-egged the pudding and made matters far more complicated than they needed to be.'

Jeffrey Archer had become trapped in a web of his own making.

Rupert Allason: A Suit Too Far

Rupert Allason had a talent for winning libel cases. Christened 'Action Man' by certain sections of the British press, the Conservative MP and successful author of spy novels (under the pseudonym of Nigel West) had launched no fewer than 16 libel cases and won the lot. Many were settled out of court and whilst Allason never disclosed the amount of his 'winnings', they were believed to have run into hundreds of thousands of pounds. His most lucrative payday was thought to have been in 1992 when he received £200,000 from the *Daily Mirror* over allegations of cowardice. He also won an apology and damages from the *Independent* in 1994 and an apology from the *Mail on Sunday* in 1993 for comments on his marriage.

So when he was alerted to what he described as a 'vicious libel' and a 'revolting slur' in a book accompanying the popular television satire *Have I Got News For You,* he decided to sue BBC Worldwide, who published the book, and Hat Trick Productions who made the programme. An accomplished amateur advocate, Allason opted to represent himself, but for once his powers of persuasion let him down and he lost the case. Having rejected an offer of £50 from the BBC and Hat Trick to settle, he was left facing a legal bill of around £50,000.

The offending passage had appeared in the diary *Have I Got 1997 For You.* Beneath a photograph of Allason was printed the caption: 'A maverick Tory MP who, when he's writing spy novels, is called Nigel West and, when he's voting against his own government, is called something quite unprintable. Indeed, given Mr Allason's fondness for pursuing libel actions, there are also excellent legal reasons for not referring to him as a conniving little shit.'

Despite 45-year-old Allason's track record, his appearance at the High Court in London in January 1998 was, he said, the first time he had appeared before a jury. He opened the case by apologizing to the jury for any shortcomings there might be in his amateur advocacy. Glancing to his right, at the bank of BBC lawyers that included Charles Gray, QC, a junior counsel and seven other suited individuals all carrying large black document cases, Allason invited the jury to study the full might of the BBC's litigation department. By contrast, he came armed only with a satchel, a glass of water, an Oxford Dictionary and a cheap plastic pen. He was clearly looking for the sympathy vote.

Allason, who had lost his Torbay seat at the 1997 general election by 12 votes, proceeded to read the passage in question from the BBC book. The court heard that the remark referred to his opposition to the Maastricht Treaty and his refusal to support the government in a House of Commons no-confidence vote on the issue in 1993. Allason argued that his opposition reflected his determination to stick to his guns and to keep his promise to his constituents of the time. He said that he did not deserve to be defamed by people who thought it was clever to sneer at those in public life.

BBC Worldwide and Hat Trick denied libel, pleading fair comment on a matter of public interest. They claimed that the book was light-hearted and funny, like the TV programme on which it was based – a show on which Allason was once a panellist. The court was treated to a screening of a May 1996 episode of *Have I Got News For You* in which Rupert Allason's team emerged as the winners. Ian Hislop, a regular team captain, editor of *Private Eye* and himself no stranger to libel proceedings, was heard to say: 'Beaten by Rupert Allason. That bodes well for the next time we meet in court.'

Allason conceded the knockabout nature of the programme and said that he had enjoyed appearing on it but would not accept that the phrase 'conniving little shit' was in the spirit of the show. 'This isn't a jolly jape,' he said. 'There are rogues and scoundrels included in this book, including Robert Maxwell, but none of them has a description approaching mine.'

He told the court that he had heard about the remark in the book through a telephone call from his 77-year-old mother Nuala. Questioning her in the witness box, there was a surreal moment when Allason asked her: 'For the sake of the court, you are my mother?' After confirming that she was, Mrs Allason recounted how, in December 1996, a friend visiting from America had told her there was a book that had 'something shocking and dreadful' in it 'about you'.

'I didn't believe what she was telling me,' continued Mrs Allason, 'so I went to the Sloane Square branch of WH Smith and bought the book. I looked it up and I was absolutely horrified by what I read. I simply couldn't believe it. To see such dreadful language in print about my son – I couldn't have been more distressed.' Asked by her son whether it was usual for people to criticize him, given his position as a public figure, she replied: 'You have been a policeman and an MP and I could not see there was any reason why they should write that about you.' Allason then asked his mother if she was proud of him. 'Yes,' she answered, 'I'm particularly proud about the time when he arrested some drug smugglers.' But before she could continue listing the more glorious moments of her son's career, Mr Justice Popplewell reprimanded Mr Allason for straying from the central facts.

When he had first heard about the contents of the book, Rupert Allason said that he immediately complained to the BBC, asking them to remove or reprint the offending page.

Colin Swash, the author of the remark, denied that there was any malice behind the entry. He agreed that the language used was 'not pleasant', but was 'the language of the grown-up playground'. He added that the words he had used were his estimation of what Mr Allason's fellow Tory MPs were saying about him at the time. He said Allason should have taken it as a joke. 'David Mellor was called a sex-mad buffoon,' said Swash, 'but I'd expect him to shrug, say something nasty about us, and then get on with life.'

Charles Gray suggested that Rupert Allason had a 'fondness for litigation' and treated libel actions as a hobby. The plaintiff denied the allegation and said there was 'nothing fun' about libel. The court was shown a second TV clip, a video of Allason appearing on a chat show hosted by Clive Anderson, himself a former barrister. When asked by the host what newspapers had written about him to deserve being sued, Allason replied: 'Usually the truth.' Questioned by Charles Gray as to what he had meant by that remark, Allason said: 'It is what is known as a joke.'

Gray went on to suggest that Allason had, in the past, enjoyed using harsh words about the reputations of others. To this, Allason answered: 'I hope that the people that I've been critical of have been crooks by and large.' Charles Gray then produced a transcript of an interview in which he said Allason had been insulting about a number of prominent public figures, including Lord Archer of Weston-Super-Mare and the former hostage Terry Waite.

In his closing speech, Rupert Allason made an impassioned plea to the jury not to let the media get away with it, but Charles Gray argued that the remark in the book was in a long line of British tradition of poking fun at people in authority. 'Think before you make an award which throttles programmes like *Have I Got News For You*,' he said.

After three hours of deliberation, the jury of six men and six women found against Rupert Allason. The verdict was unanimous. He remained impassive as the verdict was announced before slipping out of the court via a side exit without commenting.

But his adversaries had plenty to say. A spokesman for Hat Trick commented: 'It is a healthy and welcome sign that the jury decisively rejected a politician's attempt to secure large damages for a humorous comment in a book based on a programme that is enjoyed by millions.' Jimmy Mulville, managing director of Hat Trick, added: 'Mr Allason is obviously very skilled at bringing this sort of action and it would have been a bad day for the programme, and others like it, if he had succeeded.' The last word went to Ian Hislop who said of the vanquished Allason: 'I understand litigation is a bit of a hobby of his. He's going to have to find a new hobby now.'

Jonathan Aitken: A Fall From Grace

In April 1995, Jonathan Aitken, the Chief Secretary to the Treasury, issued libel writs against the *Guardian* and Granada

Television's *World in Action* over what he described as 'wicked lies' about his business activities. He promised a campaign to purge the media. 'If it falls to me,' he declared, 'to start a fight to cut out the cancer of bent and twisted journalism in our country with the simple sword of truth and the trusty shield of fair play, so be it. I am ready for the fight.' But the man who saw himself as the great crusader perished on his own sword. He ended up losing £2 million, his parliamentary seat, his wife, his reputation and, ultimately his freedom.

Jonathan Aitken had always seemed destined for the top. The great-nephew of press baron Lord Beaverbrook, he was something of a golden boy with looks, charm and superb debating skills which had won him the public schools' debating championship. Beaverbrook told him: 'You're a very bright boy with a very bright future.' Educated at Eton and Oxford, Aitken was offered his first parliamentary seat at the age of 20 and was being compared within the Conservative Party to Pitt the Younger who became Prime Minister at 24. By 22, Aitken was writing speeches for Foreign Secretary Selwyn Lloyd and three years later he became Lloyd's secretary, a move which propelled him to the very heart of the party.

He enjoyed living dangerously, writing about the delights of smoking pot at Oxford and expressing his admiration for Richard Nixon, about whom he wrote a 600-page biography. Then there were the women: Margaret Thatcher's daughter, Carol, Lady Antonia Fraser, Lady Charlotte Curzon, Elizabeth Harrison, former wife of Rex Harrison, and Arianna Stassinopoulos. Not all found him irresistible, however. Margaret Thatcher declined to promote him after he ended the relationship with Carol, while newsreader Anna Ford famously tipped a glass of red wine over him at a party in protest at the way he and his cousin Tim had taken over TV-am.

He had no such problems with money and developed close links with the Middle East. He co-founded the merchant bank Aitken Hume with the help of Saudi Arabian money and through investments on behalf of the Saudi royal family. And he recovered from the Thatcher snub to be made Minister of Defence Procurement under John Major, a job where it was assumed his knowledge of the Middle East would prove useful. Two years later, in 1994, he was promoted to the Cabinet. But his business dealings had started to give cause for concern, notably at the *Guardian* and at Granada Television's hard-hitting investigative series *World in Action*. Working together, the two teams of journalists compiled a detailed dossier on Aitken's activities. By April 1995, they were ready to go public.

The *World in Action* programme, whose allegations were also carried that morning on the front page of the *Guardian*, was screened on 10 April 1995 and was entitled 'Jonathan of Arabia'. It levelled three main accusations at Aitken, himself a former journalist. The first was that he had tried to arrange girls for a Saudi prince and his entourage at the Inglewood Health Hydro of which he was a director, near Newbury in Berkshire; the second was that he had enjoyed improper commercial relations with two Lebanese arms dealers, Fouad and Ziad Makhzoumi, while he had been Minister of State for Defence Procurement between 1992 and 1994; the third was that business associates of the Saudi royal family had paid for his stay at the Ritz Hotel in Paris in September 1993.

In the documentary, the former principal of Inglewood, Robin Kirk, and Jo Lambert, the former matron, both said that on separate occasions Aitken had asked them to provide girls, once for a sheikh and once for a group of Arabs. Inglewood had been bought by associates of Prince Mohammed bin Fahd, a son of the Saudi king. Ms Lambert recalled a telephone conversation with Aitken: 'He rang back and said was it possible to get any girls for the Arabs and I said no, I don't know any girls. If you need girls you bring them up with you. I said, where am I going to get girls in the middle of Berkshire? Do you want me to put an ad in the *Newbury Weekly News*?'

The programme also claimed that in 1994, when he was Minister of State for Defence Procurement, he met Fouad Makhzoumi. Aitken used to be a director of Mr Makhzoumi's company, Future Management Services, which was trying to arrange the supply of defence and security equipment to Lebanon. Mr Makhzoumi's lawyers insisted that the meeting was for 'social reasons'.

World in Action examined Aitken's stay at the Ritz Hotel in Paris where he met Saudi businessman Said Ayas. The programme claimed that a number of Prince Mohammed's associates were there and that all the bills were paid for by a secretary from an organization associated with the Saudi royal family called the Asturian Foundation.

Jonathan Aitken was swift to issue denials on all three counts. Regarding the Inglewood allegation, he replied: 'This is an outrageous falsehood. Not only did I never do any such thing during my 11 years as a director of the health hydro, it should also be made clear that the prince in question, Prince Mohammed bin Fahd, the son of King Fahd, never stayed at Inglewood. His one and only short visit to Inglewood was for lunch some 13 years ago. No girls were present and I made no suggestion that they should be present or available to him or his friends.' Aitken added that the matron had been dismissed for dishonesty although criminal charges were not pressed. Jo Lambert denied that she had been dismissed for dishonesty.

Turning to the Lebanese question, Aitken said: 'The fact of the matter is that I was approached in late 1992 by the Makhzoumi brothers, who have been long-standing personal friends and former banking clients of mine, asking about defence sales possibilities in Lebanon. As the minister responsible for defence exports I acted entirely correctly by turning the whole matter over to Ministry of Defence officials within the Defence Exports Sales Organisation . . . As for the linked suggestion that I improperly failed to register my former banking directorship with the Makhzoumis' company Future Management Services in the Register of Members' Interests, I am confident that I acted entirely in accordance with the register in not recording this non-remunerated directorship. There was no requirement to register such directorships until 1993.

'The third article in the *Guardian* attacking me is a confusing, old-hat rehash of the creative collaboration between the newspaper and Mr Mohammed Al Fayed's Ritz Hotel in Paris, about alleged irregularities over my stay there in September 1993. Nothing in the *Guardian* article shakes my conviction that my stay in the Ritz Hotel did not breach the rules governing the conduct of ministers as laid down in Questions of Procedure for Ministers. If there is anything new in the *Guardian*'s regurgitation of this episode it seems to be the suggestion that I was in the hotel on an expenses paid business visit arranged by a lady – a lady whom I have never met nor heard of – for the purpose of meeting three businessmen. Let me make it crystal clear that not only did I not meet any of these gentlemen in Paris, I am informed that none of them was staying at the Ritz during my visit of September 18–19.' He went on to dismiss other 'misrepresentations, falsehoods and lies' as 'clearly part of the paper's long campaign of sustained attempts to discredit me'. He concluded: 'I have done nothing wrong.'

Two months after suing for libel, Aitken resigned as Chief Secretary to the Treasury so that he could fight the action. He then lost his Thanet South seat at the 1997 general election. A month later in June, he was in the High Court for the start of his libel case, one in which Granada and the *Guardian* were represented by the scourge of the litigious, George Carman, QC.

Of the various accusations levelled against Aitken, the one which quickly became the focus of attention was the stay at the Paris Ritz whereby Aitken was accused of having his £1000 hotel bill paid for by a former Arab business associate – Said Ayas, who at the time was an aide to Prince Mohammed – in breach of ministerial guidelines. In the course of a lengthy correspondence at the start of 1994 with the then editor of the *Guardian*, Peter Preston, Aitken claimed that his Serbian wife Lolicia had paid the hotel bill and that the weekend was perfectly innocent. When, eight days later, Preston made it plain that he knew that the bill for room 526 (Aitken's) had been paid by Said Ayas in rooms 626/7, Aitken replied that the hotel had made a mistake in typing Mr Ayas's name on his account. But this, he insisted, was because Mr Ayas had booked his room, the two having arranged to meet in Paris as old friends. He added that he had found the receipt of the payment by his wife. Preston asked to see a copy of the receipt but Aitken responded instead with what he claimed was confirmation from Frank Klein, president of the Ritz, that his bill had not been paid by Mr Ayas. In fact, Mr Klein's letter had been carefully edited by Aitken and said only that Mr Ayas did not 'personally' settle the bill. The edited letter was forwarded by Aitken to Cabinet Secretary Sir Robin Butler. Both Sir Robin and Prime Minister John Major then said they were satisfied with Aitken's version of events. As it turned out, they were too easily pleased.

Aitken told the court that his wife and 14-year-old daughter Victoria had travelled from London to Paris on Thursday, 16 September 1993 by ferry and train. Aitken said that he had checked in at the Ritz in Paris on 17 September, intending to stay for one or two nights depending on when Victoria needed to go on to Switzerland. To his surprise, they had already left Paris by train for Geneva earlier that day. He said he produced a credit card to pay for the hotel room but was told it was 'not necessary'. Under cross-examination from George Carman, Aitken insisted that his wife had returned to Paris on the Sunday and paid his hotel bill using $3000 in cash which he had given her for the trip. In earlier witness statements, Aitken had said his wife was dyslexic and preferred paying with cash, rather than by credit card. Yet the court was told that Mrs Aitken had paid for her previous night's stay at a hotel in Switzerland using a credit card.

George Carman told the High Court that Aitken's evidence was 'tainted with improbability' on 13 points. He said that the former minister's account of his stay at the Ritz was a 'web of lies' in which 'improbability was heaped on improbability' so that Aitken could conceal the fact that he had improperly held a business meeting with Arab associates and allowed an Arab friend to pay his hotel bill. Mr Carman said that Aitken had 'covered his tracks' in a letter written to Sir Robin Butler and had 'pursued a conspiratorial agreement' with Said Ayas to explain the fact that the bill had been added to Mr Ayas's account. Aitken had maintained that his bill had ended up on Said Ayas's account either as the result of a genuine mistake or because he had been 'set up' by the Ritz. George Carman dismissed that suggestion, along with the one that Aitken's offer to pay by credit card had been refused by hotel staff.

The former MP was then asked about a statement from a Ritz cashier who said that Aitken's hotel bill for the weekend in question had been paid by a 'brunette lady of European aspect speaking French'. Aitken contended that the woman was his wife Lolicia who paid 4257 francs in cash for what she believed to be the full balance of his two-night stay, although it was in fact over £400 short.

Indicating the blonde tresses of Mrs Aitken, who was sitting in court, George Carman said: 'Your wife is not a brunette now, is she?'

'She's not this week,' replied Aitken, adding that his wife had tried many shades over the years. Her passport, however, described her as blonde.

The court was told that Manon Vidal, secretary of the treasurer to Prince Mohammed bin Fahd, was a French-speaking brunette. George Carman said that it was she who had paid Aitken's bill.

Aitken stuck to his guns although admitting, 'My wife has been unable to recall the precise details of what did happen – all that Carry on Arabia scene around the Ritz cashier desk on that afternoon.' He also introduced a new character – his mother-in-law. He told the court that he had made a phone call on the Sunday morning to his wife's hotel in Switzerland after she had allegedly left to return to Paris – and had spoken to his mother-in-law. The two women had shared a room together the previous night, he added. However, records from the hotel showed that Mrs Aitken had only been charged a single occupancy rate for her Saturday night stay. If Aitken were to be believed, there were a lot of incompetent hotels around.

With George Carman describing his story as 'scandalous, incredible and preposterous', Aitken also had to admit that he had failed to declare the gift of a 'magnificent' ladies' watch from a brother-in-law of the Saudi king in the House of Commons Register of Members' Interests.

Aitken was caught out again over a Granada TV film in which a crew had sought to interview him over the allegations which would be aired on the *World in Action* programme, 'Jonathan of Arabia', four days later. In a witness statement, Aitken had claimed he was harassed by *World in Action* journalists who had 'stampeded' towards him outside his home in Lord North Street, Westminster, shouting, 'Why won't you answer questions?' Aitken said his daughter, Alexandra (Victoria's twin), had been 'visibly upset' by the crew's aggressive behaviour and had burst into tears. Aitken claimed he had got into his ministerial Jaguar with his daughter, only to be pursued in a 'Keystone Cops' style car chase by the Granada journalists. But when the unedited rushes were played to the court, they showed Aitken climbing into the car without his daughter. No attempt was made to pursue him. When George Carman said, 'Even the technical geniuses from Granada Television could not have removed your daughter from the film if she was there,' Aitken blustered that it was either a different film or there were two exits from the house. Carman commented: 'As a man who claims to take up the sword of truth before this court, you have revealed yourself a stranger to the truth whenever it suits you.'

Aitken's capacity for creativity was finally exposed, not directly by the acid tongue of George Carman but by Wendy Harris of British Airways' security and investigation service. After being subpoenaed by the defence, she signed a damning witness statement which proved that, contrary to Jonathan Aitken's testimony, his wife and daughter Victoria were never in Paris between 17 and 20 September 1993. Instead, they were shown to have flown directly from London Heathrow to Geneva without stopping en route. This meant that Mrs Aitken could not possibly have paid the bill at the Ritz.

Ms Harris had discovered flight coupons on BA's microfilm records proving that Mrs Aitken and her daughter had flown from Heathrow to Geneva on flight 724 at 8.30 a.m. on 17 September. Mrs Aitken had returned alone from Geneva to Heathrow on flight 731 at 7.05 p.m. on 20 September while a booking was reserved for Victoria to return from Geneva on flight 725 at 12.05 p.m. on 13 December. Ms Harris said in her statement: 'It would not have been possible to retrieve flight coupons for a passenger unless they did travel on that flight.'

Ms Harris also discovered that Mrs Aitken had returned a hire car in Geneva at 6.35 p.m. on Sunday, 19 September – two hours after she was supposed to have been with the Ritz cashier. She had paid for the hire car by American Express, a credit card her husband claimed she never used.

Faced with this damning new evidence, Aitken threw in the towel, withdrew his libel action and went into hiding. In doing so, he effectively conceded that the other allegations against him were also true. A few hours earlier, he had announced a separation from his wife.

Reacting to Aitken's downfall, former *Guardian* editor Peter Preston, who had masterminded the investigation into the former minister's corrupt activities, branded him a 'serial liar'. He added: 'Mr Aitken was lying about the Ritz from the start and the lies unravelled and unravelled and are lying on the floor. If there is one thing that sticks in my gullet, it's that anyone would use a school-child to back up a story like this. It's disgraceful by any standards.'

Peter Preston's successor as *Guardian* editor, Alan Rusbridger, said of Aitken: 'We always wondered how low he would stoop. That was the moment we knew. Jonathan Aitken seems to have impaled himself on the simple sword of truth. For three years he has lied to newspapers, lied to the Cabinet Secretary, lied to the Prime Minister and lied to his colleagues. Now he has made his fatal mistake by lying on oath to the High Court.'

The most curious aspect to the case was that Aitken appeared to have seen off the other allegations made against him, only to be trapped over the relatively insignificant Ritz affair. Peter Preston admitted that Aitken might well have got away with his story if his wife had flown by a foreign airline such as Swissair, which it would have been impossible to subpoena. Alan Rusbridger added that the real reasons for Aitken's visit to the Ritz that weekend remained a mystery. He said that he did not know what was so important that Aitken had jeopardized his family, career and wealth in order to cover his tracks.

As Aitken found himself saddled with paying 80 per cent of the defence costs – around £800,000 – plus his own legal bill of some £1.2 million, he knew that his ordeal was far from over. In 1998, the 56-year-old Aitken was charged with perjury and perverting the course of justice. Aitken and Said Ayas were jointly charged with conspiring to pervert the course of justice between 9 April 1995 and 21 June 1997. The charge alleged that they signed witness statements and allowed them to be submitted to the High Court action against the *Guardian* and Granada Television, falsely claiming that, prior to travelling to Geneva, Mrs Aitken and Victoria had been in Paris on 17 September 1993, that they had stayed at a flat there belonging to Ayas's daughter and that Mrs Aitken had paid a bill for Mr Aitken at the Paris Ritz. Aitken faced three other charges: drafting and getting his daughter Victoria to sign a statement backing this version of events, knowing it to be false; making a statement that his wife had been in Paris and paid his hotel bill; and committing perjury by repeating this in the high court.

In January 1999, by which time he and Lolicia were divorced, the man once tipped as a future Prime Minister suffered the ignominy of being the first Cabinet Minister in history to stand in the dock of the Old Bailey. All too aware of the strength of the evidence against him, Aitken's lawyers struck a deal with the Crown Prosecution Service where he would hold his hands up to two of the charges and plead not guilty to the remaining two. This, his lawyers hoped, would earn him a reduced sentence since perjury can carry a prison term of up to seven years. In June 1999, Aitken, already declared bankrupt, was given two concurrent jail sentences of 18 months for perjury and perverting the course of justice.

As a forlorn Aitken exited the court, he was left to reflect that he could have settled the whole matter quietly in the spring of 1997. For the *Guardian* had agreed on a compromise deal whereby Aitken would have been left with a dent in his bank balance but his reputation intact. Alan Rusbridger had proposed that both parties could pay their own costs – around £200,000 each – and come up with a statement for the day after the general election, which would have ensured limited media coverage. But when the offer was put to him, Aitken rejected it. He wanted his day in court because he thought he was untouchable, being blessed with the same arrogance as his hero, Richard Nixon. Aitken believed that Nixon should never have been 'hounded out' of office and was convinced that the same thing would never happen to him. It just goes to show that 'Tricky Dicky' wasn't necessarily the best role model.

Chapter 7

Miscarriages of Justice

Stefan Kiszko: The Gentle Giant

To the east of Greater Manchester lie the Pennine moors – a bleak, sinister landscape stretching for miles, broken only by the occasional dwelling or the few roads which link Yorkshire and Lancashire. It was on Saddleworth Moor, high above Oldham, that Ian Brady and Myra Hindley buried the bodies of their child victims in the 1960s. A decade on, in 1975, and some eight miles to the north on Rishworth Moor, the Pennines once again became the centre of a child murder investigation.

It was early on the morning of 8 October 1975 that David Greenwell, a joiner from Nottingham, having spent the night in his car parked in a lay-by on the A672 Oldham-to-Halifax road outside Ripponden to save the cost of lodgings, spotted something blue flapping in the chill wind on the slopes above him. Gingerly he approached what appeared to be a bundle of clothing, only to discover, to his horror, that it was wrapped around a child's body lying face down. The blue raincoat had belonged to 11-year-old Lesley Molseed who had not been seen for three days since setting off from her Rochdale home on a lunchtime shopping errand for her mother. She had been stabbed 12 times in the chest and neck with a small knife. Her killer had then wiped the bloody blade on her thigh. Although she was fully dressed and had not been raped, there were semen stains on her clothing.

The murder of a child naturally provokes strong emotions in public and police alike. There is enormous pressure on the police to catch the killer before he or she has the opportunity to strike again. Less than three months after the gruesome discovery up on Rishworth Moor, the authorities were certain that they had tracked down Lesley Molseed's killer. His name was Stefan Kiszko and he would go on to serve 16 years in prison – for a crime he did not commit. And to make matters worse, vital police evidence which would have proved his innocence at the time was never revealed in court.

Stefan Kiszko was born in Rochdale in 1952, an only child. His parents had fled Eastern Europe at the end of the Second World War and had arrived in Britain as refugees. His mother Charlotte worked as a spinner at a cotton mill and his father Ivan laid roads. Stefan was a gentle giant who would grow to reach 6 ft 2 in and weigh 18 stone but his size and somewhat timid nature made him the victim of bullies at school. He left school in 1968 and, after taking a one-year commercial course at Rochdale College, found a job as a clerk with the Inland Revenue.

Then in 1970 Stefan Kiszko's world was shattered by the death of his father. Stefan grew wholly reliant on his mother who, in turn, smothered him with affection. He became the archetypal 'mummy's boy'. In truth, his mother was his only friend. Girls were not interested in this awkward, lumbering loner who had a curious high-pitched voice and was the only man at the tax office who didn't shave, while the local children jeered at him rather than talked to him. To them, he was a ridiculously comic character, a freak of nature.

Although Stefan Kiszko was intelligent, he was woefully immature and his health began to give cause for concern. In August 1975, he was treated at Rochdale Infirmary after injuring his ankle. A consultant there became worried that Kiszko was anaemic and he was given a massive blood transfusion. At first, it was thought that he might have been suffering from leukaemia but instead he was found to be severely hypogonadal – an under-development of the sexual organs. His penis was abnormally small and his testicles had not developed properly. To remedy the condition, he was given a series of testosterone injections. A few weeks later, Lesley Molseed was murdered.

There was no reason for the police to suspect Stefan Kiszko's involvement in the terrible crime. He had never been in trouble with the law and was known as someone who wouldn't hurt a fly. But on the two days immediately prior to Lesley's disappearance, a number of young girls in the area had reported that a man had indecently exposed himself to them. Clearly this was something which might have had a bearing on the case although at least three of the complainants later admitted that there hadn't been a 'flasher' at all – they had simply wanted a bit of attention. On the night of 5 November, another girl who had reported a flasher took her mother to Stefan Kiszko's house and identified him as the culprit.

The police brought him in for questioning and he was vague about his movements around the time of Lesley's disappearance. Officers also noted that he did not seem particularly surprised when the line of questioning progressed from acts of indecency to murder. With no other lead despite an enormous public response, the police decided to home in on Stefan Kiszko and took him in for further questioning four days before Christmas.

At first the questioning centred around the indecent exposures. Kiszko, who did not have a solicitor present, began by denying the allegations, saying: 'I couldn't do anything like that. That's why I'm having these injections.' He explained that he was having treatment because he didn't 'fancy girls' and that the injections were to 'bring me on'. This was of immediate interest to the police. The semen stains on Lesley's body had indicated that her killer had a low sperm count and now here was Kiszko admitting that he was having treatment for impotence.

As the interrogation wore on, Stefan Kiszko's answers became more damning. Tired and emotional, he confessed to indecent exposure on 4 October and to having sexual urges when he saw girls. He even confessed to exposing himself to girls on 3 October – the incidents which the girl 'victims' would later admit were entirely fictitious. Whether these confessions were the result of fatigue, the testosterone injections and the dramatic effects they were having on his body, or simply his immaturity, will never be known. Maybe it made him feel like a real man.

On the morning of 22 December, by which time he had been held in custody for over 24 hours, Kiszko asked when he could go home and then suddenly confessed to the killing of Lesley Molseed. In front of three officers, he allegedly dictated a seven-page statement which included crucial information about the murder, such as the semen stains found on her and how the blade of the knife had been wiped on the body. Kiszko signed the statement at 5.35 p.m. Only then was a solicitor hired to represent him.

Kiszko immediately told his solicitor that he had only confessed so that he could go home to his mother. He then made a second statement in which he denied murdering Lesley. Stefan Kiszko was scared and confused.

In the meantime the police found two small knives in Stefan's bedroom and in his car they discovered what they took to be child-abducting equipment – a hooded parka coat, industrial gloves, sweets and balloons. They also found a number of soft porn magazines. Kiszko was examined by police surgeon Dr Edward Tierney who, as well as taking various tissue, hair and blood samples, also took a semen sample. The result of this sample would undoubtedly have led to Stefan Kiszko's acquittal but for some inexplicable reason, it did not come to light for another 16 years.

Stefan Kiszko stood trial for the murder of Lesley Molseed at Leeds Crown Court in July 1976 and pleaded not guilty. His lawyer was David Waddington, QC, later to rise to the rank of Home Secretary. Prosecuting counsel Peter Taylor, QC, outlined the details of Kiszko's testosterone treatment, claiming that the defendant had developed a sudden sex urge after receiving the injections. 'It was manifested in relation apparently to young girls. He indulged in such behaviour over three days, culminating in the abduction and killing of Lesley.' The mother of the girl to whom Kiszko was said to have exposed himself on 4 October picked him out in court as the man her daughter had held responsible a month later.

The jury heard how, after making one confession and then retracting it, Kiszko made another admission. According to Det. Supt. Dick Holland, Kiszko said: 'I have told you the truth. I remember the girl by the shop in Broad Lane and taking her to the moors. I must have stabbed her.' Yet this alleged confession was apparently never entered as a formal signed statement. The court was also told that on the night of 23 December, Kiszko was driven across the moors to Halifax magistrates' court by Det. Supt. Holland and Det. Sgt. John Akeroyd. They claimed that when they stopped at the murder site, Kiszko started to shake and said he could hear voices. Det. Sgt. Akeroyd said that Kiszko was extremely upset.

Forensic scientist Ronald Outteridge revealed how fibres on the dead girl's clothing were similar to those from a piece of carpet found in Kiszko's car but, as the judge, Mr Justice Park, later pointed out, carpet can be commonplace and a fibre of wool hardly amounts to a fingerprint. As for the semen stains, they were mentioned by the prosecution purely to establish a sexual motive for the murder. With the technology available at the time, there was insufficient semen to enable the killer's blood group to be identified.

Much of the prosecution case revolved around Stefan Kiszko's new-found sex drive. The jury heard how he had been given his second injection on Friday, 3 October, immediately prior to what was said to be his campaign of indecent exposure, followed by murder. The police surgeon, Dr Tierney, told the court that after the testosterone treatment, Kiszko's facial and pubic hair had developed quite rapidly and how, from never having to shave, he had to shave every other day. Dr Barry Enoch, a consultant physician specializing in glandular disorders, testified that the injections would not have made the recipient more interested in children and would not on their own have led to the murder. And they certainly would not have resulted in a previously mild-mannered man such as Stefan Kiszko stabbing a girl 12 times in an orgy of violence. Anyway, he said, the dose given to Stefan Kiszko was relatively modest. But Dr Enoch agreed that it was possible for the drug to give someone a sex drive and at the same time make him feel inhibited about normal sexual contact because his sexual equipment was still inadequate. He added that it was quite common for this feeling to result in masturbation, pornography or the use of sex magazines rather than seeking sexual contact.

Stefan Kiszko's defence was that he had been at home with his mother on the Sunday lunchtime when Lesley Molseed had been abducted and had later visited his father's grave with his mother and his aunt Alfreda. He said that the only reason he had confessed to the murder in his first statement – the statement he immediately retracted once he had been given a solicitor – was because he had been terrified of Det. Supt. Holland who, he claimed, had threatened to beat him up. He went on to add that he had known nothing about the precise details of the murder until the police had described them to him and put the so-called confession in his mouth.

But although Kiszko had pleaded not guilty, David Waddington did not want to take any chances and, to this end, introduced a safety net of a defence of diminished responsibility. If this were proved and the defendant found guilty, he would be convicted of manslaughter rather than murder. However, the two lines of defence – one that Kiszko was entirely innocent, the other that if he had killed, it had been while his mind was impaired – were uneasy bedfellows and arguably did nothing to help his cause. Waddington did actually try to persuade his client to plead guilty on the grounds of diminished responsibility, but Kiszko wouldn't hear of it and insisted that he was innocent.

The key witness in helping to establish the line of diminished responsibility was forensic psychiatrist Dr Michael Tarsh. Asked to assess Stefan Kiszko's lifestyle, Dr Tarsh said that the defendant was extremely close to both his mother and his aunt and that he had no real acquaintances outside his immediate family. In fact, said Dr Tarsh, 'he led a rather drab sort of life. I think his motor car was almost like his private temple. It really meant an enormous amount to him that he could drive around, sit in it and could read magazines in it, that he could take his mother and aunt out. It was a very big thing in his life. So far as I know he had never had a friend, male or female, and apart from one or two Ukranian parties and one or two office parties, he had never been anywhere or done anything. I think he just about managed to exchange a kiss once at an office party, but otherwise he had no contact with young people at all. His sexual interest seemed to have been briefly aroused when he was 17 or 18 and he was able to masturbate. He was able to use the "Men only" type of magazine as a stimulus but then it became largely dormant by the time he was 19.

'I see him emotionally like an 11- or 12-year-old, dependent on his mother, dependent on home, friendless, not having learned to cope with the normal relationships and difficulties people go through in puberty. I think of him as a fat, socially withdrawn, socially inept, mother-fixated, unhappy person.'

Dr Tarsh was then asked by the defence under what circumstances Stefan Kiszko might have approached an 11-year-old girl whom he did not know. The expert replied that there would have had to be the rare and unusual combination of vulnerable personality, physical well-being and profound sexual stimulation. 'I don't think he would be able to control the sexual stimulation. If you take ordinary young people and give them testosterone, it doesn't make them aggressive or unable to control themselves. But this is like taking a boy of 11 with the social expectations of 25, who doesn't know how to deal with it, and expecting him to deal with it.'

'Assuming that he killed,' pressed David Waddington, 'do you think he would be fully responsible for what he did?'

'No,' answered Dr Tarsh. 'I would have considered him to be in this state of sexual exultation which first led him to approach the child. I would speculate some sort of rejection or fighting, or words on behalf of the little girl, which would have been the trigger to prompt this frenzied outburst, which clearly there was. The child has signed her own death warrant. The child has said something like, "You are a dirty old man" or "You ought to be locked up". I think he would become uncontrollably angry. If he did this under the circumstances which I have suggested, then I must find that he was unable emotionally to resist these destructive impulses and his level of control of himself was diminished, and diminished a lot.'

So Kiszko's defence lawyer had succeeded in establishing a case for diminished responsibility, but at what cost? The expert evidence that Kiszko might have become 'uncontrollably angry' had sent the message to the jury that, despite his previous gentle nature, the course of injections could have rendered him dangerous, maybe even to the point of killing.

In his summing-up, the judge told the jurors that, if they found the defendant guilty of killing Lesley Molseed, they could consider verdicts of either murder or manslaughter on the grounds of diminished responsibility because of an abnormality of mind. He went on: 'This was a crime against an innocent defenceless child of the utmost brutality and, in the course of his evidence in the witness box, the defendant may have revealed himself to you as untruthful, dishonest, perhaps cunning. Yet there is no question at all that up to the time of his treatment in hospital, being a man in name only, stunted in physique and in the development of his personality, he had never done anything wrong.'

After five and a half hours' deliberation, the jury found Stefan Kiszko guilty of murder by a 10–2 majority. He was sentenced to life imprisonment. With words which would have a hollow ring to them 16 years on, Mr Justice Park heaped fulsome praise on the police investigation headed by Det. Chief Supt. Jack Dibb and Det. Supt. Dick Holland. 'I don't want to part with this case,' said the judge, 'without expressing on behalf of the public our gratitude to the members of the police forces concerned for their great skill, dedication, and duty in sifting the mass of material they had to sift in this case and for their great skill in bringing to justice the person responsible for this dreadful crime.'

As a convicted child-killer, Stefan Kiszko was seen as the lowest form of prison life, a natural target for his fellow inmates. A month after being sentenced, he was transferred from Armley Prison, near Leeds, to high-security Wakefield Prison. On his first night there, he was beaten up by six prisoners. For his own protection, he was placed in solitary confinement but that measure failed to prevent further attacks. In May 1977, he was left needing 17 stitches to a head wound following another vicious assault. At the same time, as a result of being wrongfully imprisoned, his mental health started to deteriorate and he was put on tranquillizers. He grew steadily worse and, in 1982, by which time he had been transferred to Gloucester Prison, he was described by a prison welfare officer as 'quite mad'. He continued to protest his innocence but these were increasingly seen as the ravings of a madman.

Two people who never lost faith were his mother and aunt. Charlotte Kiszko, too, was suffering her fair share of illness, in the form of a chronic lung disease, but she was a fighter and from the outset vowed to clear her son's name. She began by contacting her local MP, the colourful Cyril Smith, but he felt that the case against her son was too strong. She pushed for an appeal which was finally heard – and rejected – in 1978. Even though the years passed and her son's condition grew worse – at one point he even accused her of being one of the people keeping him locked up – she never gave up hope that she would one day prove his innocence. It seemed that the police, politicians and the legal system were all against her until she finally found a sympathetic solicitor, Campbell Malone.

No sooner had he finished preparing a petition for a reappraisal of the case which, among other things, was highly critical of David Waddington's defence strategy back in 1976 than Campbell Malone heard that the same David Waddington had been appointed Home Secretary. The petition was delivered to the Home Office in June 1990 but no reply was received for five months. And even then it was decidedly non-committal. So Malone pushed a little harder, suggesting that the Home Secretary's own previous involvement in the case was a factor behind the slow progress. Nine days later, he was informed that the police had been asked to look into Stefan Kiszko's conviction.

The job fell to Det. Supt. Trevor Wilkinson of West Yorkshire Police who set about re-examining the forensic evidence from the case. At the forensic science laboratory in Wetherby, he looked into the records on Lesley Molseed and came across a hand-written note which said that the semen stains on Lesley's clothes had contained sperm. But Stefan Kiszko was sterile and would never be able to produce sperm. So the semen on the girl's body could not possibly have come from Kiszko. Mysteriously, the five slides containing all the semen samples from Lesley's clothing had vanished.

The discrepancy between Kiszko's semen sample and that on the body of Lesley Molseed was never revealed to the defence at the time of the trial. Fortunately, police surgeon Dr Tierney had kept his original notes which confirmed that Det. Chief Supt. Jack Dibb – head of the murder inquiry – had been aware of the tests. Had the results been deliberately suppressed by the police for fear of wrecking the case against Stefan Kiszko? With Jack Dibb now dead, it is a question which will probably never be answered.

The new evidence secured Stefan Kiszko's release. On 18 February 1992, the Court of Appeal quashed his conviction for the murder of Lesley Molseed. 'The years in prison were a nightmare and a hell, to be honest,' he told reporters. 'This is because of the way you are treated if you are a prisoner for that nature of offence. While in prison, I had not been able to draw the strength from within myself. Other prisoners called me all sorts of names, but I always believed in my own innocence. I didn't lose faith that I would be acquitted. I always believed the courts would come on my side.'

He was less charitable towards the police. 'They just wanted somebody to go down as a mug in this case. In a way I was framed because the detectives said: "Just get it wrapped up for Christmas and end it some way or other."'

He went on to repeat his claim that police officers handed him a pre-written statement in which he confessed to the murder. He said the investigating officer read it to him and told him to sign it. 'I just signed it any old way. I was under the impression these officers were going to hit me or do something violent. They were very tall and very strong. I feel angry towards the police because of the way they handled all this. They should never have arrested me.'

On a happier note, he hugged his mother and said how much he was looking forward to being at home with her.

Their happiness was to be short-lived. On the night of 21 December 1993 – 18 years to the day when he was led away by detectives – Stefan Kiszko died of heart failure. He was 41. Six months later, Charlotte Kiszko, having never recovered from the loss of her beloved son, also died – a tragic end to a tragic case.

Charles Stielow: Forty Minutes From Death

Charles B. Phelps was a wealthy, elderly farmer who lived with his devoted housekeeper Margaret Wolcott at an isolated house near West Shelby in Orleans County, New York. On the night of Sunday, 21 March 1915, the pair were shot dead during a robbery. The finger of suspicion pointed at Charles Stielow and his brother-in-law, Nelson Green, two poorly educated, hard-up farm-hands who lived near Phelps and sometimes used to work for him, but there appeared to be insufficient evidence to get the case to stick.

So Orleans County hired a private detective, George Newton, in the hope that he would be able to obtain something more incriminating. Newton soon came up trumps, producing a confession in which Stielow admitted his part in the robbery but said that Green had done the shooting. At their trials in July 1915, Stielow was convicted of first-degree murder and Green then pleaded guilty to second-degree murder in order to save his skin. Sure enough, Green got off comparatively lightly with 20 years in prison while Stielow was condemned to die in the electric chair and was sent to Sing Sing to await execution.

In the death house at Sing Sing, Stielow started to claim that he had been tricked into making the confession and that he was really innocent. Such protestations are hardly rare among prisoners about to face the electric chair but Spencer Miller Jr, the Deputy Warden of Sing Sing, was impressed by Stielow's statements and launched an investigation. Miller was particularly puzzled by the scholarly nature of Stielow's supposed confession – remarkable in view of the fact that Stielow was unable to read or write. It was quickly apparent that the confession he was alleged to have authenticated contained words not in his limited vocabulary and phrases beyond his comprehension. Furthermore, it was rumoured that the detectives responsible for Stielow's arrest and conviction had been handsomely rewarded by Orleans County. On the strength of the doubts about the authenticity of the confession, State Governor Whitman granted no fewer than three reprieves, sparing Stielow from the electric chair.

As part of the campaign to free Stielow, his supporters brought new evidence before the Supreme Court in July 1916. They realized that if they could discredit private detective George Newton, they might be able to prove Stielow's innocence. If the tape recorder had been invented, Stielow would have been a free man but, without such technology, they had to rely on making a dictaphone record of a conversation which had apparently been overheard between Newton and a New York detective and in which Newton supposedly boasted of illegally extracting the confession from Stielow. But all the record could offer was other people's voices recreating the conversation which had allegedly taken place between the two detectives. Every word could have been invented, as the judge was quick to point out when he rejected the fresh evidence as hearsay. On 26 July, the judge turned down the appeal for a new trial and ordered that Stielow be executed three days later, at 6 a.m.

After cheating death three times, it looked as if the fates would finally catch up with Charles Stielow on this occasion. But his supporters were not about to give up without a fight. They headed for New York City and at one o'clock on the morning of 29 July (five hours before the time of execution), they took the unprecedented step of waking up Justice Charles Guy at his home in Convent Avenue and asked him to consider the evidence in the Stielow case.

The vast majority of judges would have taken a dim view of being roused in the middle of the night but Justice Guy did not seem to mind at all and pored over the pile of affidavits as promised. But by 5 a.m. – one hour before Stielow was due to die – he realized that the volume of paperwork was such that he would not have time to go everything in sufficient detail. Nevertheless he could see from what he had read already that Stielow's campaigners had the basis of a good case and so he telephoned through to Sing Sing to say that he was issuing a writ postponing the execution until 11 p.m. The phone message reached Sing Sing just 40 minutes before Stielow was due to walk to the chair. He had already been sent to the execution chamber to prepare for the end. In those primitive days of telephone communications, it would only have needed a minor storm to pull down the lines with the result that the message would not have got through. The weather, at least, was on Charles Stielow's side.

Having finished reading through the statements relating to the case, Justice Guy was satisfied that Stielow should be spared for the time being. Even so, the car taking the judge's official order broke down on the way to Sing Sing and did not arrive until 10 p.m. – only an hour before the postponed execution. Stielow was living dangerously.

The following month, a junk dealer by the name of Erwin King was charged with a separate robbery – a crime for which his accomplice, Clarence O'Connell, was already serving time. The word was that King had been in the vicinity of the Phelps residence on the day of the murder so an undercover detective, Thomas Fogarty, was put in jail with King to see whether the latter would incriminate himself. Fogarty managed to win King's confidence to the extent that King confessed to the Phelps robbery but insisted that O'Connell had been the gunman. However, O'Connell denied any part in the Phelps raid and King quickly withdrew his confession. With it went Charles Stielow's hopes of a retrial.

Yet again Stielow was left to contemplate imminent death. The latest execution date was 11 December but, after more appeals, the Governor decided on 3 December to commute the sentence to life imprisonment.

The battle to free Stielow continued and 17 months later the case was reviewed by a special commission. On 8 May 1918, the commission declared Charles Stielow innocent of all charges and he was finally allowed to walk free from Sing Sing.

Oscar Slater: A Victim of Character Assassination

On 21 December 1908, Marion Gilchrist, a wealthy spinster of 82, sent her servant, Helen Lambie, out to buy a Glasgow evening newspaper. She was away for some ten minutes and, on her return, she saw a neighbour, Arthur Adams, standing outside the door to Miss Gilchrist's flat. He said that he had been disturbed by a noise from within. As Helen Lambie entered the flat, a man emerged and walked calmly past her and Adams. Making his exit, the stranger also passed 14-year-old Mary Barrowman. Inside the flat, Helen Lambie found the body of Miss Gilchrist lying by the fireplace. She had been savagely attacked. Curiously, although the dead woman was known to have had jewellery worth several thousand pounds hidden in her flat, the only item which seemed to be missing was a diamond brooch in the shape of a crescent. On the evening of Christmas Day, a bicycle dealer informed the Glasgow police that a German Jew, under the assumed name of Oscar Slater, had been trying to sell a pawn ticket for a diamond brooch. On making further inquiries, the police were confident that they had got Miss Gilchrist's murderer when in fact Slater's only crime was to lead a somewhat shady lifestyle and to be a stranger in a foreign land.

It has to be said that the first signs were encouraging for the police. Thirty-seven-year-old Slater (his real name was Leschziner) did seem to bear an approximate resemblance to the description of the man seen leaving Miss Gilchrist's flat and the pawned brooch was roughly the same value as the missing one. Even more promising was that when officers raided the lodgings where Slater lived with his mistress, they discovered that the couple had left Glasgow by train, bound for Liverpool from where, on 26 December, they had sailed on the *Lusitania* to New York under the name of Mr and Mrs Otto Sando. Fleeing to the United States under an assumed name appeared to be the action of a guilty man. So when Slater reached New York, he was immediately arrested and his seven trunks of luggage were impounded.

But no sooner had it been built than the police case started to fall apart. The pawn ticket was found on Slater and the brooch recovered, but Slater had pawned it a month before Miss Gilchrist's murder. And anyway, it wasn't even the deceased's brooch. It was one which Slater had owned for years and had frequently pawned in the past. Thus the most crucial piece of evidence against Slater had evaporated overnight. However the police were not to be deterred and two officers from Glasgow, accompanied by the three witnesses – Adams, Lambie and Barrowman – set sail for New York. The police hoped that the witnesses would identify Slater as the man they had seen leaving the flat on the evening of the murder so that he could be extradited and brought back to Scotland to stand trial. All three affirmed that Slater was very like the man they had seen but it later transpired that both Adams and Barrowman had been shown photographs of Slater before attending the identification parade! Also, while they were waiting in the corridor beforehand, he had actually been led past them and was obviously the prisoner. The whole thing was a farce, although for Oscar Slater it was to prove no laughing matter.

The police were determined to forge ahead and the matter of extradition was resolved by the accused's willingness to return to Britain to face trial. On 21 February 1909 he was back in Glasgow.

By then, the rest of the case against Oscar Slater had all but disintegrated. Even if they were to forget about the brooch and the dubious witness identifications – and they were not about to – the police reckoned that Slater's flight from Scotland was proof enough of his guilt. Yet in the Bohemian clubs which he frequented it was widely known that Slater was planning to emigrate to the United States around the turn of the year. His departure date had originally been scheduled for 1 January but his mistress and their servant testified that he had received two letters on the morning of 21 December one from a Mr Rogers, a friend of Slater's in London, telling him that Slater's wife was pestering him for money, and the other from a Mr Devoto, a former business associate, asking Slater to join him in San Francisco. For some reason, neither of these letters were produced in court nor did the prosecution or defence attempt to disprove or verify their existence even though they offered a perfectly reasonable explanation as to why Slater had brought forward his departure date to 26 December. Not only were the police conspiring against Slater but his own lawyers were proving hopelessly inadequate.

The police had also failed to unearth anything remotely incriminating from their search of Slater's luggage. Three hats were found, but none which corresponded with the one which the three witnesses had claimed to have seen on the head of the killer. A light-coloured raincoat was discovered among Slater's possessions but there was no evidence of blood in the pockets. Since the murder weapon was not found at the scene of the crime, the culprit must have taken it away with him. The witnesses did not report seeing such an implement so it is not unreasonable to assume that it was secreted in his pockets. The murder being a particularly violent one, there would have been significant traces of blood, yet there was none. Similarly, no credible murder weapon was discovered in the seven trunks. A hammer was found but, in the words of Sir Arthur Conan Doyle, who campaigned for Slater's innocence: 'It was an extremely light and fragile instrument, and utterly incapable in the eyes of commonsense of inflicting those terrific injuries which had shattered the old lady's skull. It was said by the prosecution to bear some marks of having been scraped or cleaned, but this was vigorously denied by the defence, and the police do not appear to have pushed the matter to the obvious test of removing the metal work, when they must, had this been indeed the weapon, have certainly found some soakage of blood into the wood under the edges of the iron cheeks or head.'

Oscar Slater's trial began at the High Court in Edinburgh on 3 May. Helen Lambie stuck doggedly to her evidence despite outrageous discrepancies, while Arthur Adams insisted that Slater 'closely resembled' the man he had seen. In effect, their descriptions were simply of an odd-looking foreigner. Another witness, Mrs Liddell, a member of the

Adams household, positively identified a man she had seen loitering in the street a few minutes before the murder as being Slater. Yet closer examination of her testimony reveals that, when first confronted with the defendant at an identification parade, she said that he 'slightly' resembled the man she had seen. She subsequently claimed to be certain that it was Slater and maintained that she had a clear view of his face, even though she refused to commit herself as to whether or not the man in the street was clean-shaven and her description of his clothing differed greatly from that given as the murderer's.

Both Slater's mistress and his servant stated quite definitely that the defendant was at home shortly after seven o'clock on the evening of the murder. Miss Gilchrist was beaten to death around 7 p.m. but the distance to Slater's flat was such that, if he had been the killer, he could not possibly have arrived home until 7.30 p.m. at the earliest. Even allowing for the fact that his mistress might have been prepared to lie to save his skin, there was no reason for his servant to have done so, particularly since he had recently given her notice to quit. In spite of this evidence, the Lord Advocate told the jury: 'The prisoner is hopelessly unable to produce a single witness who says that he was anywhere else than at the scene of the murder that night.'

The prosecution also presented as fact the supposition that the murder weapon was a small hammer, thereby further linking the killing to Slater. In truth, the wounds on the victim could have been inflicted by a variety of instruments, including a burglar's jemmy. He also suggested that because Slater dealt in precious stones – he made his money by peddling jewellery – he would have been able to dispose of the proceeds from a robbery. The criminal, added the prosecution, was clearly someone unfamiliar with the layout of the house and who did not know where Miss Gilchrist kept her jewels. 'That answers to the prisoner,' trumpeted the Lord Advocate, perhaps unaware that the description also fitted 99.9 per cent of the population of Scotland. And in spite of his promises to the contrary, the Lord Advocate never did show how Slater was supposed to have known about the presence of Miss Gilchrist's collection of jewels.

The only area in which the prosecution was on fairly safe ground was that of blackening Slater's character. There is little doubt that he was a decidedly unscrupulous character – a habitual liar who repeatedly changed his name, who most probably lived off immoral earnings and who was considerably in debt. However, he had no criminal record and using aliases and being in debt did not make him a murderer. The judge, Lord Guthrie, appeared perfectly happy to allow the prosecution to assassinate Slater's character without even offering the mildest rebuke. The prosecution case was, at best, flimsy and was based upon the wild coincidence that the man who had been erroneously linked with the missing brooch had still turned out to be the murderer after all. The Lord Advocate left no room for doubt and wound up his closing speech with the words: 'My submission to you is that his guilt has been brought fairly home to him, that no shadow of doubt exists, that there is no reasonable doubt that he was the perpetrator of this foul murder.'

If Slater had been as well served by the defence as the police were by the Lord Advocate, he might well have got off. However, Slater's lawyer, Mr McClure, did not go in for dramatic rhetoric but preferred to let the evidence speak for itself quietly. Indeed, it was so quiet that it was obviously inaudible to the jury. He pointed out how it had always been the defendant's intention to travel to America and how, the day after the murder, Slater had told witnesses of his travel plans, even to the point of revealing his sailing time and port of departure. As Mr McClure said, these were hardly the deeds of a fugitive from justice. Furthermore, the defence reminded the jury that Slater had continued to wear the clothes in which he was supposed to have committed the murder for the rest of that evening – again, hardly likely considering the killer would have been heavily blood-stained. But McClure failed to expose other glaring holes in the Crown case which had offered no explanation as to how Slater had known about the existence of Miss Gilchrist's jewels, had broken into her flat or disposed of the missing brooch. Slater's lawyer also omitted to press home to the jury the fact that his client had returned voluntarily to Britain to stand trial and had not simply been forced back by the process of extradition. Worse still, McClure refused to put Slater into the witness box. Slater, who apparently spoke broken but quite intelligible English, was keen to give evidence but, for some reason best known to himself, McClure kept him under wraps. The decision sent out nothing but negative signals to the jury, who assumed that the defendant must have had something to hide. Indeed, McClure's only attempt to show that his client wasn't quite the blackguard portrayed by the prosecution was to reveal how one of his last deeds before leaving Glasgow for America had been to go to the trouble of obtaining an English £5 note to send to his parents in Germany as a Christmas present. The message was that anyone who cared so much for his parents could not be all bad.

But the message did not seem to convey itself to Lord Guthrie who, in his summing up, was highly scathing about Slater's character. Perhaps this influenced the jury as, after just 70 minutes' deliberation, they returned a verdict of guilty. Of the 15 jurors, it subsequently emerged that nine had found Slater 'guilty', one had found him not guilty and five were for 'not proven'. Under English law at that time, a new trial would have been needed, but under Scottish law the majority verdict was acceptable.

Slater was horrified. 'I know nothing about the affair, absolutely nothing,' he cried. 'I never heard the name. I know nothing about the affair. I do not know how I could be connected with the affair. I know nothing about it. I came from America on my own account.'

Slater was duly sentenced to death but a petition signed by 22,000 members of the public who sympathized with Slater's plight saw the sentence reduced to life imprisonment just a day before the intended execution.

Sir Arthur Conan Doyle felt so strongly about the case that he was determined to clear Slater's name. He received invaluable assistance from John Trench, a Glasgow police officer who had worked on the Slater investigation. Trench revealed that, shortly after the discovery of Miss Gilchrist's body, Helen Lambie had told senior officers that she actually knew the man whom she saw leaving the flat. Far from being a sinister-looking stranger, he was a regular visitor to Miss Gilchrist's flat – Dr Francis James Charteris. Yet the police had decided to ignore this obvious line of inquiry, preferring to pursue a lowly foreigner rather than a respected local medic. According to John Trench, they had virtually dictated Lambie's written statement.

By 1927, Oscar Slater had languished in Peterhead jail for 18 years. That year, Lambie, then living in America, confirmed John Trench's version of events. This led to renewed interest in the case, as a result of which Mary Barrowman also back-pedalled on much of her evidence. Within two weeks, Slater was freed but without any official declaration that he had been wrongly convicted. So Conan Doyle organized an appeal which Lambie refused to attend. As a result of the appeal, Slater was awarded £6000 in compensation and the guilty verdict was set aside on the grounds that the judge had misdirected the jury. Oscar Slater died in 1948.

Isidore Zimmerman: Too Little, Too Late

The story of Isidore Zimmerman is a roller-coaster ride of human emotions. Convicted for a crime of which he was innocent, he was just two hours from being executed when his sentence was commuted to life imprisonment. He spent another 23 tortuous years in jail before finally being freed. For the next 21 years, he pressed the US government for compensation, to which he was undoubtedly entitled. Eventually he was awarded $1 million, of which two-thirds was immediately swallowed up in legal fees. Three and a half months later he died of a heart attack.

For the first 20 years of his life, Isidore Zimmerman had made no headlines whatsoever but all that changed on 10 April 1937 when there was a hold-up at the Café Boulevard at 144 Second Avenue on Manhattan's Lower East Side. In the course of the robbery, police officer Michael Foley was shot dead.

Six men were arrested and two more, apparently to conceal their own involvement in the crime, falsely accused Zimmerman of supplying weapons to the gang. Zimmerman was one of seven charged with first-degree murder. He pleaded 'not guilty' and at the trial, which featured 12 defence attorneys and 84 witnesses, he hardly warranted a mention. Nevertheless he was found guilty and sentenced to death.

Little did Zimmerman know but he would turn out to be the lucky one. Of the other six defendants, five died in the electric chair and one in jail. Zimmerman himself spent nine months on death row and, on 26 January 1939, ate what he thought was his last meal, had his head shaved and said goodbye to his family. But two hours before he was due to be electrocuted, he learned that Governor Herbert Lehman had commuted his sentence to life imprisonment on the grounds that he had been convicted largely on the testimony of two accomplices who, in return for their help, hadn't even been indicted.

Zimmerman continued to protest his innocence from behind bars but his pleas did not go down well either with the authorities or his fellow inmates. He would later claim that his ordeal in prison included severe beatings, long periods of solitary confinement in 'strip cells' and diets of bread and water. He was considered a nuisance.

There were times when Zimmerman felt like giving up but he galvanized himself into further bouts of letter-writing, not knowing whether the letters would actually be delivered. Among those to whom he wrote was lawyer Maurice Edelbaum, who was so impressed by Zimmerman's plausibility and by the fact that he seemed to have a genuine grievance that he agreed to take on the case without a fee. This for a lawyer is the supreme sacrifice.

At last, in 1962, Zimmerman won the right to a new trial and the State Court of Appeals overturned his conviction. The reason given was that a prosecutor in the office of Thomas E. Dewey, the Manhattan District Attorney, had deliberately used perjured testimony and had suppressed evidence which might have proved Zimmerman's innocence. 'I feel like I'm back from the grave,' said Zimmerman on his release. 'I wrote a million letters and tried a million actions but nothing happened till Mr Edelbaum came into the picture.'

After everything he had been through, Zimmerman thought he was entitled to compensation. He wanted $10 million to make up for the traumas he had endured during 24 years in jail for a crime he hadn't committed, but the process became bogged down as the government baulked at paying out such a sum. Finally, on 30 June 1983, 66-year-old Zimmerman was awarded $1 million, reduced to $660,000 after expenses. Zimmerman could not conceal his disappointment, stating that he was 'very unhappy' that the judge had rejected his claim for $10 million. 'I should have gotten much more,' he said, 'because what I sacrificed can never be replaced.'

He never had the chance to spend it. In October, less than four months after the belated award, Isidore Zimmerman died of a heart attack at his home in Queens – the final twist on the roller-coaster ride.

Sacco and Vanzetti: The Jury is Still Out

Few cases have stimulated as much debate within American legal circles as that of Nicola Sacco and Bartolomeo Vanzetti, two Italian immigrants executed in 1927 for killing a cashier and a guard in the course of a payroll robbery. Over the past 72 years, their innocence has been championed by numerous individuals who claim that Sacco and Vanzetti were convicted because of their background and anarchist leanings rather than on the basis of any firm evidence against them. Books still appear on the subject on a regular basis, each offering the final solution, yet rarely agreeing on a verdict. To this day, nobody has been able to prove conclusively whether or not Sacco and Vanzetti were guilty or whether they were the victims of a gross miscarriage of justice.

The period around the end of the First World War was a troubled time in American history, which saw intense political repression of foreign-born radicals. The purge was known as the 'Red Scare'. The authorities clamped down hard on anarchist militants, particularly any supporters of Luigi Galleani's Italian language journal, *Cronaca Sovversiva*, the most influential anarchist journal in the United States. The journal, notorious for its extreme views and its encouragement of violent revolution, had been forced to cease publication when the US government joined the Great War in 1917, on account of its hardline anti-war stance. Its editors were arrested and, when the war ended, deported to Italy. Between 1919 and 1920, the Red Scare was at its height. During this time, the US government's acts of repression – many of them illegal – prompted acts of retaliatory violence from the anarchists as the restored *Cronaca* whipped its readership into a revolutionary frenzy. Terrorist atrocities were rife and a former editor of the journal was strongly suspected of having blown himself up during an attempt on Attorney-General Palmer's home in Washington, DC, in June 1919. That particular terrorist act saw Congress vote funds for anti-radical investigations and launch the career of J. Edgar Hoover as the director of the General Intelligence Division in the Department of Justice. The Sacco–Vanzetti case would become one of Hoover's first major responsibilities.

Sacco, a shoemaker who had emigrated to the United States in 1908, and Vanzetti, a fish peddler, were known supporters of *Cronaca*. Although neither had a criminal record, they were thought to have been involved in industrial disruption, political agitation and anti-war propaganda. In short, as far as the US government was concerned, they were undesirable aliens.

At 3 p.m. on 15 April 1920, a cashier and a guard working for the Slater and Morrill Shoe Company were transferring $16,000 from one of the company's factories to another. Their journey took them along the main street of South Braintree, Massachusetts, a small industrial town to the south of Boston. Suddenly, two men standing by a fence drew guns and opened fire, fatally wounding both the cashier (Parmeneter) and the guard (Berardelli). As the employees were being gunned down, a car containing two or three more men pulled up. The gunmen snatched up the cash boxes, leaped into the car and made their getaway across railroad tracks. The car was found abandoned in woods two days later.

The raid bore many similarities to a robbery carried out in nearby Bridgewater on 24 December 1919. Both jobs featured a gang and a car and in both instances, eye-witnesses thought the culprits were Italians. In the Bridgewater robbery, the car had sped off towards Cochesett and so the police began concentrating their investigation on any Italian owning or driving a car in Cochesett. With motoring still in its infancy, the list was by no means long. They found a likely suspect in a man named Boda, whose car was in a garage awaiting repairs. The garage proprietor was told to inform the police as soon as anybody came to collect the car.

Boda happened to be a friend of Sacco and Vanzetti's and, like them, a foreign-born radical. But the trap set to ensnare Boda instead brought the police Sacco and Vanzetti when, on 5 May, they had the misfortune to collect his car. They were not under suspicion for the Braintree murders at first but since both men were carrying guns when arrested, officers began to question them further. In Sacco's pocket, they found a draft of a poster advertising a forthcoming anarchist meeting at which Vanzetti was to be the principal speaker. When the police started questioning the pair about their political tendencies, Sacco and Vanzetti became nervous. This was perfectly understandable, not only because of the general climate of the day in America but also because a colleague of theirs, Andrea Salsedo, had mysteriously died while being held by the Department of Justice. Against this backdrop of fear, Sacco and Vanzetti lied about their radical activities and their answers, although given in relation to questions about their politics rather than about the double murder, were used to incriminate them in the payroll robbery. As Robert D'Attilio, author of *Sacco–Vanzetti: Developments and Reconsiderations*, noted: 'These falsehoods created a "consciousness of guilt" in the minds of the authorities, but the implications of that phrase soon became a central issue in the Sacco–Vanzetti case. Did the lies of the two men signify criminal involvement in the Braintree murder and robbery, as the authorities claimed, or did they signify an understandable attempt to conceal their radicalism and protect their friends during a time of national hysteria concerning foreign-born radicals, as their supporters were to claim?'

Sacco and Vanzetti were initially charged with possessing firearms without permits. They were then questioned about the Bridgewater robbery. Sacco had a concrete alibi for the time of the hold-up and was not charged, but Vanzetti was. In the meantime, the police decided they also had enough evidence against the pair to charge them with the Braintree killings.

In a move contrary to the usual custom of Massachusetts courts, Vanzetti was tried first in the summer of 1920 on the less serious charge – the Bridgewater robbery. Although he too had a strong alibi supported by a number of witnesses, he soon knew he was fighting a losing battle. Most of his witnesses were Italian, who spoke poor English, and their testimony, given largely in translation, failed to convince the American jury. Vanzetti did not help his cause by refusing to take the stand to defend himself. His reluctance was due to the fact that he was terrified about having to reveal his radical activities, knowing full well that being found guilty of political extremism amounted to much the same as a conviction for robbery or murder in 1920. The jury took his silence to be an admission of guilt and he was given 15 years' imprisonment – a harsh sentence for a first offence in which nobody was actually hurt.

Being tried and convicted for a separate robbery beforehand clearly jeopardized Vanzetti's prospects in the murder trial. In such troubled times, it would be hard enough for him and Sacco to get a fair hearing anyway, but being found guilty of the Bridgewater robbery made it doubly difficult. The lack of trust placed by the jury in the Italian witnesses also indicated that there would be a mountain of hostility to overcome, a theory reinforced by the severity of the judge's sentence. Sacco and Vanzetti could not help thinking there was one law for Italian immigrants and another for Americans.

In the face of this, their supporters recognized the need for a fresh defence strategy at the murder trial. On the advice of militant anarchist Carlo Tresca, a new counsel was brought in – Fred H. Moore, a renowned socialist lawyer. Moore opted for a totally different approach, one which stretched beyond the question of robbery and murder. He wanted the jury – and the American nation as a whole – to see the wider picture, to recognise that the prosecution had a hidden motive. And that motive, claimed Moore, was to assist the federal and military authorities in suppressing the Italian anarchist movement, to which Sacco and Vanzetti belonged. Moore wanted the defendants to acknowledge their anarchism in court, not to try and hide it, and to show that their arrest and prosecution stemmed solely from their extremist tendencies rather than from any firm police evidence. The only reason they were on trial, contended Moore, was because they were Italian radicals.

Moore set about his task with a vengeance, organizing public meetings and distributing tens of thousands of pamphlets throughout the United States. He got in touch with international organizations, solicited the support of labour unions and generally tried to attract maximum publicity for the plight of Sacco and Vanzetti. He even tried to enlist the aid of the Italian government since the defendants were still, nominally at least, Italian citizens. Moore's aggressive campaign transformed what might otherwise have been yet another American murder trial into an international *cause célèbre*.

The first indication that it would require more than a smart defence lawyer to get the two men off the hook came with the realization that the trial judge was to be Judge Webster

Thayer, the same man who had punished Vanzetti so harshly for the Bridgewater robbery. Judge Thayer's impartiality was understandably called into question after he had referred to the defendants in court as 'anarchistic bastards'. The dice were stacked against them in every respect. The trial took place in May 1921 at Dedham in Norfolk County, a quiet residential area where citizens looked upon immigrants with suspicion. Most of the jury were selected by sheriff's deputies from Masonic gatherings and from people deemed by the deputies to be 'substantial' and 'intelligent'. They were unlikely to have much sympathy with extremists, especially Italian ones. Their mistrust of outsiders extended to Fred Moore, who hailed from the west.

Moore also succeeded in antagonizing the judge, who didn't seem to bat an eyelid when Sacco and Vanzetti were described in court as 'dagos' and 'sons of bitches'. Sacco and Vanzetti spoke only broken English and consequently misunderstood many of the questions put to them at the trial. Nor were they best served by an interpreter whose conduct was so dubious that the defendants eventually brought in their own interpreters to check his questions and answers.

The prosecution contended that Sacco did the shooting while Vanzetti was in the getaway car, the rest of the gang having remained at liberty. Five witnesses were trotted out to state that Sacco was one of the gunmen. The principal among these was Mary Splaine who worked in the shoe factory. Despite having only seen the gunman fleetingly and from a distance of 60 feet, amazingly she was able to recall his identity in precise detail 13 months after the shooting, right down to the shade of his eyebrows and the exact length of his hair. What made her powers of identification all the more remarkable was that, at the preliminary hearing, just a few weeks after the robbery, she had been unable to pick him out. When confronted with this contradiction in court, she at first blamed the stenographer, before withdrawing that accusation and simply insisting that Sacco was the gunman. So determined had the police been to nail Sacco that, shortly after his arrest and in violation of approved police methods for the identification of suspects, they had brought him alone into Mary Splaine's presence. Yet in spite of getting such a good look at him, she still couldn't identify him three weeks later at the preliminary hearing. Miraculously, her memory was to improve.

She was by no means the only prosecution witness whose original identification of Sacco was vague but whose testimony was unshakable by the time of the trial. Another witness, Lola Andrews, actually told a friend that the police had pestered her to identify Sacco and Vanzetti in jail. She told the friend: 'The government took me down and wanted me to recognize these men and I don't know a thing about them. I have never seen them and I can't recognize them.' But in court she was able to, and the District Attorney hailed her testimony as 'convincing'.

The witnesses who put Vanzetti in the car were equally unreliable. Le Vangie, a gate tender for the New Haven railroad, positively identified Vanzetti as the driver of the getaway car as it raced over the tracks. He said the driver was young with light-coloured hair; Vanzetti was middle-aged, dark and with a black moustache.

The defence called witnesses who swore that Sacco was in Boston on 15 April 1920, obtaining a passport to return to Italy following the death of his father. An official at the Italian consulate in Boston supported this story, saying that he had dealt with Sacco's request and at a time of day when it would have been impossible for the defendant to get to Braintree in time to commit the robbery. Vanzetti's alibi relied on customers who said he had served them that day. None of the stolen money was traced to either man.

The District Attorney was particularly eager to convince the jury that Sacco's .32 Colt was the murder weapon. He produced so-called expert testimony to back up the claim, but this too was highly suspect. Captain Proctor of the state police said after the case that he could not be certain that any of the five bullets found in the victims' bodies were definitely from Sacco's gun. Furthermore, he had told the District Attorney this before the trial. Yet with carefully phrased questions, the DA had managed to present possibility as fact. With so many outside factors contributing to conspire against them, it was therefore hardly a surprise when, on 14 July 1921, after a six-week trial, Sacco and Vanzetti were found guilty of robbery and first-degree murder and sentenced to death.

The guilty verdict marked the start of a six-year campaign to save Sacco and Vanzetti – a chain of motions, appeals and petitions to both state and federal courts in an effort to gain a new trial. Among the evidence presented by the defence was Captain Proctor's new statement but the redoubtable Judge Thayer belittled his testimony – a curious change of heart since he had attached such importance to it at the trial. The defence also presented a claim of perjury by prosecution witnesses, allegations of prejudice by Judge Thayer and of misconduct by the police, and various initiatives seeking to lay the blame at someone else's door. Convicted bank robber Celestino Madeiros was said to have confessed to the Braintree murders but stronger evidence suggested that the real culprits were the infamous Morelli gang. All of these motions – including the one accusing himself of bias – were ruled upon and rejected by Judge Thayer.

By 1924, Fred Moore had been replaced as Sacco and Vanzetti's lawyer. His confrontational tactics had not endeared him to the people of conservative Massachusetts and even the anarchists who were supposed to be on his side became alarmed at the way he collected money from impoverished workers to fund the appeals. And when he offered a large reward to trace the real killers – a move contrary to anarchist ideals – he fell foul of Sacco and Vanzetti themselves. His replacement was Boston lawyer William Thompson who, whilst he didn't share their political views, did firmly believe in their innocence.

Thompson may have endeavoured to play down the political significance of the case but it was like trying to stop a steamroller with a feather. The Sacco–Vanzetti affair had generated so much interest and nationalistic fervour that there was no hope of reducing it to the status of just another murder investigation. Throughout America, liberals and ordinary individuals, worried about whether justice had really been done, joined forces with anarchists, socialists, communists, immigrants of all nationalities and Italians in general to protest against the verdict. Felix Frankfurter, then a law professor at Harvard University and who later rose to the rank of Supreme Court judge, worked tirelessly to rally 'respectable' opinion behind the two men. Demonstrations took place in such diverse cities as London, Paris, Mexico City and Buenos Aires, all in the hope of securing a retrial. But ranged against the supporters of Sacco and Vanzetti were conservatives and patriots hell-bent on defending the honour of American justice, who saw the protests as a flagrant attack on the American nation. To these people, Sacco and Vanzetti were nothing more than common criminals and their followers rabble-rousers. They could not be allowed to succeed at the expense of the American judicial system. To admit defeat would be to admit that there was a basic flaw in the American way of life. And that would never do.

On 9 April 1927, after countless appeals and stays of execution, the Supreme Judicial Court of Massachusetts rejected an appeal for a new hearing and confirmed the death sentences.

Legal Blunders

However, the protests continued to be so vociferous that the Governor of Massachusetts, Alvan T. Fuller, finally bowed to pressure and agreed to consider whether clemency might be an option. He appointed an advisory committee, known as the 'Lowell Committee' because its leading light was A. Lawrence Lowell, president of Harvard. The committee concluded that the trial and judicial process had 'on the whole' been just and that clemency was not warranted.

Sacco and Vanzetti still protested their innocence but were prepared to face death as martyrs to the cause. On learning of his fate, Vanzetti declared: 'If it had not been for this, I might have live [sic] out my life talking at street corners to scorning men. I might have die [sic], unmarked, unknown, a failure. Now we are not a failure. This is our career and our triumph. Never in our full life can we do such a work for tolerance, for justice, for men's understanding of man, as we now do by an accident: our words, our lives, our pains – nothing! The taking of our lives – lives of a good shoemaker and poor fish peddler – all! The last moment belongs to us – that agony is our triumph!'

Sacco and Vanzetti were electrocuted in Massachusetts on 23 August 1927. 'Long live anarchy,' shouted Sacco as he entered the death-chamber. In London, thousands gathered in Hyde Park to mourn the executions.

Doubts have persisted ever since that Sacco and Vanzetti were innocent pawns sacrificed in the US government's battle against militant extremists. If their deaths would help crush the radicals, so be it. The end justifies the means. Theories have abounded. Some say that both men were innocent; others that Sacco was guilty and Vanzetti innocent. However, those demanding a pardon for the pair have been unsuccessful to date, the nearest to an official admission of a miscarriage of justice being in July 1977 when Michael Dukakis, Governor of Massachusetts, issued a proclamation removing 'any stigma and disgrace from the names Sacco and Vanzetti'. Henceforth, he declared, 23 August, the day of their execution, would be designated in Massachusetts as Sacco and Vanzetti Memorial Day. Two months later, the official files on the case were released under the 50-year ruling. Anyone hoping for dramatic new evidence, hitherto suppressed, was sorely disappointed, although it did emerge that Professor Frankfurter, who championed Sacco and Vanzetti's cause so eloquently, had had his phone tapped, an indication that there was something more sinister afoot than a straightforward murder trial. So many years after the event, it now seems increasingly unlikely that the truth of their guilt or innocence will ever be known, but the names of Nicola Sacco and Bartolomeo Vanzetti will surely remain synonymous with the struggle of oppressed minorities and political activists throughout the world.

Wrongful Convictions

Convicted of the 12 August 1925 murder of Ward Pierce, cashier at the Art Metal Shop, Buffalo, New York, Edward Larkman was sentenced to death. Ten hours before he was due to be executed in January 1927, by which time his head had already been shaved and he was saying farewell to his wife, his sentence was commuted to life imprisonment by Governor Alfred Smith because 'the State did not establish its case against Larkman beyond a reasonable doubt'. Two years later, Anthony Kalkiewicz, arrested for taking part in another Buffalo hold-up, confessed that he was one of the gang of five who killed Ward Pierce. Larkman was released and in 1933 he was formally pardoned when it was revealed that the police, knowing that the killer had worn sunglasses, had made him put on a pair of sunglasses and stand alone at the identity parade to be picked out by an eyewitness.

*

Freddie Pitts, a 28-year-old pulp cutter, and Wilbert Lee, a 20-year-old Army private, were two black men charged with the August 1963 murder of two white service-station attendants at Port St Joe, Florida. Beaten by police officers into a confession, they pleaded guilty at the suggestion of their court-appointed lawyer. Twice they were convicted of murder and they remained on death row for nine years even after another man had confessed to the crime and the chief prosecution witness had retracted her story, saying that the police had coerced her into naming Pitts and Lee as the killers. The prosecutors and other state officials knew of her retraction but kept quiet about it. Pitts and Lee were finally pardoned in September 1975 when lawyer Arthur Kennedy read a draft copy of Gene Miller's book about the case, *Invitation to a Lynching*, and persuaded the Governor to look into it.

*

Arrested for the 1955 murder of an eight-year-old girl in Canton, Illinois, Lloyd Miller was bullied by the police into signing a confession. Incriminated by a pair of blood-stained jockey shorts, he was found guilty and sentenced to death. Between 1958 and 1963, he was scheduled for electrocution seven times before earning a stay of execution. Further investigation of the evidence revealed that Miller didn't wear jockey shorts and that anyway the so-called blood was really paint. The prosecution had known this but had never disclosed it. Miller was freed in 1967.

*

In June 1988, Marie Wilks, seven months' pregnant, was murdered after being abducted when her car broke down on the M50 near Tewkesbury, Gloucestershire. Eddie Browning, a club bouncer with a string of minor convictions, was found guilty of the killing despite the fact that he was not picked out by any witnesses, including a police inspector, and there was no forensic evidence suggesting the victim had been in his car. Yet he was alleged to have severed her jugular vein before bundling her into his car and driving up the motorway. Overnight, Browning became one of the most hated men in Britain, but six years later, at his second appeal, his conviction was quashed after the police inspector's evidence was found, under hypnosis, to be contradictory and detectives were shown to have ignored as many as 1500 other lines of inquiry. Freeing Browning, the judges concluded that 'no one identified him or his specific car at the scene'.

*

William Wellman, who was black, was sentenced to death for the 1941 rape of an elderly white woman in Iredell County, North Carolina. He was already seated in the electric chair, ready for execution, when Governor J. Melville Broughton issued a reprieve on hearing that another man had confessed to the crime. Wellman was granted a full pardon after an investigation showed that he had signed a payroll receipt 350 miles away in Virginia on the day of the rape.

Mahmood Mattan: Justice 46 Years Too Late

In February 1998, the Court of Appeal quashed the murder conviction of Mahmood Mattan, a Somali living in Cardiff, Wales, who had been found guilty of killing pawnbroker Lily Volpert back in 1952. The Mattan family were delighted that his name had finally been cleared, but for Mattan himself it was all too late. He had been executed for the crime 46 years earlier.

Mahmood Mattan was born in what was then British Somaliland in 1923. In the early 1940s, he moved to Cardiff in South Wales where he found work as a seaman. It was a well-trodden route. Somalis had settled in the dockside Tiger Bay area of Cardiff since the late nineteenth century, many of them working on the coal ships which set off from what was then a bustling port. Although probably best known as the birthplace of singer Shirley Bassey, Tiger Bay had a fearsome reputation in the 1940s and 1950s. It was a district of deprivation with a high crime rate and racial tension was rife. Gang fights with razors were pretty much the norm on a Saturday night.

In 1947, Mattan married a local girl, Laura Williams, one of 11 children. They had known each other for just three months. Her family did not agree with her choice of husband and for much of their marriage the couple were forced, by racial prejudice, to live in separate houses in the same street. The rule in Tiger Bay – or Bute Town as it is now known – was that the different races kept apart. Although no one would admit it, this was a form of apartheid. Maltese, Greek, West Indian, West African, Arab, Italian – these nationalities all lived in the Bay area but they didn't mix in the same house. If, like Laura, you were a white girl married to a black man, you were subjected to racial hatred on a daily basis. She had buckets of water thrown over her and had to listen to neighbours screaming at her: 'Black man's whore!' Even the Somalis had tried to pay her money not to marry Mattan.

Two years after the wedding, Mattan quit his job as a seaman and instead found employment as a labourer. By March 1952, he had just been paid off by a steelworks. He was regarded as something of a rogue, who loved to gamble on greyhounds and was a regular card player. But he had no history of violence.

Forty-one-year-old Lily Volpert kept a small shop at 203 Bute Street in the heart of Tiger Bay. A short plump lady, only 4ft 10in tall, Miss Volpert officially ran a general outfitters but everyone in the area knew that she also operated as an unofficial pawnbroker and money-lender. As a result, she kept valuables as well as cash on the premises. In a district as rough as Tiger Bay, it was a risky business. She generally closed the shop at 8 p.m. but all the locals knew that she would open up after that if there was a knock on the door. She didn't like to turn trade away.

One such knock came on the night of 6 March 1952, at about 8.05 p.m., a few minutes after Lily Volpert had shut up shop. At the time she was having supper in the back room with her mother Fanny, widowed sister Doris and Doris's ten-year-old daughter Ruth. Lily got up to answer the call, leaving her family to their meal. Even when she hadn't returned 15 minutes later, they apparently thought nothing of it. Some customers took longer to deal with than others. In fact, they weren't aware of anything untoward having taken place at the front of the shop until the police arrived. They had been summoned by a neighbour, William Archibald, who lived three doors away. At 8.15 p.m., he had tried the front door of Volperts and had seen Lily lying dead on the floor, her throat slashed from ear to ear. A huge trail of blood was smeared across the floor, indicating where she had managed to crawl for a few feet.

The victim's sister told police that shortly before the murder she had seen a coloured man – either a West Indian or a 'bushy-haired' Somali – hanging around outside the door of the shop with a torch in his hand. Although Mahmood Mattan did not have hair which by any stretch of the imagination could be described as bushy, a couple of hours after the murder, on a routine search, officers entered his lodgings at 42 Davis Street. By then, his wife had gone back to live with her mother while they waited for a council house to become available. The police told him that a coloured man had been spotted at the scene of the crime. Mattan flew into a rage. 'Why coloured man?' he screamed. 'You lie. All policemen are liars!'

Despite the fact that Lily Volpert's killer would have been

covered in blood when her jugular was severed, the police found no bundle of blood-stained clothes nor any sign of the wad of 100 £1 notes said to be missing from the dead woman's desk. All they found was a razor with a broken blade and no blood on it and a small amount of loose change. Mattan said that he no longer shaved with that razor and that it had been broken for some time. The only blood they ever found on Mattan was on one of his shoes.

Mattan was brought in to take part in an identity parade. Lily Volpert's sister failed to pick him out.

But the police had more luck with Harold Cover, a 32-year-old Jamaican, who seemed happy to tell them what they wanted to hear. In his original statement, he said that he had seen two Somalis near the shop around the time of the murder. He described the one he saw coming out of the shop as being 5ft 10in tall, aged 30 to 40, wearing no hat or coat but a brown suit. Cover particularly noticed that the man had a gold tooth. Mattan was 5ft 8in, aged 29 and, according to the police, had worn a dark overcoat that night. And he did not have a gold tooth. Nevertheless, Cover identified the man coming out of the shop as Mahmood Mattan. He was the only person to place Mattan in Bute Street on the night of the killing.

This was sufficient for the police and, on 15 March, Mattan was charged with the murder of Lily Volpert. His trial lasted just three days. The key prosecution witness was Harold Cover. In his original statement to the police, he said that he had seen Mattan leaving the shop at 8 p.m. at the latest. However Miss Volpert's family were sure that she was still alive between 8.05 and 8.10 p.m. In court, Cover conveniently changed the time at which he had seen Mattan making his exit. His first statement, which also included the discrepancies in his description of the man he had seen, was never shown to the defence since the rules of 'disclosure', which now require the prosecution to make their evidence known to the defence, did not apply in those days.

Nor did the jury ever hear how six separate witnesses – including the victim's mother, sister and niece – all of whom said they had seen coloured men outside or inside the shop at the vital time, failed to pick out Mattan at identity parades. Mattan had no solicitor at the parades and his lawyers were not informed of these significant non-identifications. As a result, potentially valuable witnesses were never called upon to give evidence on Mattan's behalf. Similarly, the sister's description of a 'bushy-haired' Somali, when Mattan had tight curls, was never relayed to the jury.

One woman who did testify was May Gray, a second-hand clothes dealer. Three days after the Volpert family had offered a £200 reward in return for information leading to the killer, and a whole week after the murder, she came forward to reveal that on the night of Lily Volpert's death, Mattan had come into her shop and showed her a wallet containing 100 £1 notes. Under cross-examination, Mrs. Gray could not explain how it was possible to cram so many notes into a small wallet like Mattan's. She also confessed that she had a strong dislike of Mattan and his family.

And what of the incriminating shoe? It amounted to nothing more than microscopic flecks of blood of unknown age. Mattan had bought the pair second-hand. No forensic tests were carried out on the blood. Today, the blood evidence would not even be considered reliable enough to be admitted into court.

Unfortunately, the illiterate Mattan did himself no favours in the witness box. He offered an alibi that was easily disproved and simply claimed that every prosecution witness was lying, even about relatively trivial matters. His solicitor later admitted: 'Mattan was a fool to himself.' Over 40 years on, his widow would remark: 'He was hanged for being cheeky.'

Mattan came across in court as decidedly shifty, which simply reinforced the view around Tiger Bay about anyone who was part of a mixed marriage. The race card was even played by his own lawyer, Thomas Rhys-Roberts, who, turning to the jury in his closing speech, called his client 'a half-child of nature, a semi-civilized savage'. Laura Mattan later said that 'Rhys-Roberts was the best witness the prosecution could call.' To make matters even tougher for Mattan, his counsel was pitched against Edmund Davies, QC, a man thought by many to be the finest lawyer produced by Wales this century. It was a hopeless mismatch. In his final address to the jury, Davies said: 'Did you think he (Cover) spoke with the tongue of truth? If you are satisfied about Harold Cover, it is my duty to submit to you that this is the end of the case.' Wrongly, as it would turn out, the jury were satisfied about Cover and, after deliberating for just over an hour and a half, returned a verdict of guilty. Mattan was sentenced to death.

Although Mattan was convicted solely on the word of Cover and a few vague spots of blood of indeterminate age, Mr Justice Oliver, refusing him leave to appeal, pronounced that the evidence was quite sufficient for the jury to convict. At 9 a.m. on 3 September 1952, less than seven weeks after the death sentence was passed, Mahmood Mattan was hanged at Cardiff Prison. He had maintained his innocence to the last, his final request being that his body should not be taken from the prison until his name was cleared. Twenty-three-year-old Laura Mattan stood praying outside the prison walls in the rain as her husband was hanged.

She never doubted his innocence for one second and, as the years passed, a more general disquiet began to grow about the conviction, never more so than in 1969 when Harold Cover, the prosecution's star witness, was jailed for life for the attempted murder of his own daughter by cutting her throat with an open razor. It also emerged that, even before Mattan's trial, Cover had a history of violence. In the wake of Cover's conviction, the then Home Secretary, James Callaghan, was approached by the Mattan family but did not refer the case to the Court of Appeal.

Mahmood Mattan's command of English had been distinctly shaky, which had rendered some of his replies in court quite bizarre, yet he had foolishly refused the services of an interpreter, Bernard de Maid. In 1995, the same Bernard de Maid, now a Cardiff solicitor, took up the Mattans's case. He said of Mattan: 'It was almost as if he felt he could not be found guilty regardless of what he said and did. He had wrongly presumed that no British court of law could convict him of something he had not done.'

Together with his wife Lynne, Bernard de Maid uncovered the fact that vital evidence had been withheld from the defence at the time of the trial and that Harold Cover had only identified Mahmood Mattan after the £200 reward – enough to buy a house in the city – had been offered by the victim's family. As the case began to swing Mrs Mattan's way, she had her husband's remains exhumed from the felon's grave at Cardiff Prison and reburied in a cemetery in the city. She knew that he would finally be vindicated.

By the time the case went to the Court of Appeal, Laura Mattan was seriously ill with cancer. She heard Michael Mansfield, QC, pour scorn on Harold Cover's evidence. Without it, he said, only the embers of the prosecution case remained. The court was told how Cover's original description matched that of another Somali, Tehar Gass, right down to his distinctive gold tooth. It emerged that one of the investigating officers, Detective Inspector Loudon Roberts, who died in 1981, was aware that Cover's description did not match that of Mr Mattan, but that this evidence was not put before the jury. Gass was interviewed about the killing at the time and admitted visiting the shop earlier on the day of the murder.

Once again, the jury was not told of this. Gass was subsequently accused of another murder in 1954, after the stabbing of wages clerk Granville Jenkins, but was found to be insane. After his release from Broadmoor, he was deported to Somalia. Gass was known to have had an obsession with knives. In the light of these developments, John Williams, QC, for the Crown, conceded that there were so many inconsistencies in Harold Cover's evidence that he was no longer a credible witness. The evidence given by the other chief prosecution witness at the 1952 trial, May Gray, was also dismissed as unreliable.

The three judges ruled that the case against Mahmood Mattan was 'demonstrably flawed' and quashed the conviction. Lord Justice Rose said that Mr Mattan's death and the length of time taken to dismiss the conviction were matters of profound regret. 'The court can only hope that its decision today will provide a crumb of comfort for his surviving relatives.'

'I feel that I have waited forever for this day,' said Mrs Mattan afterwards. However, her main emotion was one of anger that it had taken such a short time to destroy the case against her husband, a case described by Cardiff West MP Rhodri Morgan as a 'legalized lynching'. Harold Cover, who also attended the hearing, left insisting that he had always told the truth about the case. So, too, had Mahmood Mattan.

Dr Sam Sheppard: A Ruined Life

It was the case which was said to have inspired the 1960s television series *The Fugitive*. But whereas Dr Richard Kimble, wrongfully convicted for the murder of his wife, managed to escape custody and pursue the mysterious one-armed man half-way across America, Dr Sam Sheppard, also wrongfully convicted for killing his wife, had to conduct his campaign to track down the elusive bushy-haired intruder from behind bars. Both men were eventually exonerated but, in Sheppard's case, the whisperings and dark mutterings continued. He took up medical practice again but soon found that mud has a nasty habit of sticking. What patients he had generally eyed him with suspicion and, to make matters worse, no insurance company would cover him in case he was sued for negligence. In the end, persistent public innuendo forced him out of his chosen profession. He divorced his second wife, married a 19-year-old and embarked on a short-lived career as a professional wrestler, calling himself 'Killer Sheppard'. But his health declined, he turned to drink and in April 1970, just four years after his conviction was overturned, he died of liver failure at the age of 46.

Yet it was a life which had promised so much. Sam Sheppard came from a respectable, middle-class family; his father, Dr Richard Sheppard, was an eminent member of society in Cleveland, Ohio. Dr Sheppard Sr was the founder of the 110-bed Bay View Hospital, housed in a converted Cleveland mansion, and worked there as a general surgeon and osteopath. Sam was employed there too as a neurosurgeon. His brothers Richard and Stephen were also doctors at the hospital and, to avoid obvious confusion, he was known to all as 'Dr Sam'.

Sam Sheppard had known Marilyn Reese since high school. They were childhood sweethearts for whom marriage was an inevitable progression. Together they bought a splendid home overlooking Lake Erie and when they had a son, Sam (originality in choosing names wasn't a strength of the Sheppard family), their happiness seemed complete. Marilyn was a Sunday school teacher at the Bay Methodist Church and, outwardly at least, they appeared the perfect 1950s American couple, all white teeth and smiles. But on the night of 3 July 1954, their lives entered a state of terminal decay.

The Sheppards were a gregarious pair and enjoyed nothing more than having people around for dinner. That evening, they had entertained their friends Don and Nancy Ahern. They left around 12.30 a.m. and Sam proceeded to fall asleep on the couch in front of the late-night movie. Preferring not to disturb him, Marilyn crept upstairs to bed.

According to Sheppard, he was awoken by his wife's screams. He rushed upstairs but as he entered the bedroom, he received a vicious blow to the back of the head. When he came to, still dazed, he saw his wife lying on her twin bed. Blood pouring from a wound on her head had formed a red pool on the bed linen. There was more blood on the walls. The room had been ransacked. He checked her pulse but felt none. He ran into the next room to check that their son (nicknamed 'Chip' to distinguish him from his father) was unharmed. No sooner had he ascertained that the boy was still fast asleep than he heard noises downstairs. He ran to investigate but arrived just in time to see someone disappearing out of the back door. Although still feeling groggy, he gave chase and, remarkably, caught up with the intruder on the beach, only to be knocked unconscious for a second time.

As Sheppard would later testify, 'I believed that I was disorientated and the victim of a bizarre dream.' He staggered back home where, instead of calling the police, he telephoned a neighbour, J. Spencer Houk, the mayor of Cleveland, pleading: 'For God's sake, Spen, get over here! I think they've killed Marilyn.' The Houks were over within minutes and found Sheppard slumped wearily in a chair. He pointed upstairs and Mrs Houk went to the bedroom to confirm the awful truth. Marilyn was dead.

Spencer Houk called the police. By now it was 5.57 a.m., dawn on the Fourth of July. It was a glorious day, a day for celebration everywhere except in this little corner of Cleveland. As officers swarmed all over the murder scene, the mayor's son discovered Dr Sam's canvas medical bag on the hill leading down to the beach. Its contents were handled by a number of people before the police were able to check for fingerprints.

At 8 a.m. Coroner Samuel Gerber arrived. A great favourite with reporters because he told them what they wanted to know, he put the time of death at between three and four o'clock in the morning, Marilyn's watch having stopped at 3.15 a.m. He revealed that the victim had sustained no fewer than 35 wounds to the head and he said of the killer: 'He rained blow after blow on her with savage fury.' It was stirring stuff, and all good copy for the newshounds. He went on to state that the murder weapon was a blunt instrument of some kind. But Dr Gerber was worried, not only by the savagery of the attack on Marilyn Sheppard but also by the state of the room. He confided to the officers at the scene: 'It's in such a mindless disarray that it looks like some amateur attempt to make it appear as if the crime was committed while a robbery was taking place.' The inference of his words was clear enough: Sam Sheppard was under suspicion.

The police weren't finding it easy to question Sam Sheppard. He was in hospital where his brother Steve maintained that he was in no fit state to be questioned. An independent doctor supported this diagnosis, saying that Dr Sam had suffered serious damage to the spinal cord in the neck region, bruises on the right side of his face, lacerations to the mouth and chipped teeth. They were not the sort of injuries which could have been self-inflicted.

Sam Sheppard attended his wife's funeral wearing an orthopaedic collar and sitting in a wheelchair. He wept openly at the graveside. He was able to disclose that the man he had chased from the house had bushy hair and was wearing a white shirt and he offered a reward of $10,000 for information leading to the capture of the killer. However, the police were growing increasingly impatient. Despite Dr Gerber's view that there were no signs of a break-in on the night of the murder, the police had no real reason to suspect that a man with such an unblemished record and with no obvious motive should suddenly batter his wife into an early grave. But they were becoming frustrated by their lack of access to Sheppard. They were desperate to quiz him at length and began to view his brother Steve's continued protection of the key witness as an indication that perhaps Sam Sheppard had something to hide. 'We expected co-operation from the family,' stormed Dr Gerber, 'but we don't seem to be getting it. Here's a witness surrounded by his whole family of doctors.' Prosecutor John Mahon echoed those sentiments: 'In my 23 years of criminal prosecution, I have never seen such flagrant stalling.'

To all intents and purposes, Sheppard was a pillar of the community. He denied ever being unfaithful to his wife, but when the police started digging it didn't take them long to come up with some dirt. It emerged that the supposedly happily married, devoted family man had had more than one extra-marital affair, the latest being with Susan Hayes, a former nurse at Bay View.

Sam Sheppard did not have to give evidence at the inquest but agreed to do so. He repeated his story as to what had happened on the night of the murder but also made two fatal errors. He said that he and Marilyn had had a happy marriage, that they had never 'seriously' discussed divorce and, when questioned about his involvement with Susan Hayes, he insisted that there was no sexual relationship with his former work colleague. But the day after the inquest, the Cleveland papers carried banner headlines in which Susan Hayes admitted that she and Dr Sam had been having an affair for two years and that they had talked about getting married.

The news of Sheppard's infidelities rocked middle-class Cleveland. By behaving so appallingly, he had betrayed them all. Former friends dropped him like a red-hot brick and he became a social outcast. Married men simply didn't have affairs in the 1950s. Although there was still precious little evidence to show that he had murdered his wife and no motive beyond the fact that he had enjoyed a couple of affairs, a whispering campaign started up against him. The press joined in with headlines such as 'Quit Stalling Bring – Him In' and soon the whispering had become a deafening roar. In the face of such overwhelming public opinion, the police finally relented and charged Sam Sheppard with murder.

The whole of Cleveland seemed to want to watch the trial. It began in October 1954 and lasted two months. Virtually all of the evidence against Sheppard amounted to nothing more than speculation. The one damning item was Sheppard's wrist-watch which had been found in the canvas bag tossed in the shrubbery along with his fraternity ring and some keys. The face of the watch was speckled with blood and, said the prosecution, it could only have got there because the defendant had been wearing it while bludgeoning his wife about the head. However, the remainder of the evidence consisted solely of a succession of potentially incriminating questions, but questions to which the prosecution did not have the answers.

There was the mystery of Sheppard's missing T-shirt. When Mayor Houk and his wife had arrived at the house, Sheppard was stripped to the waist. When asked by the police about his shirt, he could not produce it. The prosecution contended that this was because he had destroyed it, since it would undoubtedly have been covered in blood. Yet the shirt was never recovered.

Dr Gerber stated that a bloody imprint found on Marilyn Sheppard's pillow had been made by a surgical instrument, the like of which Sam Sheppard would probably have owned. But Dr Gerber could not be more specific about the type of instrument and nor was the instrument in question ever found.

Morphine had been taken from Sheppard's medical bag. What was the significance of this? Again, the prosecution had no real answer, just idle speculation.

And what had happened in the two hours between the estimated time of death and the call to Spencer Houk?

Dr Steve Sheppard said that, on arriving at the murder scene, he had noticed a cigarette end floating in the upstairs toilet – a clear indication that there had been an intruder since the Sheppards didn't smoke. Yet later the cigarette had gone, the result of police incompetence. Sam Sheppard claimed that the police had tried to frighten him or trick him into confessing at a time when he was in no physical or mental state to stand up to intensive interrogation, and two separate witnesses stated that they had seen a man with a white shirt and bushy hair near the Sheppard home, although their testimony was somewhat tarnished by their admission that they had only come forward after hearing of the reward.

Certainly Sam Sheppard's curious behaviour in the immediate aftermath of the attack on his wife had raised doubts as to his innocence while his affairs indicated that he was not entirely truthful. Mrs Houk talked of rows between the Sheppards and Mrs Ahern said that Marilyn Sheppard had told her about their marriage problems, including Sam's purchase of a watch for Susan Hayes. Mrs Ahern also revealed that a friend had said the Sheppards were considering divorce. The last remark was a clear instance of hearsay yet Judge Edwin Blythin, whose summing-up was heavily loaded against the defence, unaccountably allowed it to stand. The prosecution had succeeded in pushing ahead with the trial before the defence had time to prepare its case properly, particularly with regard to examining the murder scene. But it was still the job of the prosecution to prove that Sam Sheppard had committed the murder and they had singularly failed to do so. However, the jury saw it differently and, whilst finding him not guilty of first-degree murder, found him guilty of second-degree murder. Even then, it had been a close-run thing.

Sam Sheppard was sentenced to life imprisonment, condemned by the moral guardians of Cleveland. He was being punished for cheating on his wife.

The verdict had dramatic repercussions on the Sheppard family. Both his mother and his father-in-law committed suicide shortly afterwards and his father died of a broken heart. Even a member of the jury killed himself. Despite these tragedies, there was no obvious softening of attitude towards Sheppard. The general consensus of opinion among the people of Cleveland was that he had got what he deserved.

Given the fact that it had been conducted in such a hostile atmosphere, the feeling among Sheppard's lawyers was that it had been an unfair trial. Over the next few years, they tried on no fewer than 12 occasions to move for a re-trial but without success. Meanwhile Sam Sheppard languished in jail. The charismatic doctor whose trial had made so many headlines was rapidly becoming a forgotten man. And the further he drifted from the public eye, the more remote his chances became of overturning the conviction.

All that changed with the appointment of a new lawyer, F. Lee Bailey. A flamboyant character with a knack for pulling rabbits out of the hat in court, rather like Perry Mason, Bailey courted the media and set about reawakening interest in the Sheppard case. He was helped by the arrival of a new woman in Sam Sheppard's life – a pretty 33-year-old German divorcée named Ariane Tebbenjohanns who liked to wrap herself in mink. She and Sheppard had been exchanging letters for some time and when she revealed that she was coming over to Ohio to visit the prisoner in person, Bailey saw it as a heaven-sent opportunity to drum up some much-needed publicity. He tipped off the press, who eagerly snapped up the story of the murderer and his new love.

More importantly, Bailey received fresh evidence from leading criminologist Dr Paul Kirk and an affidavit from columnist Dorothy Kilgallen, who cast grave aspersions on the impartiality of Judge Blythin at the trial. She said that the judge, who was now dead, had told her during the trial that it was an open and shut case. When she had asked him what he meant, he replied: 'He is guilty as hell. There is no question about it.'

In 1964, Bailey's hard work paid off. District Judge Carl Weinman ordered Sam Sheppard's release pending a fresh trial. He found five separate violations of Sheppard's constitutional rights in the events leading up to the first trial and described the courtroom proceedings in 1954 as a 'carnival', adding, 'If ever there was a trial by newspaper, this is a perfect example.'

Freed after ten years, Sam Sheppard wasted no time in marrying Ariane. Touched by the genuine romance, public feeling was finally beginning to shift. Maybe Sam Sheppard wasn't the devil in disguise after all. People began to question whether, in view of the inconclusive evidence at his trial, he deserved another chance. Was it right to deny his new bride, who had done nothing wrong, the opportunity for future happiness?

The Supreme Court granted Sam Sheppard's request for a second trial and it began in October 1966, this time without the prejudicial publicity which had set the tone for the previous trial and without Judge Blythin in charge of proceedings. The new judge was Justice Francis Talty, a man with a reputation for fairness. Lee Bailey knew that his task was not only to expose the shallowness of the evidence but also to discredit the chief prosecution witnesses. If he could do so, he reckoned his client would be home and dry. The two men he had to break down were Dr Gerber and Sgt Robert Schottke, both of whom had seen their careers enhanced by Sheppard's conviction and both of whom were convinced that Sheppard was guilty. The good doctor had actually taken to giving lectures on the case, putting himself forward as the man whose evidence had sent Sam Sheppard down. Lee Bailey was just the man to cut Dr Gerber down to size.

After taking him through his testimony about the blunt instrument said to have been used to kill Marilyn Sheppard, Bailey expressed surprise that, considering the thoroughness with which the investigation was supposed to have been conducted, the aforementioned instrument was never found. Gerber reluctantly had to admit to that particular failing. The jury detected his unease. He was also forced to admit that, despite a nationwide search, he could not produce any surgical implement which might have caused the imprint on the pillow, a piece of evidence in which he had placed such store at the original trial. Bailey then confronted him with a remark which he was alleged to have made on the morning after the killing. According to Bailey, Gerber had told police officers: 'Well, men, it is evident the doctor did this, so let's go get the confession out of him.' Gerber indignantly denied the allegation, but Bailey had planted sufficient seeds of doubt in the jury's mind.

As for Sgt Schottke, Bailey was able to pinpoint a basic flaw in the police investigation procedure regarding the Sheppard case. Having found the canvas bag which contained Sheppard's watch, ring and keys, the police had omitted to check the items for the presence of any fingerprints other than Sheppard's. 'So,' said Bailey, 'you did not find out exactly what prints were there before accusing the defendant of murder?'

'No,' mumbled the sergeant. Like Dr Gerber, his credibility had been demolished by Bailey's skilful cross-examination.

Two down, but still one to go – Dr Gerber's assistant, Mary Cowan. She was in possession of what seemed to be the most damning piece of evidence of all – a transparency of Sheppard's blood-spattered wrist-watch. Questioned by the prosecution, she said that the face of the watch contained specks of flying blood and stated categorically that they could only have got there during the violent attack on Marilyn Sheppard. She and the evidence appeared unshakable but then Lee Bailey came up with one of those courtroom revelations on which he had built his reputation. Examining the transparency again, he spotted tiny specks of blood on the inside of the watch-strap. How did Mary Cowan account for that? Surely the particles of blood could not possibly have got on the inside of the strap at the time that Sam Sheppard was supposed to be smashing in his wife's head? Bailey had a far more plausible explanation and called Dr Paul Kirk to the stand. Dr Kirk said that he had no doubt as to how the blood had got on the watch – it had been when Sam Sheppard had touched his wife's body to detect whether or not there was a pulse.

That discovery was to prove the telling blow. In a rousing closing speech, Bailey memorably described the prosecution evidence as 'ten pounds of hog wash in a five pound bag'. Even if the jury didn't understand what he meant, they were obviously impressed by his unique turn of phrase and returned a verdict of not guilty against Sam Sheppard.

So, after ten years behind bars for a murder he did not commit, Sam Sheppard was finally set free. But life could never return to normal and sadly, neither his marriage, his happiness nor indeed his life were to last long.

Although Sam Sheppard had been cleared, there were inevitably still a few doubters and, even after his father's death, son 'Chip' fought to clear the family name. It was a long, slow process, but one eventually resolved by the advent of DNA testing. Permission was obtained to exhume Sam Sheppard's body and, in 1997, after nine months' testing, Dr Mohammad Tahir was able to announce that DNA evidence showed conclusively that Sam Sheppard's blood had not been present at the murder scene. He was proved beyond doubt to have been an innocent man.

Bibliography

Bland, James, *Crime Strange But True* (Warner Books, 1995)

Burn, Gordon, *Somebody's Husband, Somebody's Son* (Pan, 1990)

Cawthorne, Nigel, *Sex Killers* (Boxtree, 1994)

Fuhrman, Mark, *Murder in Brentwood* (Zebra Books, 1997)

Gaute, J. H. H. and Odell, Robin, *The New Murderers' Who's Who* (Headline, 1989)

Goodman, Jonathan (ed.), *The Pleasures of Murder* (1984)

Goodman, Jonathan (ed.), *The Christmas Murders* (1986)

Honeycombe, Gordon, *More Murders of the Black Museum* (Hutchinson, 1993)

Jeffreys, Diarmuid, *The Bureau* (Pan, 1995)

Jones, Frank, *White-Collar Killers* (Headline, 1993)

Lloyd, Georgina, *One Was Not Enough* (1986)

Pile, Stephen, *The Book of Heroic Failures* (Futura Books, 1982)

Rose, Jonathan (with Steve Panter and Trevor Wilkinson), *Innocents* (Fourth Estate, 1997)

Vincent, Adrian, *Fatal Passions* (Warner Books, 1992)

Wallechinsky, David and Wallace, Amy, *The Book of Lists* (Aurum Press, 1994)

Index